INTE

A JOURNAL OF MORMON SCRIPTURE

VOLUME 2 · 2012

INTERPRETER FOUNDATION

OREM, UTAH

Interpreter: A Journal of Mormon Scripture

The goal of the Interpreter Foundation is to increase understanding of scripture through careful scholarly investigation and analysis of the insights provided by a wide range of ancillary disciplines, including language, history, archaeology, literature, culture, ethnohistory, art, geography, law, politics, philosophy, etc. Interpreter will also publish articles advocating the authenticity and historicity of LDS scripture and the Restoration, along with scholarly responses to critics of the LDS faith. We hope to illuminate, by study and faith, the eternal spiritual message of the scriptures—that Jesus is the Christ.

Although the Board fully supports the goals and teachings of the Church, Interpreter Foundation is an independent entity and is neither owned, controlled by nor affiliated with The Church of Jesus Christ of Latter-day Saints, or with Brigham Young University. All research and opinions provided on this site are the sole responsibility of their respective authors, and should not be interpreted as the opinions of the Board, nor as official statements of LDS doctrine, belief or practice.

This journal is a weekly publication. Visit us at MormonInterpreter.com

TABLE OF CONTENTS

The Role of Apologetics in Mormon Studies

Daniel C. Peterson

The following essay was presented on 3 August 2012 as "Of 'Mormon Studies' and Apologetics" at the conclusion of the annual conference of the Foundation for Apologetic Information and Research (FAIR) in Sandy, Utah. It represents the first public announcement and appearance of Interpreter: A Journal of Mormon Scripture, which had been founded only slightly more than a week earlier, on 26 July. In my view, that rapid launch was the near-miraculous product of selfless collaboration and devotion to a cause on the part of several people—notable among them David E. Bokovoy, Alison V. P. Coutts, William J. Hamblin, Bryce M. Haymond, Louis C. Midgley, George L. Mitton, Stephen D. Ricks, and Mark Alan Wright—and I'm profoundly grateful to them. This essay, which may even have some slight historical value, is something of a personal charter statement regarding that cause. It is published here with no substantial alteration.

Founded in California in 1979 by John W. Welch, FARMS, or the Foundation for Ancient Research and Mormon Studies, became part of Brigham Young University in 1997.

It did so at the invitation of President Gordon B. Hinckley, who remarked at the time that "FARMS represents the efforts of sincere and dedicated scholars. It has grown to provide strong support and defense of the Church on a professional basis. I wish to express my strong congratulations and appreciation for those who started this effort and who have shepherded it to this point."

Plainly, FARMS had gained a reputation for doing apologetics, though it must be said that apologetics was never its sole focus. It has always fostered scholarship that cannot plausibly be characterized as apologetic; Professor Royal Skousen's meticulous, landmark work on the text and textual history of the Book of Mormon is perhaps the most notable example of such scholarship, but it's far from alone.

Our official motto, though, was drawn from Doctrine and Covenants 88:118: "By study and also by faith."

In his essay "Advice to Christian Philosophers," Alvin Plantinga of the University of Notre Dame, indisputably among the preeminent Christian philosophers of our time, argued that "we who are Christians and propose to be philosophers must not rest content with being philosophers who happen, incidentally, to be Christians; we must strive to be Christian philosophers."[1] Elder Neal A. Maxwell exhorted Latter-day Saint academics in much the same spirit: "The LDS scholar has his citizenship in the Kingdom," he said, "but carries his passport into the professional world—not the other way around."

However inadequately, we who were affiliated with FARMS from its early years tried to work and to act in that spirit.

In 2006, much to our delight and (though we had requested the change) to our surprise, the organization was rechristened as the Neal A. Maxwell Institute for Religious Scholarship. Elder Maxwell had always been an enthusiastic supporter of our work and personally interested in it; his passing, two years before, had saddened us, and others, enormously.

At the dinner during which the new name was formally announced, President Boyd K. Packer, of the Quorum of the Twelve praised two specific aspects of the Institute's work: the Islamic Translation Series and the Institute's defense of the Kingdom. It was very much in the spirit of Elder Maxwell him-

---

1. Alvin Plantinga, "Advice to Christian Philosophers," *Faith and Philosophy* 1/3 (July, 1984): 271.

self, who wanted to permit critics of the Church "no more un-contested slam dunks."

As recently as 21 April 2010, the Maxwell Institute's Mission Statement positioned the organization as "Describ[ing] and defend[ing] the Restoration through highest quality scholarship" and "Provid[ing] an anchor of faith in a sea of LDS Studies."[2]

In a posthumous tribute to his friend C. S. Lewis, the English philosopher and theologian Austin Farrer wrote a passage that became a favorite of Elder Maxwell's, and that Elder Maxwell used on several public occasions. It also served for many years as a kind of unofficial motto for several of us who were involved with, first, FARMS and, then, its successor organization, the Maxwell Institute:

> Though argument does not create conviction, lack of it destroys belief. What seems to be proved may not be embraced; but what no one shows the ability to defend is quickly abandoned. Rational argument does not create belief, but it maintains a climate in which belief may flourish.[3]

In referring to such "argument," Austin Farrer had in mind what is commonly called—very commonly among Catholics and Evangelicals, though far less commonly among Latter-day Saints—*apologetics.*

Derived from the Greek word ἀπολογία ("speaking in defense") *apologetics* is the practice or discipline of defending a position (usually, but not always, a religious one) through the use of some combination or other of evidence and reason. In modern English, those who are known for defending their positions (often minority views) against criticism or attack are

---

2. As cited by Ericson, "Where is the 'Mormon' in Mormon Studies?" 7.

3. Austin Farrer, "Grete Clerk," in *Light on C. S. Lewis*, ed. Jocelyn Gibb (New York: Harcourt and Brace, 1965), 26.

frequently termed *apologists*.[4] In my remarks today, I'll be using the word *apologetics* to refer to attempts to prove or defend religious claims. But the fact is that every argument defending any position, even a criticism of Latter-day Saint apologetics, is an apology. "By itself, 'apologist' does not tell whether the cause is noble or disreputable."[5]

Some people turn their noses up at the thought of apologetics. As Richard Lloyd Anderson notes, being called an "apologist" is commonly "a put-down, meaning one who trashes truth."[6] "'Apologetics,'" writes Paul J. Griffiths, currently Warren Professor of Catholic Thought at the Divinity School of Duke University,

> has . . . become a term laden with negative connotations: to be an apologist for the truth of one religious claim or set of claims over against another is, in certain circles, seen as not far short of being a racist. And the term has passed into popular currency, to the extent that it has, as a simple label for argument in the service of a predetermined orthodoxy, argument concerned not to demonstrate but to convince, and, if conviction should fail, to browbeat into submission.[7]

"In almost all mainstream institutions in which theology is taught in the USA and Europe," Griffiths reports,

---

4. For reflections on what was then the place of apologetics within the overall program of the Neal A. Maxwell Institute for Religious Scholarship, see Daniel C. Peterson, "The Witchcraft Paradigm: On Claims to 'Second Sight' by People Who Say It Doesn't Exist," *FARMS Review* 18/2 (2006): ix–xviii.

5. Richard Lloyd Anderson, personal communication (31 July 2012), in the possession of the author.

6. Richard Lloyd Anderson, personal communication (31 July 2012), in the possession of the author.

7. Paul J. Griffiths, *An Apology for Apologetics: A Study in the Logic of Interreligious Dialogue* (Maryknoll, NY: Orbis Books, 1991), 2.

apologetics as an intellectual discipline does not figure prominently in the curriculum. You will look for it in vain in the catalogues of the Divinity Schools at Harvard or Chicago; liberal Protestants have never been wedded to the practice of interreligious apologetics, and while the Roman Catholic Church has a long and honorable tradition of apologetics, interreligious and other, its approach to theological thinking about non-Christian religious communities has moved far from the apologetical since the Second Vatican Council, and especially since the promulgation of the conciliar document *Nostra Aetate*.[8]

Apologists, some critics declare, are not concerned with truth; what apologists do isn't real scholarship, and anyhow, as one hostile Internet apostate put it, apologetics is "a fundamentally unethical and immoral enterprise." Or, alternatively, in the words of another anonymous Internet ex-Mormon, "Each of us is either a man or woman of faith or of reason.... All apologetics is, is *faux* logic, *faux* reason designed to lure the wonderer back into the fold. Those of faith are threatened by defectors to reason." "Apologists," he continued in a subsequent post,

> try to shill an explanation to questioning members as though science and reason really explain and buttress their professed faith. It [*sic*] does not. By definition, faith is the antithesis of science and reason. Apologetics is a further deception by faith peddlers to keep power and influence.

I'm willing to wager, by the way, that although these critics want believers to stop responding, they do not intend to stop criticizing. There is no question that any team will score more easily if the opposing team's defensive players leave the field,

---

8. Griffiths, *An Apology*, 2.

but I'm unaware of any athlete with the chutzpah to make the request.

But this attitude seems, anyway, to reflect a fundamental misunderstanding—like any other form of intellectual enterprise, apologetics can be done competently or incompetently, logically or illogically, honestly or not—and it certainly ignores the venerable tradition of apologetics, which has enlisted some very notable writers, scholars, and thinkers (e.g., Socrates/Plato, St. Justin Martyr, Origen of Alexandria, St. Augustine, al-Ghazālī, Ibn Rushd [Averroës], Moses Maimonides, St. Anselm, St. Thomas Aquinas, Hugo Grotius, John Locke, John Henry Newman, G. K. Chesterton, Ronald Knox, C. S. Lewis, Dorothy Sayers, Richard Swinburne, Alvin Plantinga, Peter Kreeft, Stephen Davis, N. T. Wright, and William Lane Craig). It's dubious (at best) to summarily dismiss these people or their apologetic writings as "fundamentally unethical and immoral" and flatly irrational. Within The Church of Jesus Christ of Latter-day Saints, although the term has rarely been used, there has been apologetic activity from the very beginning. (The brothers Parley and Orson Pratt, Oliver Cowdery, Orson Spencer, John Taylor, B. H. Roberts, and Hugh Nibley represent some of the high points.)

Still, a few faithful members of the church profess to disdain apologetics as well.

Some, for instance, seem to believe it inherently evil. They appear to use the word *apologetics* to mean "trying to defend the church but doing so badly," whether through incompetence, dishonesty, or mean-spiritedness. But, again, *apologetics*, as such, is a value-neutral term. Just like historical writing, carpentry, and cooking, apologetics can be done well or poorly. Apologists, like attorneys and scientists and field laborers, can be pleasant or unpleasant, humble or arrogant, honest or dishonest, fair or unfair, civil and polite, or nasty and insulting.

The very recent decision by the current leadership of the Maxwell Institute to forego explicit defense and advocacy of Mormonism—to renounce explicit apologetics—may have been influenced by concerns about the arrogant mean-spiritedness of one or two of those most prominently associated with its apologetic side. But, from what I can tell—and I'll freely admit that I and others have found explanations of the Institute's announced "new course" somewhat inscrutable—it seems certain that the principal factor was a desire to become more purely "academic," and to reconceive its audience as not merely *including* professional scholars but as primarily if not exclusively *composed* of full-time academics and academic libraries.

Whereas, much earlier, FARMS had been encouraged by a prominent Church leader not to forget "the Relief Society sister in Parowan," the Maxwell Institute's new audience has been expressly said not to include "the typical Mormon in Ogden."

"The Neal A. Maxwell Institute for Religious Scholarship," says the Institute's public announcement that it had dismissed the editors of the *Mormon Studies Review* (or *FARMS Review*) and suspended publication of that journal, "is continually striving to align its work with the academy's highest objectives and standards, as befits an organized research unit at Brigham Young University. . . . We are going to assemble a group of scholars in the area of Mormon studies to consult with us on how best to position *Mormon Studies Review* within this area of study."

So what is "Mormon studies"? What is this field in which the new *Mormon Studies Review*, when and if it reappears after a suitably long period of detoxification, is going to better position itself?

"The term *Mormon studies* means different things to different people," M. Gerald Bradford, the current director of the Maxwell Institute, wrote in an article published by the *FARMS Review* in 2007. "For some . . . it is synonymous with Mormon historical studies. . . . I use the term to refer to a range of efforts likely to contribute directly to work on the tradition in various religious studies programs."[9]

Mormon studies, it seems, is a subset of the broader field of "religious studies." But what is this field of "religious studies"?

On the whole, it's quite different from the way in which Brigham Young University has historically approached Mormonism. "In the wider academic world," writes Dr. Bradford,

> within religion programs in private, nonaffiliated, and public colleges and universities, such study is conducted in a diverse intellectual environment. At BYU the subject is approached from a perspective of institutional and individual commitment. While BYU does offer a few courses on other religions, it does not maintain a religious studies program. It is devoted, in other words, to teaching students the "language of faith" more than the "language about faith."[10]

"It proceeds," he says of religious studies, "on the basis of maintaining a distinction between descriptive and structural studies on the one hand and attempts at grappling with religious value judgments and truth claims on the other."[11] It constitutes "an important and influential alternative to theological approaches that have been, and continue to be, the way religion is most often studied and taught in this country."[12] In religious studies, says Dr. Bradford, "before attempting to resolve questions of truth or value, the goal should be to show the influence and power of these ideas and practices in the real world and to discern how they interact with other aspects of human

---

9. M. Gerald Bradford, "The Study of Mormonism: A Growing Interest in Academia," 120, n. 2.

10. Bradford, "Study of Mormonism," 125–26.

11. Bradford, "The Study of Mormonism," 127–28.

12. Bradford, "The Study of Mormonism," 129.

existence."[13] Thus, there should be no surprise that, in Dr. Bradford's lengthy *FARMS Review* article entitled "The Study of Mormonism: A Growing Interest in Academia," strikingly little attention—indeed, almost none—is given to apologetics.[14]

"Fundamentally," observes my friend and colleague William Hamblin, who has published extensively on Islam, ancient holy warfare, and Solomon's temple in myth and history,

> religious studies examines religion as a human phenomenon, with the (often unspoken) assumption that religious belief and practice is entirely explainable without positing the existence of God or his intervention in human history and life. This is a self-imposed limitation on the discipline, in which it is mimicking . . . the empiricism and materialism of the natural sciences. This assumption makes some sense in some ways, since religion is indeed an integral part of of all human societies and cultures, and can be studied by examining its human context and its impact on human cultures, societies, and individuals.[15]

A couple of almost randomly chosen religious studies programs should serve to illustrate the orientation of the field:

The website of the religious studies program at Utah Valley University, in Orem, explains that

> The program is intended to serve our students and community by deepening our understanding of religious beliefs and practices in a spirit of open inquiry. Its aim is neither to endorse nor to undermine the claims of religion, but to create an environment in

---

13. Bradford, "The Study of Mormonism," 131.

14. M. Gerald Bradford, "The Study of Mormonism," 119–74.

15. http://mormonscriptureexplorations.files.wordpress.com/2012/07/mormon-studies1.pdf

which various issues can be engaged from a variety of perspectives and methodologies.[16]

A corresponding entry for the religious studies program at the University of North Carolina at Chapel Hill informs students that

> Writing for religious studies takes place within a secular, academic environment, rather than a faith-oriented community. For this reason, the goal of any paper in religious studies should not be to demonstrate or refute provocative religious concepts, such as the existence of God, the idea of reincarnation, or the possibility of burning in hell. By nature, such issues are supernatural and/or metaphysical and thus not open to rational inquiry.[17]

In this light, notice how the 2012 Mission Statement of the Maxwell Institute reads, and contrast it with the one I quoted above from 2010:

> By furthering religious scholarship through the study of scripture and other texts, Brigham Young University's Neal A. Maxwell Institute for Religious Scholarship seeks to deepen understanding and nurture discipleship among Latter-day Saints while promoting mutual respect and goodwill among people of all faiths."

"Understanding" will be "deepened" through "the study of scripture and other texts"—some of these other texts being those of the Middle Eastern Texts Initiative, which I conceived and founded and which deals with such materials as the *Physics* of Ibn Sina, Moses Maimonides' *Medical Aphorisms*, and *The Incoherence of the Philosophers* by al-Ghazali. "Scholarship"

---

16. http://www.uvu.edu/religiousstudies/aboutprogram/mission.html.

17. http://www.unc.edu/wcweb/handouts/religious_studies.html

will also, the Statement indicates, "nurture discipleship among Latter-day Saints."

Gone is the language about "defend[ing] the Restoration" and "provid[ing] an anchor of faith in a sea of LDS Studies." The focus, now, is on "how best to position *Mormon Studies Review* [and, presumably, the Maxwell Institute as a whole] within this area of study."

It's been explained to me and a few others that, in fact, the Maxwell Institute will continue to do apologetics, in the sense that solid scholarship will create a favorable impression in the minds of the scholars who read it. But this seems to stretch the meaning of the term *apologetics* well beyond customary bounds. Fielding a successful football team and hiring an effective grounds crew to keep the flowers blooming on BYU's campus also tend to make favorable impressions upon outsiders, and I support them, but they don't seem in any real sense "apologetic."

One enthusiastic proponent of Mormon studies has pointed out what should be obvious, given the general nature of the broader field of religious studies, that "those engaged in Mormon studies do not necessarily have to be Mormon themselves."[18]

Let me say right away that I believe there is a place for such studies. I, myself, in my writing on Islam, work from within a similar methodology. And I don't object to such approaches when the topic is Mormonism. That's why I'm currently serving as president of the Society for Mormon Philosophy and Theology, which actively involves non-Mormon and—how can I say this without given offense where none is intended?—non-communicant Mormon scholars as well as believing Mormon scholars in its conferences and its journal and on its board.

---

18. Ericson, "Where is the 'Mormon' in Mormon Studies?" 6.

In fact, during the last conversation that I had with the director of the Maxwell Institute before I left for six weeks overseas—I was dismissed by email roughly a week into my trip, while in Jerusalem—I was informed of the new course to which the Maxwell Institute is now committed. To illustrate what the "new course" might look like, three volumes recently published by a new Mormon-oriented venture called Salt Press were offered to me as prime examples of the kind of writing that the Institute *ought* to be sponsoring. As it happens, I *agree* that that's the kind of thing we should have been sponsoring. In fact, I serve on Salt Press's Editorial Board.

I see no reason why both apologetics and Mormon studies shouldn't be encouraged, nor even why they can't both be pursued by the same organization, published in the same journal, cultivated by the same scholar. There is, I believe, a place for both.

I see apologetics as a form, a subgenre, of Mormon studies. If I didn't, I would never have permitted the renaming of the *FARMS Review* as the *Mormon Studies Review*, because that name change would have represented a fundamental change of mission for the journal—as, in fact, I'm now informed that it *did*.

I'm for inclusion, rather than exclusion. But there can be no question that Mormon studies, as it's conceived in secular academic programs, is quite distinct from apologetics or "defense of the faith." And, unlike me, some see the two approaches as utterly incompatible, one being academically legitimate and the other not—just as the kind of religious education practiced at BYU would be disdained at many colleges and universities.

A few observers, commenting on the recent shake-up at the Maxwell Institute, have claimed that it represents a generational change: A newer, perhaps better trained, certainly kinder and gentler cohort of scholars is arriving on the scene that is embarrassed if not disgusted by the things their predecessors have done, and that is eager to replace sordid polemics and distasteful pseudo-scholarship with solid, dispassionate Mormon studies. Time will tell whether this change of generations will really bring the predicted transformation. But it's demonstrably untrue that academic discomfort with apologetics is a novelty, without precedent. Hugh Nibley, widely venerated now, was reviled and resented by some of his fellow Latter-day Saint academics not so very long ago.

Richard Lloyd Anderson, one of our most distinguished Latter-day Saint scholars and the premier authority on the Witnesses to the Book of Mormon, told me many years ago of being labeled early in his career by fellow Mormons as an apologist rather than a real scholar. "Today," he has told me in a private email

> Latter-day Saint scholars are rescuing "apologist" from the trash bin, but it probably will continue as a standard sneer in uninformed circles. I would rather not be so described, but I am convinced intellectually and spiritually that Joseph Smith was authorized by angels to restore Christ's Original Church. Rather than feel insulted by a misused label, I keep paradoxical satisfaction that the ancient and millennial gospel of light has caused me to be exiled to intellectual outer darkness. Yet the Lord promised his ancient Twelve: "Whosoever therefore shall confess me before men, him will I confess also before my Father which is in heaven" (Matt. 10:32).
>
> This conflict will not soon end. But I still will hope for more accurate descriptions. My thesaurus lists "advocate" as a synonym for "apologist." These terms have few differences in objective meaning, but the connotative distinction for me is very meaningful.[19]

---

19. Richard Lloyd Anderson, personal communication (31 July 2012), in the possession of the author.

I'm not sure, unfortunately, that Latter-day Saint scholars have rescued the term *apologist* from the trash bin, as Professor Anderson says. I haven't given up hope, but I'm not sure that we'll be *able* to do it.

In an article entitled "Where is the 'Mormon' in Mormon Studies?" that appeared in the 2011 inaugural issue of the *Claremont Journal of Mormon Studies*, Loyd Ericson, a proponent of Mormon studies who has been vocally overjoyed at recent changes—both of direction and of personnel—at the Maxwell Institute, suggested that some people might need to be excluded from the field of Mormon studies. We're "force[d] . . . to ask the questions," he wrote, "of who should be allowed to participate, how should be it be done, and what should be the objects of these studies. Should boundaries of exclusion be drawn? Or should all—including the evangelizing, the apologists, the revisionists, and the anti-Mormons—be allowed to mingle in the broadest field of Mormon Studies?"[20]

Of "the Mormon apologists"—who, he wrote under quite different circumstances back in 2011, are "easily best represented by Daniel Peterson and his colleagues in the Maxwell Institute at Brigham Young University"—Ericson cautions that "While they may at least seem to work within academic standards, there still exists an uneasiness among many about including them into Mormon Studies because of the belief of many academics that Mormon and/or religious studies is a forum for studying, and not promoting or defending, religious beliefs."[21]

Ericson allowed, hypothetically, that there might be a "uniquely Mormon methodology" that one could employ in Mormon studies. "This methodology," he says,

---

20. Ericson, "Where is the 'Mormon' in Mormon Studies?" 13.
21. Ericson, "Where is the 'Mormon' in Mormon Studies?" 6.

would include a faith or religiously based testimonial as part of one's argument or discussion. Examples of this might include appealing to one's own spiritual confirmation of the historical reality of Joseph Smith's First Vision when discussing the beginnings of Mormonism, basing an understanding of the context of the Book of Mormon off of one's belief in its ancient origins, or the claim that the growth of the LDS Church is due to the Holy Spirit influencing others to convert to God's true church.[22]

His statement is fascinating. Notice how it equates "appealing to one's own spiritual confirmation of the historical reality of Joseph Smith's First Vision when discussing the beginnings of Mormonism" and "claim[ing] that the growth of the LDS Church is due to the Holy Spirit" with "basing an understanding of the context of the Book of Mormon off of one's belief in its ancient origins." All of these are subsumed under the notion of "includ[ing] a faith or religiously based testimonial as part of one's argument or discussion."

One's personal spiritual experiences would never constitute appropriate or acceptable evidence in an academic argument, however appropriate they surely are in church, and FARMS and Maxwell Institute authors have never appealed to them in that way. Nor would it be suitable to claim, in a purely secular academic argument, that the Holy Spirit is the cause of any religious trend or event. Methodological naturalism reigns supreme in the general academic world, and for good reason.

But an important element in the FARMS and Maxwell Institute approach, certainly a facet of the approach taken by many authors, has been to presume the antiquity of the Book of Mormon, the Book of Abraham, and the like, or at least to

---

22. Ericson, "Where is the 'Mormon' in Mormon Studies?" 10.

consider ancient settings. We wanted to see what can be learned about the texts on that basis, to get an idea of how productive such a viewpoint is. Moreover, Hugh Nibley, the patron saint of FARMS, argued at length in such essays as "New Approaches to Book of Mormon Study," which first appeared in 1953 and was then incorporated into his Collected Works via the 1989 anthology *The Prophetic Book of Mormon*, that the proper way to examine the provenance of a disputed text is, first, to assume that it's genuine. He quotes the eminent German scholar Friedrich Blass: "We have the document, and the name of its author; we must begin our examination by assuming that the author indicated really wrote it."[23]

In an online exchange with me back in 2010, Loyd Ericson argued that any apologetic effort attempting to defend the antiquity of the Book of Mormon, the Book of Moses, and the Book of Abraham inescapably makes faulty assumptions about the verifiability of those texts. Why? Because the versions of these scriptures that we have today are in English and date from the nineteenth century, and because we do not possess (and, hence, cannot examine) the putative original-language texts from which they are claimed to have been translated. Accordingly, he said, they cannot plausibly be read, used, tested, or analyzed as ancient historical documents. They can only be read as documents of the nineteenth century, as illustrations of, and in the light of, that period. This, he claimed, is an insurmountable problem.

But, as I argued in an essay published in the late *FARMS Review* in 2010, it isn't. Scholars routinely test the claims to historicity of translated documents for which no original-language manuscripts are extant and, also routinely, having

---

23. Hugh Nibley, *The Prophetic Book of Mormon* (Salt Lake City: Deseret Book and FARMS, 1989), 55.

satisfied themselves of their authenticity, use them as valuable scholarly resources for understanding the ancient world.[24]

A few members of the Church appear to reject apologetics in principle, regarding it as inevitably, no matter how charitably and competently it is done, more detrimental than beneficial. They seem to do so on the basis of something resembling fideism, the view that faith is independent of reason, and even that reason and faith are incompatible with each other. "The words *reasoning* and *evidence* trouble me," one active Church member said to me during an Internet discussion. They seem, he said,

> to imply that things like Hebraisms and the NHM inscription will validate my commitment to Mormonism. This is absolutely and patently untrue and false. Reasoning and so-called evidences are illusions, in a world that requires faith. There is no rationale for angels, gold plates, and a corporeal Divine visit(s). There is no rationale for a resurrection, atonement, or exaltation. These things defy reason and logic. There is no possible evidence for these things either. My faith, my redemption, my happiness/peace are the reasons and evidence for my devotion.

Now, obviously, to treat God solely as a hypothesis, a conjecture, or a topic for discussion is very different from reverencing or submitting to God in a spirit of religious devotion. There are few if any for whom reason is sufficient without faith. Ideally, from the believer's perspective, God comes to be known in a personal I-Thou relationship, as an experienced challenge and as a comfort in times of sorrow, not merely as a chance to show off in a graduate seminar or, worse, to grandstand on an Internet message board. And many of those who know God in that way—certainly this must be true of simple, unlettered

---

24. See Daniel C. Peterson, "Editor's Introduction: An Unapologetic Apology for Apologetics," *FARMS Review* 22/2 (2010): xii–xv.

believers across Christendom and throughout its history—may neither need nor desire any further evidence. Moreover, most would agree—I certainly would—that it is impossible, using empirical methods, to prove the divine. And it is surely true that faith is best nurtured and sustained, not by immersion in clever arguments, but by the method outlined in Alma 32. Emulation of the Savior, loving service, faithful home and visiting teaching, generous fast offerings, earnest missionary work, prayerful communication—these are the fundamentally significant elements of a Christian life. There are relatively few people for whom apologetics is a necessary, let alone a sufficient, path to faith.

For the vast majority of people, today as in premodern times, faith isn't a matter of reason or argumentation, but of hearing the testimonies of others and of coming to conviction on the basis of personal experiences. Each Fast Sunday, Latter-day Saints are privileged to hear often beautiful testimonies that offer neither syllogisms nor objective data. Missionaries quickly discover that it is testimony that changes hearts, not chains of scriptural references, let alone a weighty volume of apologetics.

But that is not to admit that evidence and logic are wholly irrelevant to religious questions. Apologetics is no mere luxury or game. Someone who has been confused and bewildered by the sophistry of antagonists—and often, though not always, that is exactly what it is—might well justly regard apologetic arguments as a vital lifeline permitting the exercise of faith, as a way (in the words of one message board poster) of "keeping a spark going long enough to rekindle a fire." Testimony can see a person through times when the evidence seems against belief, but studied conviction can help a believer through spiritual dry spells, when God seems distant and spiritual experiences are distant memories. Even faithful members who are untouched by crisis or serious doubt can be benefited by solid apologetic arguments, motivated to stand fast, to keep doing the more fundamental things that will build faith and deepen confidence and strengthen their all-important spiritual witness. Why should such members be deprived of this blessing?

"I am well aware," says the Oxford philosophical theologian Brian Hebblethwaite in the very first paragraph of his 2005 book *In Defense of Christianity*,

> that reason is not the basis of faith. Christian faith is not founded on arguments. Most believers have either grown up and been nurtured in what have been called "convictional communities" and have simply found that religious faith and participation in religious life make sense to them, or else have been precipitated into religious commitment and practice by some powerful conversion experience. Few people are actually reasoned into faith. The arguments which I intend to sketch here are more like buttresses than foundations, reasons that can be given, as I say, in support of faith.[25]

I like that image of foundation and buttresses.

Furthermore, in my judgment, that active Church member is simply wrong. There is, in fact, a rational case to be made for such propositions as the actual existence of the gold plates of the Book of Mormon and the resurrection of Christ.[26]

---

25. Brian Hebblethwaite, *In Defense of Christianity* (Oxford: Oxford University Press, 2005), 1.

26. On the corroborating witnesses to the gold plates, Richard Lloyd Anderson has long been the preeminent authority. See, for example, his classic *Investigating the Book of Mormon Witnesses* (Salt Lake City: Deseret Book, 1981) and a number of his other substantial studies; also *David Whitmer Interviews: A Restoration Witness*, ed. Lyndon W. Cook (Orem, UT: Grandin, 1991), and John W. Welch and Larry E. Morris, eds., *Oliver Cowdery: Scribe, Elder, Witness* (Provo, UT: Maxwell Institute, 2006). As an example of writing about the plates themselves, see Kirk B. Henrichsen, "How Witnesses Described the 'Gold Plates,'" *Journal of Book of Mormon Studies* 10/1 (2001): 16–21. There

Will apologetic arguments save everybody? No. The Savior himself aside, *nothing* will—and, in fact, at least a few determined souls will apparently forgo salvation despite even his gracious atonement. But the fact that some remain unmoved by them no more discredits apologetic arguments as a whole than the enterprise of medicine is rendered worthless by the fact that some patients don't recover. Certain illnesses are fatal.

The children of God have different temperaments, expectations, capacities, personal histories, interests, and paths, and we dare not, or so it seems to me, close a door on someone's journey that, though perhaps unnecessary to us, might be invaluable for that person. The fact that I can swim scarcely justifies my standing on the shore watching while someone else drowns because she can't. As C. S. Lewis put it, speaking of and to well-educated British Christians,

> To be ignorant and simple now—not to be able to meet the enemies on their own ground—would be to throw down our weapons, and to betray our uneducated brethren who have, under God, no defence but us against the intellectual attacks of the heathen. Good philosophy must exist, if for no other reason, because bad philosophy needs to be answered.[27]

If the ground is encumbered with a lush overgrowth of critical arguments, the seed of faith of which Alma speaks cannot take root. It's the duty of the apologist, in that sense,

---

are numerous articles on ancient parallels to the Book of Mormon plates, among them William J. Hamblin, "Sacred Writing on Metal Plates in the Ancient Mediterranean," *FARMS Review* 19/1 (2007): 37–54. For Christ's resurrection, see any number of publications by such authors as Gary Habermas and William Lane Craig, as well as Stephen T. Davis, *Risen Indeed: Making Sense of the Resurrection* (Grand Rapids, MI: Eerdmans, 1993), and N. T. Wright, *The Resurrection of the Son of God* (Minneapolis: Fortress, 2003).

27. C. S. Lewis, "Learning in War-Time," in *The Weight of Glory and Other Addresses* (New York: HarperCollins, 2001), 58.

to clear the ground in order to make it possible for the seed to grow. Faith is still necessary. (I'm unaware of anybody who claims that religious belief derives purely from reason; for that matter, I'm confident that unbelief doesn't, either.) Apologetics is simply a useful tool that, much as Austin Farrer wrote, helps to preserve an environment that permits such faith to take root and flourish.

"Be ready," says the First Epistle of Peter, "always to give an answer to every man that asketh you a reason of the hope that is in you with meekness and fear" (1 Peter 3:15). That's the King James Version rendering of the passage. "Always be prepared," reads the *New International Version*, "to give an answer to everyone who asks you to give the reason for the hope that you have. But do this with gentleness and respect." The Greek word rendered "answer" in both translations is *apologia*, which is manifestly cognate with the English word *apologetics*.

A skeptic of apologetics might, of course, respond that the author of 1 Peter is telling Christians to be willing to testify of Christ and their hope for salvation, something quite distinct from a call to use reason to defend a particular religious claim. And, obviously, the biblical apostles would indeed want us to stand as witnesses for Christ. But does 1 Peter 3:15 exclude the use of rational argument in such testifying?

It seems highly unlikely. The word that is translated as "reason" by both the King James Version and the New International Version, cited above, is the Greek λογος, or *logos*. It is an extraordinarily rich term, and much has been written about its meaning.[28] *Logos* can refer to speech, a word, a computation or reckoning, the settlement of an account, or the independent personified "Word" of God (as in most translations of John 1:1). A central meaning, however, is "reason," and it is from *logos*

---

28. Not least of which is Faust's meditation on John 1, which, he finally decides, should be rendered "In the beginning was the Deed" (*Im Anfang war die Tat*). See Johann Wolfgang von Goethe, *Faust*, act 1, scene 3, lines 1210–37.

that the English word *logic* derives—as do the names of any number of fields devoted to systematic, rational inquiry (e.g., *anthropology, archaeology, biology, cosmology, criminology, Egyptology, geology, meteorology, ontology, paleontology, theology,* and *zoology*). It is rendered in the Latin Vulgate Bible's version of 1 Peter 3:15 as *ratio* ("reason," "judgment"), which is obviously related to our English word *rational*. Furthermore, when Paul spoke before King Agrippa at Caesarea Maritima— arguing that, among other things, Christ's resurrection fulfilled the predictions of Moses and the other prophets—he was making his "defense," and he used a Greek verb closely and directly related to *apologia*: *apologeisthai*. The *Apology* of Plato, similarly, reports the speech that Socrates offered before his Athenian accusers.

It seems that 1 Peter's exhortation to "be ready always to give an answer to every man that asketh you a reason of the hope that is in you" charters and legitimates the use of reasoned argument in support of the gospel of Jesus Christ. Frankly, the idea that active Latter-day Saints might (or even should) feel no obligation to use what they know in order to defend the church against its critics, or to help struggling Saints, strikes me as exceedingly strange. Our responsibility as members of The Church of Jesus Christ of Latter-day Saints to love and serve the Lord with all our heart, might, *mind*, and strength implies such an obligation, and our temple covenants absolutely *entail* that we sustain and defend the kingdom of God.[29]

In a sense, the scholar, thinker, teacher, or writer who places his or her skills on the altar as an offering to God is no different from the bricklayer, knitter, carpenter, counselor, administrator, dentist, accountant, youth leader, farmer, physician, linguist, genealogist, or nurse who donates time and labor and

---

29. See Doctrine and Covenants 4:1–4, and note the clear missionary context of the passage. Compare Mark 12:28–31, which draws on Deuteronomy 6:4–9 and Leviticus 19:18.

specific abilities in the service of God and the Saints and humanity in general.

> Now the body is not made up of one part but of many. If the foot should say, "Because I am not a hand, I do not belong to the body," it would not for that reason cease to be part of the body. And if the ear should say, "Because I am not an eye, I do not belong to the body," it would not for that reason cease to be part of the body. If the whole body were an eye, where would the sense of hearing be? If the whole body were an ear, where would the sense of smell be? But in fact God has arranged the parts in the body, every one of them, just as he wanted them to be. If they were all one part, where would the body be? As it is, there are many parts, but one body. The eye cannot say to the hand, "I don't need you!" And the head cannot say to the feet, "I don't need you!" (1 Corinthians 12:14–21, NIV)

As C. S. Lewis put it, "All our merely natural activities will be accepted, if they are offered to God, even the humblest, and all of them, even the noblest, will be sinful if they are not."[30]

Now, one might conceivably argue that while, as a Christian, one is under a divine mandate to bear witness, one is not obliged to use reason to defend specific truth claims, or that, whatever covenants they may have taken upon themselves, Latter-day Saints are not obligated to defend their specific church by the use of such rational arguments as they can muster.

The scriptures, however, seem to teach otherwise. Jesus himself, for example, appealed to miracles and to fulfilled prophecy as evidence that his claims were true. To his disciples, he said, "Believe me that I am in the Father, and the Father in me: or else believe me for the very works' sake" (John 14:11). To

---

30. Lewis, "Learning in War-Time," 54.

the two Christian disciples walking along the road to Emmaus immediately after his resurrection, he said: "O fools, and slow of heart to believe all that the prophets have spoken: Ought not Christ to have suffered these things, and to enter into his glory? And beginning at Moses and all the prophets, he expounded unto them in all the scriptures the things concerning himself" (Luke 24:25–27).

Speaking to other Jews, the original Christian apostles likewise employed fulfilled prophecy and the miracles of Jesus—particularly his resurrection—to demonstrate that Jesus was the Messiah. Consider, for example, how, in his sermon on the day of Pentecost, Peter appeals to all three:

> Men of Israel, listen to this: Jesus of Nazareth was a man accredited by God to you by miracles, wonders and signs, which God did among you through him, as you yourselves know. This man was handed over to you by God's set purpose and foreknowledge; and you, with the help of wicked men, put him to death by nailing him to the cross. But God raised him from the dead, freeing him from the agony of death, because it was impossible for death to keep its hold on him. David said about him:

> I saw the Lord always before me.
> Because he is at my right hand,
> I will not be shaken.
> Therefore my heart is glad and my tongue rejoices;
> my body also will live in hope,
> because you will not abandon me to the grave,
> nor will you let your Holy One see decay.
> You have made known to me the paths of life;
> you will fill me with joy in your presence.

Brothers, I can tell you confidently that the patriarch David died and was buried, and his tomb is here to this day. But he was a prophet and knew that God had promised him on oath that he would place one of his descendants on his throne. Seeing what was ahead, he spoke of the resurrection of the Christ, that he was not abandoned to the grave, nor did his body see decay. God has raised this Jesus to life, and we are all witnesses of the fact. (Acts 2:22–32, NIV)

In dealing with non-Jews, the apostles attempted to demonstrate the existence of God by appealing to evidence of it in nature. Thus, for instance, in Acts 14, when the pagans at Lystra were so impressed by the miracles of Barnabas and Paul that they mistook them for, respectively, Zeus and Hermes, the two apostles were horrified.

They rent their clothes, and ran in among the people, crying out, and saying, Sirs, why do ye these things? We also are men of like passions with you, and preach unto you that ye should turn from these vanities unto the living God, which made heaven, and earth, and the sea, and all things that are therein: who in times past suffered all nations to walk in their own ways. Nevertheless he left not himself without witness, in that he did good, and gave us rain from heaven, and fruitful seasons, filling our hearts with food and gladness. (Acts 14:14–17)

Addressing the saints at Rome, Paul declared that

the wrath of God is being revealed from heaven against all the godlessness and wickedness of men who suppress the truth by their wickedness, since what may be known about God is plain to them, because God has made it plain to them. For since the creation of the world God's invisible qualities—his eternal power and divine nature—have been clearly seen, being understood from what has been made, so that men are without excuse. (Romans 1:18–20, NIV)

Such appeals to the evidence of nature are also found in the Old Testament: "The heavens declare the glory of God," says the Psalmist; "the skies proclaim the work of his hands" (Psalm 19:1, NIV). Historical evidence also plays a role. Addressing the Saints at Corinth, the apostle Paul ticks off a list of witnesses to the resurrection of Jesus as evidence for the truth of what they have been taught:

For what I received I passed on to you as of first importance: that Christ died for our sins according to the Scriptures, that he was buried, that he was raised on the third day according to the Scriptures, and that he appeared to Peter, and then to the Twelve. After that, he appeared to more than five hundred of the brothers at the same time, most of whom are still living, though some have fallen asleep. Then he appeared to James, then to all the apostles, and last of all he appeared to me also. (1 Corinthians 15:3–8, NIV)

During his stay in Athens, Paul "reasoned in the synagogue with the Jews and the God-fearing Greeks, as well as in the marketplace day by day with those who happened to be there" (Acts 17:17, NIV.) And, most notably, he presented a logical case to some of the city's Epicurean and Stoic philosophers on Mars Hill, near the Acropolis, even citing proof texts from pagan Greek poets in support of his doctrine (Acts 17:18–34)

It's clear that both Jesus and the apostles were perfectly willing to supply evidence and to make arguments for the truth of the message they preached. Did this mean that they didn't trust the Holy Ghost to bring about conversion? Hardly.

Instead, they trusted that the Holy Ghost would work through their arguments and their evidence to convert those whose hearts were open to the Spirit.

Moreover, according to the Book of Mormon, a similar mixture of preaching, testifying, and appealing to reason was employed by the inspired leaders of the pre-Columbian New World. Consider the case of the antichrist called Korihor:

> And he did rise up in great swelling words before Alma, and did revile against the priests and teachers, accusing them of leading away the people after the silly traditions of their fathers, for the sake of glutting on the labors of the people. Now Alma said unto him: Thou knowest that we do not glut ourselves upon the labors of this people; for behold I have labored even from the commencement of the reign of the judges until now, with mine own hands for my support, notwithstanding my many travels round about the land to declare the word of God unto my people. And notwithstanding the many labors which I have performed in the church, I have never received so much as even one senine for my labor; neither has any of my brethren, save it were in the judgment-seat; and then we have received only according to law for our time. And now, if we do not receive anything for our labors in the church, what doth it profit us to labor in the church save it were to declare the truth, that we may have rejoicings in the joy of our brethren? Then why sayest thou that we preach unto this people to get gain, when thou, of thyself, knowest that we receive no gain? (Alma 30:31–35)

Alma even appeals to a simple kind of natural theology to make his point:

And then Alma said unto him: Believest thou that there is a God? And he answered, Nay. Now Alma said unto him: Will ye deny again that there is a God, and also deny the Christ? For behold, I say unto you, I know there is a God, and also that Christ shall come. And now what evidence have ye that there is no God, or that Christ cometh not? I say unto you that ye have none, save it be your word only. But, behold, I have all things as a testimony that these things are true; and ye also have all things as a testimony unto you that they are true; and will ye deny them? Believest thou that these things are true? Behold, I know that thou believest, but thou art possessed with a lying spirit, and ye have put off the Spirit of God that it may have no place in you; but the devil has power over you, and he doth carry you about, working devices that he may destroy the children of God. And now Korihor said unto Alma: If thou wilt show me a sign, that I may be convinced that there is a God, yea, show unto me that he hath power, and then will I be convinced of the truth of thy words. But Alma said unto him: Thou hast had signs enough; will ye tempt your God? Will ye say, Show unto me a sign, when ye have the testimony of all these thy brethren, and also all the holy prophets? The scriptures are laid before thee, yea, and all things denote there is a God; yea, even the earth, and all things that are upon the face of it, yea, and its motion, yea, and also all the planets which move in their regular form do witness that there is a Supreme Creator. And yet do ye go about, leading away the hearts of this people, testifying unto them there is no God? And yet will ye deny against all these witnesses? And he said: Yea, I will deny, except ye shall show me a sign. And now it came to pass that Alma said unto him: Behold, I am grieved because of

the hardness of your heart, yea, that ye will still resist
the spirit of the truth, that thy soul may be destroyed.
(Alma 30:37–46)

And the same mixture of preaching, testimony, and reasoning has been enjoined upon members of the Church of Jesus
Christ of Latter-day Saints in this modern dispensation as well.
"Behold," the Lord told William E. McLellin in a revelation
given through the Prophet Joseph Smith on 25 October 1831,
at Orange, Ohio,

> verily I say unto you, that it is my will that you should
> proclaim my gospel from land to land, and from city
> to city, yea, in those regions round about where it has
> not been proclaimed. . . . Go unto the eastern lands,
> bear testimony in every place, unto every people and in
> their synagogues, reasoning with the people. (Doctrine
> and Covenants 66:5, 7)

McLellin was to proclaim the gospel, yes, and to bear testimony, but he was also to reason with his audience—which
sounds very much like a description of a type of apologetic argumentation. Indeed, it is difficult to conceive of a method of
testifying that in no way includes the faculty of reason. Even
to say something as simple as "I have felt divine love, so I'm
confident that there is a God who loves me" represents an el-
ementary form of logical argument. Likewise, according to a
revelation given at Hiram, Ohio, in November 1831, "My ser-
vant, Orson Hyde, was called by his ordination to proclaim the
everlasting gospel, by the Spirit of the living God, from people
to people, and from land to land, in the congregations of the
wicked, in their synagogues, reasoning with and expounding
all scriptures unto them" (Doctrine and Covenants 68:1).

Leman Copley, too, called along with Sidney Rigdon and
Parley P. Pratt on a mission to his former associates among the

Shakers by a revelation given at Kirtland, Ohio, in March 1831, was told to "reason with them, not according to that which he has received of them, but according to that which shall be taught him by you my servants; and by so doing I will bless him, otherwise he shall not prosper" (Doctrine and Covenants 49:4).

On 1 December 1831, in the wake of a series of newspaper articles written by an apostate named Ezra Booth, the Lord told the members of His little church:

> Wherefore, confound your enemies; call upon them to meet you both in public and in private; and inasmuch as ye are faithful their shame shall be made manifest. Wherefore, let them bring forth their strong reasons against the Lord. Verily, thus saith the Lord unto you— there is no weapon that is formed against you shall prosper; and if any man lift his voice against you he shall be confounded in mine own due time. (Doctrine and Covenants 71:7–10)[31]

Not surprisingly, the Church's contemporary missionary program, too, encourages and trains its representatives to give reasons, as the missionaries have always been expected to do. *Preach My Gospel*, the contemporary guide to missionary service, lists scriptural passages by the scores at appropriate places in its lessons for investigators.[14] Missionaries are plainly intended to use these to reason with those they are teaching, to explain the claims of the Restoration and to support and ground them in revealed scripture.

This is what we humans normally do in conversation. When someone asks why we're voting for Barack Obama or supporting Mitt Romney, or why we think the Dodgers the

---

31. One could argue that even God himself does not appear to disdain the use of reason with his children. See, for example, such passages as Doctrine and Covenants 45:10, 15; 50:10–12; 133:57; Isaiah 1:18.

best team in baseball, we typically give reasons. Simply reply-
ing "Because!" seems, somehow, lacking.

Paul J. Griffiths, a trained scholar of Buddhist studies
whom I've quoted previously, published a book in 1991, entitled
An Apology for Apologetics, in which he "defend[s] the need for
the traditional discipline of apologetics as one important component of interreligious dialogue."[32] He does so against what he
calls a scholarly orthodoxy that "suggests that understanding
is the only legitimate goal; that judgement and criticism of religious beliefs or practices other than those of one's own community is always inappropriate; and that an active defense of the
truth of those beliefs and practices to which one's community
appears committed is always to be shunned."[33] In his strongly
expressed opinion, "such an orthodoxy (which tends to include
the view that the very idea of orthodoxy has no sense) produces
a discourse that is pallid, platitudinous, and degutted. Its prod-
ucts are intellectual pacifiers for the immature: pleasant to suck
on but not very nourishing."[34]

Professor Griffiths argues for what he calls the principle
of the "necessity of interreligious apologetics."[35] This is how he
formulates it:

> If representative intellectuals belonging to some spe-
> cific religious community come to judge at a particular
> time that some or all of their own doctrine-expressing
> sentences are incompatible with some alien religious
> claim(s), then they should feel obliged to engage in
> both positive and negative apologetics vis-à-vis these
> alien religious claim(s) and their promulgators.[36]

---

32. Griffiths, *An Apology*, xi.
33. Griffiths, *An Apology*, xi.
34. Griffiths, *An Apology*, xi-xii.
35. Griffiths, *An Apology*, 1.
36. Griffiths, *An Apology*, 3.

Professor Griffiths distinguishes negative apologetics from positive apologetics in precisely the same way that I have. As an example of negative apologetics, which he describes as a defense of a proposition or belief against criticism, he points out that a critic of Buddhism might argue that the two propositions *There are no enduring spiritual substances* and *Each human person is reborn multiple times* are mutually contradictory. In response, a negative Buddhist apologetic will seek to show that there is no contradiction between them.

Critics of Christianity often argue that the existence of massive natural evil in the world is incompatible with the existence of a benevolent God. A negative Christian apologetic will argue that the fact of natural evil actually can be reconciled with belief in a loving God.

In a Latter-day Saint context, negative apologetics will seek to rebut, to neutralize, claims such as *Oliver Cowdery denied his testimony* or *Joseph Smith's introduction of polygamy shows him to be a man of poor character* or *Mormonism is racist.* Attacks against the claims of the Restoration began even before the publication of the Book of Mormon and the organization of the Church, and Latter-day Saints have been responding to them for nearly two centuries now. Regardless of whether the responses are have been sophisticated or not, or are judged adequate or inadequate, they constitute negative apologetics.

Positive apologetics seek to demonstrate that a given religious or ideological community's practices or beliefs are good, believable, true, and/or, in some cases, superior to those of some other community. While negative apologetics is defensive, positive apologetics is offensive—by which, incidentally, despite my richly deserved reputation for vicious and unethical polemics, I don't mean to say that it necessarily gives offense.

Griffiths argues that religious communities have an epistemic or even ethical duty to engage in apologetics.[37] Why? Because, since religious groups typically claim that their teachings are true, they are obliged to respond when, as usually happens, somebody else claims that, in fact, their teachings are wholly or partially false. We should not be indifferent to the truth or falsity of what we claim, and all the more so when our claim involves matters of ultimate importance. This means that religious communities have a duty to engage in negative apologetics, to defend or justify their assertions.

Mainstream Buddhists, for example, who espouse what has been called the doctrine of "No Self," believe that the notion of a continuing substantial "soul," such as most Christians affirm, creates and perpetuates suffering. If challenged by Buddhist thinkers on the question, it is the duty of the Christian community to justify its affirmation or to withdraw it.[38]

In fact, knowing of the existence of competing doctrines that contradict its own teachings, representatives of a religious community might proceed to a positive apologetics, seeking to demonstrate that one or more of their claims are, in fact, very believable, or even, perhaps, superior to rival views. There is, in fact, arguably an ethical imperative to do so, because religions commonly hold that adherence to their doctrines is important, and maybe even essential, to salvation. Just as a person on the shore holding a life rope has an obligation to help a drowning man, so do those who have the saving doctrines or practices have an obligation to help those who might otherwise perish.

---

37. Then next few paragraphs depend essentially upon Griffiths, *An Apology*, 15–17.

38. The entire sixth chapter of Griffiths, *An Apology*, is devoted to laying out first a kind of model Buddhist position on this matter, followed by a model Christian position, and then, as a Christian believer, seeking to illustrate a way in which an apologetic encounter between representative Buddhist and Christian intellectuals might proceed. See Griffiths, *An Apology*," 85–108.

Griffiths also argues that apologetics can substantially benefit the faithful, because of what he describes as

> the tendency of members of religious communities not to think in any very self-conscious way about the implications of the views into which they have been acculturated. These views are part of their blood and bone, among the presuppositions of their existence as human beings.[39]

Religious communities are, he says, typically forced into more nuanced understandings of their own doctrines and practices "primarily by pressures from outside or by criticisms from dissident groups within." He cites as an example the creedal formulae generated by the ancient ecumenical councils of the Christian church.[40] A Latter-day Saint might cite the impetus given to Mormon historians by Fawn Brodie's assertion that the Joseph Smith's First Vision was a fiction invented relatively late in the Prophet's life. Several earlier accounts of the Vision were discovered as part of an effort to counter her claim. Apologetics, says Griffiths, who is a scholar of Buddhism, "is a learning tool of unparalleled power. It makes possible a level of understanding of one's own doctrine-expressing sentences and their logic, as well as those of others, which is not to be had in any other way."[41]

Moreover, Griffiths argues, a failure to take contradiction between competing truth claims seriously, a kind of "can't we all just get along" indifference to resolving disputes, will have very serious consequences. "The result," he says, "would be both relativism and fideism: religious communities would become closed, impermeable, incommensurable forms of life."[42]

With Paul Griffiths, I'm convinced that apologetics is an important part of scholarly discourse in religious studies, that

---

39. Griffiths, *An Apology*, 25–26.
40. Griffiths, *An Apology*, 26.
41. Griffiths, *An Apology*, 36.
42. Griffiths, *An Apology*, 42.

it should be considered a kind of religious studies, and, therefore, of *Mormon* studies.

Accordingly, I'm delighted to announce the launch of a new venture in Mormon studies, *Interpreter: A Journal of Mormon Scripture*—the product of a team that came together only a few days back, after my return from overseas less than two weeks ago. Its first article is now online.

It will not be purely an apologetic journal, but it won't exclude or disdain apologetics, either.

Published online, it will be available in various ways, including print on demand, and will represent something far more sophisticated, technologically speaking, than we have yet seen in the field of Mormon studies. Being primarily published online, it will also be free to post articles, reviews, and notes as they're ready to be made public. At a certain point, we'll close the issue and commence a new one.

This will, I think, be an exciting venue for faithful Latter-day Saint thought and scholarship, as well as for readers. It will require some stretching, perhaps, but we intend to keep firmly in mind not merely the scholarly elite but the Relief Society sister in Parowan and the ordinary Mormon in Ogden.

Daniel C. Peterson (PhD, University of California at Los Angeles) is a professor of Islamic studies and Arabic at Brigham Young University and is the founder and editor-in-chief of the University's Middle Eastern Texts Initiative. He has published and spoken extensively on both Islamic and Mormon subjects. Formerly chairman of the board of the Foundation for Ancient Research and Mormon Studies (FARMS) and an officer, editor, and author for its successor organization, the Neal A. Maxwell Institute for Religious Scholarship, his professional work as an Arabist focuses on the Qur'an and on Islamic philosophical theology. He is the author, among other things, of a biography entitled Muhammad: Prophet of God *(Eerdmans, 2007).*

ATTACKING RATHER THAN
EXPLAINING

Cassandra Hedelius

*Abstract: In his book on Mormonism, the Reverend Andrew
Jackson claims to explain "the teaching and practices of the
LDS Church," with an intended audience of non-Mormon
Christians but also "interested Mormons." He doesn't succeed
well. Although his presentation of Mormon history is mostly fair,
his discussion of the faith of Latter-day Saints devolves into the
usual anti-Mormon tropes, to which he adds a celebration of a
simplified evangelical theology. What might have been a useful,
straightforward account of The Church of Jesus Christ and its
history ended up, instead, as a clumsy attack. Reverend Jackson
eventually re-released his book under a different title as a warning against what he considers Mitt Romney's reticence to publicly
explain his faith to the Reverend's specifications. The later itera-
tion of Reverend Jackson's opinions was not even revised beyond
a new introduction, making plain his basic antagonistic agenda.*

Review of Andrew Jackson, What Latter-day Saints Teach and
Practice: Mormonism Explained, *Wheaton, IL: Crossway Books
[a publishing ministry of Good News Publishers], 2008. 208 pp.,
with four appendixes, name index, and scripture index. $29.64
(paperback).*

Although *Mormonism Explained* is not the typical sectarian countercult diatribe on the faith of Latter-day Saints,
the Reverend Andrew Jackson[1] has provided a vigorous attack

---

1. For Reverend Jackson's education, employment, and travel, see http://
drandrewjackson.com/about/resume. Subsequent comments on these matters

on the Church of Jesus Christ. Instead of relying, with a few exceptions,[2] on the dishonest and largely incompetent sectarian countercult criticisms, he builds his case on a somewhat more sophisticated literature. He indicates that "the primary non-Mormon books," grounding his explanation/attack on the Church of Jesus Christ, "were Dr. Craig Blomberg's writing in *How Wide the Divide? A Mormon & Evangelical in Conversation*, the book *The New Mormon Challenge: Responding to the Latest Defenses of a Fast-Growing Movement*, and Richard and Joan Ostling's well-researched book *Mormon America: The Power and the Promise*" (p. 14). However, he ignores all the detailed responses to these books that have appeared, even though he is aware of the Neal A. Maxwell Institute for Religious Scholarship at Brigham Young University (see p. 186). The results of Jackson's endeavor are rather disappointing. Part of his problem is that, as I will demonstrate, he lacks the qualifications and disposition to deal openly, honestly, and competently with what he calls "Mormonism."

Setting Out Credentials

Who is Reverend Jackson? And, in his own opinion, what led and qualifies him to opine on Mormon things? His webpage indicates that he has been an associate pastor of two large churches: he worked at Kempsville Presbyterian Church in Virginia Beach (1986–1996) and then, with a Doctor of Ministry degree,[3] at the Word of Grace Church in Mesa,

---

are taken from his website.

2. Reverend Jackson recommends Bill McKeever and Eric Johnson, *Mormonism 101* (Grand Rapids, MI: Baker Books, 2000), as well as their Mormonism Research Ministry (MSM) website (see pp. 188 and 186, respectively, in Jackson, *Mormonism Explained*). He also recommends the Institute for Religious Research (IRR), and Sandra (and the late Jerald) Tanner's Utah Lighthouse Ministry (ULM) websites (p. 186).

3. In 1984 Reverend Jackson was awarded a Master of Divinity degree from Fuller Theological Seminary, after which he began employment as an evangelical pastor. In 1996, he was granted a Doctor of Ministry degree by Gordon-Conwell Theological Seminary, whose main campus is located in South Hamilton,

Arizona (1996–2008). He has a master's degree and PhD from respected seminaries. He is well traveled, having visited twenty-four countries. His special fondness for Turkey, with its connections to the New Testament, inspired him to lead and later organize biblical tours to Turkey.

How, then, came Reverend Jackson to acquire an interest in and expertise on the Church of Jesus Christ? He knew we'd ask that:

> What are my qualifications to write a book on Mormonism? Many Latter-day Saints—although not all—will dismiss my book simply because I am not Mormon and have never been a Mormon. They seem to believe that only Mormons should have the privilege of writing about what the LDS teach and practice. For many Mormons, any "outsider" is seemingly suspect, if not outright labeled a deceiving enemy of their claimed restored gospel. Being called a religious bigot or Mormon-hater is not always the most pleasant experience. (p. 10)

Granted that he may have had some unpleasant experience with individual Mormons, it's quite a stretch to tar the whole of Mormonism with that same brush. If one is merely explaining Mormonism, why expect to be seen by Latter-day Saints as a bigot? He's on the attack already, implying that Latter-day Saints can't handle even a fair and neutral explanation. Latter-day Saints have no objections to competent, civil exchanges with both sectarian and secular scholars, as his own reading of *How Wide the Divide?* ought to have shown him.

Reverend Jackson "admits" he does "not fully understand this Mormon mind-set" (p. 10), which he wrongly believes

---

Massachusetts. The D-Min degree is intended to enhance the careers of working pastors. Because it is not an academic degree, there are often minimal residency requirements, nor is a dissertation required.

treats all examination of LDS faith as the work of bigots filled with hatred. He adds that Mormons' negative reaction to criticism "strongly smacks of an unhealthy martyr complex, a form of anti-intellectualism, and a fear of scholarly evaluation or critique, whether by Mormons, non-Mormons, or ex-Mormons" (p. 10). The well thus tidily poisoned, Jackson gets specific:

> Although I am not Mormon, I did not write this book in complete ignorance, in distant abstraction, or from a socially or theologically detached position. I have lived among and interacted with Mormons and Mormon culture for over a decade now as I serve as a pastor in a church in downtown Mesa, Arizona, which is one block down from the historic Arizona temple. As many of you know, the city of Mesa was pioneered and founded by the Mormons in January 1878. In fact, the large grassy park that separates our church campus and the Arizona temple is named "Pioneer Park," memorializing the early Mormon pioneers of Mesa. As a result of living in the East Valley of the Phoenix area, I have many Mormon neighbors, acquaintances, and friends. (p. 10)

Many use the "some of my best friends are ... " gambit, but most don't write authority-claiming books about their friends, or imbibe special insights from park names. Reverend Jackson's familiarity is not thorough enough to prevent him from calling one of the Three Witnesses "David Whittier" (p. 33), claiming that "no proxy temple marriages [sealings?] are performed for the dead" in LDS temples (p. 202 n. 28), or stating that the Kirtland Temple is owned by the "Restored Latter-day Saints" (p. 193 n. 55). These kinds of silly mistakes, obvious to any of his Mormon "neighbors, acquaintances, and friends," and also easily correctable had he actually engaged with Mormons, are invisible to most non-LDS readers. In addition, genuine friends don't claim to be *explaining* another's faith, when in fact they are making war against those beliefs.

Whom or What to Consult for the "Official" LDS Teachings?

Reverend Jackson complains about the difficulty in determining what exactly he ought to "research" on Mormonism, given that "average Mormons—*not unlike many Christians*—are simply not able to accurately and thoroughly provide a systematic explanation of their beliefs" (p. 11, emphasis added), LDS missionaries are also not trained in theology (p. 11), and LDS lay leaders are often not much more help (p. 11). He turned to email exchanges with volunteers at the Foundation for Apologetic Information and Research (FAIR) but was frustrated by their disclaimer of *official* status to speak for the Church of Jesus Christ (p. 12).

Despite this attention, Reverend Jackson is careless in keeping straight what is indeed official and what is mere speculation. Well aware that the only official source of LDS doctrine is the standard works and clarifications provided by the united First Presidency and Quorum of the Twelve (p. 79), he states that "absolutely no one else in Mormonism—no matter how significant or educated—has the right to officially speak on behalf of the LDS Church" (p. 79). Why then, while professing such concern to find Mormonism's official statements, did he rely so heavily (at least forty citations) on Elder Bruce R. McConkie's *Mormon Doctrine* (p. 12)? Why not instead refer mainly to the LDS scriptures? And why prioritize the perspectives of non-Mormons such as the Ostlings[4] and Craig Blomberg[5] over the nonofficial perspectives of knowledgeable Mormons? If one aims to explain, isn't the insider perspective of greater worth?

Instead of explaining Mormonism through its official sources, which would have been the most appropriate course,

---

4. The Ostlings are cited sixteen times.
5. Craig Blomberg is cited thirteen times.

and then supplementing with commentary from knowledgeable sources, labeled as such, when necessary, Reverend Jackson has turned this on its head. His citations to scripture are haphazard and unhelpful, sometimes referencing an entire chapter or section as support for a statement of his own (p. 28 n. 52), omitting a citation to scripture when one should have been specified (p. 190 n. 11) or mis-citing scripture entirely (p. 198 n. 39 and p. 195 n. 6). He resorts frequently to critical works by the Ostlings, Blomberg, and others, without that those sources have been shown to be problematic in their use of historical facts (Ostling) and presentation of LDS doctrine (both). In the end it seems his complaining about unofficial sources and anti-intellectual Mormons was a blind designed to inoculate himself against any charge that his book only explains what people say about Mormons, sometimes from a very hostile point of view.

In summary, Reverend Jackson is a cut above the latest regurgitation of the work of Walter Martin or the Tanners, but that's a low standard, as readers of the *FARMS Review* know.

The Audience for . . .

In his introduction to *Mormonism Explained*, Reverend Jackson states that he wrote the book "primarily for the broad Christian audience," but also for "interested non-Christians and Mormons" (p. 9). Why would Latter-day Saints need a Protestant pastor's help in understanding their own faith? He justifies:

> Many—if not most—Mormons were born into LDS families, live their daily lives inside the culture and world of Mormonism, and really do not think a lot about the intricacies and theological validity of LDS teaching and practices. They seem content and happy being Mormon, and exert little energy in thinking through and evaluating the details or truthfulness of their faith. (pp. 9–10)

Of course, this may be correct in many cases. But this line of argumentation could easily be applied to his own flock, since most evangelicals are not trained in theology, probably cannot articulate their faith in anything approaching a systematic way, and may not spend much time evaluating the truth of what they believe. Like many sectarian critics of The Church of Jesus Christ of Latter-day Saints, Jackson does not realize that it is wise to allow others to define their own faith.

. . . and the Protestant Pitch

Nothing in the introduction to *Mormonism Explained* in-dicates a real bias of intention one way or the other, except for the well-poisoning dismissal of "anti-intellectual" Mormon critics of non-Mormons who dare to write about the church. But just a few pages further on one notices slip-ups here and there, all in the same direction—easy to guess which. For ex-ample, Reverend Jackson uncritically repeats the Ostlings' (and hence Wesley Walters's) conclusion that Joseph Smith was "found guilty of disorderly conduct and treasure-hunting" (p. 25), a charge that has been shown to be false. Jackson is also confident that the Three Witnesses to the plates left the Church (p. 27), but he neglects to mention that two returned and that none of the three ever denied their testimonies of the truth of the Book of Mormon and the manner of its coming forth. He also implies that Joseph Smith confessed to seriously "wayward teen years" (p. 21), leaving out the highly relevant instruction that we needn't suppose any sin greater than levity. Jackson cites the *Encyclopedia of Mormonism* to support his tenden-tious statement that Joseph Smith established the Council of Fifty because he "desired to establish God's political kingdom over non-Mormons in preparation for the second coming of Christ" (p. 48), though the essay he cites makes it clear that the Council did not, and did not intend to, "challenge existing systems of law and government (even in Nauvoo)."[6] Despite these lapses, Reverend Jackson's brief summary of LDS history in part 1 of his book (pp. 17–59) isn't terrible. It covers a lot of ground with broad strokes and is for the most part a straightforward account, especially when compared to the usual sectarian version of LDS history. But it soon becomes clear that he is not content to merely explain Mormonism—instead, he can't help but argue evangelicalism. In this, the book becomes just another banal sectarian exercise in boundary maintenance.

Apostasy?

In part 2, "What Mormonism Teaches and Why" (pp. 63–122), Jackson is emphatically on the attack against Latter-day Saints, as he is when he addresses in part 3 (pp. 125–72) what he calls "The Salvation of Mormonism" (which is his awkward way of referring to how the Saints understand redemption from death and sin). In these portions of his book, he measures the faith of the Saints from the perspective of a narrow slice of contemporary Protestant theology. In doing so he distorts LDS belief in an effort to score points with fellow Protestants and to justify the silly charge that the Church of Jesus Christ is "a major cult" and hence not Christian at all. He complains:

> Since the LDS Church continually accuses Christians of wrongly and unjustly excluding it from being Christian and strongly publicizes its dismay and disgust toward Christians who identify it as *a major cult,* the Mormons' exclusive assertion that they are the earth's only true church is not only bold, but to many Christians also offensive, prideful, and very disingenuous. (p. 65, emphasis added)

---

6. See Kenneth W. Godfrey, "Council of Fifty," *Encyclopedia of* Mormonism, ed. Daniel H. Ludlow (New York: MacMillan, 1992) 1:327.

Reverend Jackson is troubled because Latter-day Saints believe that soon after the death of the original apostles there was a gradual apostasy from the fullness of the gospel of Jesus Christ and that the Church of Jesus Christ has been restored by God through the Prophet Joseph Smith. He understands this to mean that the Church of Jesus Christ "bases its absolute exclusive status on its belief that *a complete and universal apostasy*— a falling away from God—took place immediately following the death of the New Testament apostles" (p. 65, emphasis added). He cites no source for the "and universal" description because there is none. It may suit Reverend Jackson's purpose to outrage his evangelical audience by telling them that Mormons believe that Christian faith "totally disappeared from the face of God's globe" in "the second and third centuries AD" (p. 65), but the LDS Church does not teach it. In fact, Joseph Smith said that many individuals described in Foxe's *Book of Martyrs* were "honest, devoted followers of Christ,"[7] and in recent years LDS general conference has seen a swelling in laudatory references to figures like Wycliffe and Tyndale, specifically emphasizing their sincerity and Christianity.[8]

According to Reverend Jackson, "the LDS Church believes that every major branch of global Christianity—Protestant, Roman Catholic, and Eastern Orthodox—is unsound and incomplete in its teachings and practices" (p. 64). Does he believe that each of these has always been and is now entirely and fully *sound* and *complete*? If so, how does he explain the Protestant Reformation or his own Calvinist faction or

---

7. Edward Stevenson, *Reminiscences of Joseph, the Prophet* (Salt Lake City: the author, 1893), 6.

8. See, for example, Boyd K. Packer, "On Zion's Hill," at http://www.lds.org/general-conference/2005/10/on-zions-hill?lang=eng; Robert D. Hales, "Preparation for the Restoration and the Second Coming: 'My Hand Shall Be Over Thee,'" at http://www.lds.org/general-conference/2005/10/preparations-for-the-restoration-and-the-second-coming-my-hand-shall-be-over-thee?lang=eng.

the other Protestant churches, sects, denominations, and movements spawned by Martin Luther's efforts to reform Roman Catholicism?

Reverend Jackson insists that the LDS Church must demonstrate that all vestiges of Christian faith evaporated in the second and third centuries. If it can't manage to do that, he assumes that there was no need for a restoration, only a bloody protest and reformation, and that the faith of the Saints is fatally flawed. This explains his marshaling of Stephen Robinson's remarks about the "blind spot in Christian history"—when the lights went out on the primitive church and we hear the sounds of a muffled struggle and then find a Christianity radically altered (p. 69)—as evidence *against* an apostasy. He has Professor Robinson admitting that "we" don't know much about those blind hundred years, and there is therefore no evidence of apostasy, only Mormon guesswork (p. 69).

Against the teaching about the apostasy that he invents and then ascribes to Mormons, Reverend Jackson claims that "Christians today stand strong, trusting in God's absolute faithfulness and sovereignty, knowing that he will build his church on the rock of Jesus Christ, and the gates of hell cannot stand up against it" (p. 69). Does Jackson believe that God intended for his church to take the turbulent course from Orthodoxy to Roman Catholicism to Protestant Reformation to present? Surely Jackson rejects the authority that Catholicism and Orthodoxy claim for themselves. If God did indeed intend history to produce Reverend Jackson's current church and beliefs in the way that it did, how is that much different from the actual LDS belief that Christianity left its moorings and needed to be set right?

Reverend Jackson neglects to explain why he thinks there had to be a Protestant Reformation, given such things as indulgences and inquisitions, crimes and crusades, and so forth. He merely claims that "most Christians believe that even during the most corrupt medieval period of the Roman Catholic Church, there were still true and genuine followers of Jesus Christ" (p. 194 n. 16). The LDS view, of course, quite agrees. It does not, however, believe that those "genuine followers of Jesus Christ" in the so-called Great Church were somehow proto-Protestants, or that their genuine belief made a restoration of gospel fullness unnecessary.

Are Latter-day Saints Even Christian?

"It is," Reverend Jackson says, "clear that Mormonism has set itself totally apart from all Christian churches, whether Protestant, Roman Catholic, or Eastern Orthodox, and itself affirms that it is not Christian as Christianity has always been historically understood" (pp. 75–76). He relies upon and strongly endorses Craig Blomberg's *New Mormon Challenge* chapter concluding that Mormons are not Christian (p. 75). But certainly the Emperor Constantine's "church" was neither Protestant nor at all like the evangelical movement that emerged in the United States after World War II.

According to Reverend Jackson, Professor Robinson has provided the Mormon answer to the crucial question of "whether Mormons are Christians" by admitting that "Latter-day Saints do not seek to be accepted as historically 'orthodox' Christians or as Evangelicals" (p. 76). This out-of-context quote is a favorite of countercultists online (you can google it) because, by itself, it leaves the impression that Robinson admits the Church of Jesus Christ is not Christian. But all Robinson did was correctly distinguish the faith of the Saints from other versions of Christian faith. The Saints have always believed that their faith in Jesus Christ as Lord and Redeemer is unique and not reducible to some exterior theological categories, since it depends on divine special revelations and not the chains of speculations emitted over time by churchmen or theologians.

In addition, when Roman Catholics point out that their faith must not be confused with Orthodoxy or Protestantism, such an assertion is not to be read as an admission that they are not Christians. And when Protestants insist they are not Roman Catholics, they are not admitting they are not Christians.

Failure to Engage in a Real Conversation

There are a number of assertions in *Mormonism Explained* that don't explain much and that obscure important issues. I will list a few.

- Reverend Jackson evidences no effort to grapple with the efforts of Latter-day Saints to defend their faith, and he also simply dismisses their scriptures. There is, for example, no mention of Terryl Givens's treatment of the recovery of the Book of Mormon,[9] nor is the scholarship published by the Maxwell Institute ever engaged. He argues, instead, that "the unfolding saga of the book of Abraham affirms that Mormons embrace their scriptural books—including the *Book of Mormon*—not based on historical authenticity but through an irrational faith" (p. 91). Unwillingness to alert readers to a competent literature contradicting one's points is sloppy or duplicitous, but in any case weak.

- Specific elements of the faith of the Saints are brushed aside by Jackson. For example, he states the "belief in a preexistent heavenly family originates *mainly* in modern LDS revelation and not in the teaching of the Bible" (p. 100, emphasis supplied). The weasel word *mainly* hides the fact that belief in a premortal life was known among early Christians but was subsequently suppressed

9. See Terryl L. Givens, *By the Hand of Mormon: The American Scripture That Launched a New World Religion* (New York: Oxford University Press, 2002).

in the same way that deification has been rejected or ignored by most contemporary Protestants.

• Although he is familiar with work of writers like Stephen Robinson and Robert Millet, as well as the publications of the Maxwell Institute, Jackson betrays no sign that he has taken any of this literature seriously. Hence the following: "Latter-day Saints believe that each person's eternal destiny will match what he or she has merited through good or bad works; the person will be rewarded or condemned according to what God determines he or she deserves" (p. 131). Here we see the common cavil directed at the faith of the Saints, who are often falsely accused of "works righteousness," or the absurdity that they believe they can save themselves from death and sin. Jackson does not acknowledge that the Book of Mormon teaches emphatically that God is the sole author of salvation and that only through the merits and mercy of the Holy One of Israel can mortals in any sense be saved.

The Hostile Agenda

Reverend Jackson eventually gives up any pretense of "explaining" and falls back on cheerleading for his own views. In challenging the LDS understanding of deification, he asserts that

> Christians are clear and resolved. We are created finite humans who worship a one-of-a-kind eternal God, filled with God's eternal hope and power that enables us to escape the corruption of this evil world (2 Peter 1:4). As followers of Christ, we have hearts set on fire with the future hope of enjoying God for eternity. . . .
>
> It is unthinkable, repulsive, and even blasphemous to Christians for anyone to spread the teaching that humans can become fully equal to the eternal God we worship. (p. 122)

In rebutting the idea that God might require behavioral standards such as the Word of Wisdom, in addition to other more crucial commandments, Jackson is right that "our human righteousness—no matter how heroic it might be—falls short of the glory of God. Biblical salvation is righteousness, peace, and joy in the Holy Spirit" (p. 157). Does he imagine that the Saints are not aware that even the best of humans fall short of divine excellence? Do none of his many Mormon friends belie this caricature of Mormons as so prideful as to think otherwise?

What started out as a promising effort to explain Mormon beliefs and practices in terms others could understand ends up as just another evangelical inoculation against the Church of Jesus Christ.

The Most Recent Iteration

All of this makes it thoroughly unsurprising that when events—the Mitt Romney campaign—presented an opportunity to sell more books and publicize his message, Reverend Jackson retitled and reissued his ersatz *Mormonism Explained* as *The Mormon Faith of Mitt Romney.*[10] This time around, it suited both his agenda and his marketing strategy to be much more forthcoming as to his intentions.

On 4–5 January 2012, several publications ran a press release trumpeting the stern warning "Conservative Christian Cautions Mitt Romney: 'Want Our Vote? Don't 'Spin' Your Mormon Faith!'"[11] The "Conservative Christian" was Reverend Jackson. The press release announcing the book's publication

---

10. Andrew Jackson, *The Mormon Faith of Mitt Romney: What Latter-day Saints Teach and Practice* (n.p.: Kudu Publishing, 2012). Kudu is a self-publishing, print-on-demand, electronic publisher.

11. Matthew Green, "Christian Conservative Cautions Mitt Romney: 'Want Our Vote? Don't 'Spin' Your Mormon Faith!,'" at http://www.ereleases.com/pr/christian-conservative-cautions-mitt-romney-want-vote-spin-mormon-faith-71829.

affects a helpful tone, advising Romney that if he does not tell voters "how his Mormon faith will affect his presidency" he faces trouble, but that voters will "embrace an honest heart that speaks straight to them, without pretense or spin." Time will tell the soundness of Jackson's political judgment; what is immediately apparent is that the pretense and spin are Jackson's own. The press release directs readers to another document, "10 Key Questions Reporters Should Ask Mitt Romney About His Mormon Faith," released by the book's publisher. This document not only suggests entrapping Romney with Professor Stephen Robinson's so-called admission that Mormons are non-Christian, but it also demands that Romney disclaim any intention of being sworn in on the Book of Mormon because he finds the Bible so error-laden. In other words, the guise of friendly advice was merely an excuse to call more attention to Romney's faith in ways that will cement uninformed dismissals of Latter-day Saints as beyond the pale of Christianity. Jackson leaves no doubt about this plan in his introduction to *The Mormon Faith of Mitt Romney*: "I believe," he proclaims, "voters have a right to know from Mitt Romney how his Mormon faith will shape and affect his presidency. What is there to be afraid of?" What, indeed? Perhaps his own fervent hope, expressed a mere six paragraphs later:

> I do not worry about the LDS church growing in influence if Mitt Romney becomes our president because it is my belief that it would actually have the reverse effect. It will expose the specifics of the official teaching and practices of Mormonism as greatly lacking in the light of biblical truth. Could a Romney presidency help the LDS church reassess its historical teaching, and actually move it toward more biblical foundations? It is possible, and it is my prayer.

That's the game. Disguise a contrived exposé as a neutral, expecting it will shame the Church of Jesus Christ into jettisoning distinctive truth claims, and reform along lines more to Jackson's liking.

Little has changed between *Mormonism Explained* and *The Mormon Faith of Mitt Romney* (though, to his credit, Reverend Jackson did correct a few obvious errors), and so we can draw two important conclusions. First, protestations of evenhandedness and good faith are worth little from Reverend Jackson when he gives his opinion about the faith of Latter-day Saints. Today's purported benign is tomorrow's shot across the bow. Second, Jackson lacks confidence in his own artillery. If mere were sure to isolate and "reform" Mormonism, why the inability or unwillingness to avoid obvious mistakes through engagement with LDS scholars and scholarship? Why all the question-begging? Why the obvious failure to grapple with LDS responses to evangelical accusations, despite citing several books chock-full of such answers?

Reverend Jackson's endeavors show how evangelical anti-Mormonism must engage in such tactics, or else it would quickly run out of steam. He may well have genuinely intended to write the benign explanation his first title promised, only to realize it would present his non-Mormon audience with a more rational and appealing case than he could stomach. It is gratifying to know that in the baser tactics of our critics, we can discern an acknowledgement that fair explanation would leave their position so perilous that they will not hazard making it.

Cassandra S. Hedelius studied political science and mathematics at the University of Oklahoma and law at the University of Colorado. She has practiced domestic and business law for profit, and researches and writes about Mormonism for pleasure. Her main focus is the interaction of the LDS Church with modern media and political activism, with additional interest in religious freedom and public policy.

Evaluating Three Arguments Against Joseph Smith's First Vision

Steven C. Harper

Abstract: Historically there have been just three basic arguments against the authenticity of Joseph Smith's first vision. They all begin with the a priori premise that such a vision simply could not have happened. The arguments originated with the Methodist minister to whom Joseph related his vision, author Fawn Brodie, and the Reverend Wesley Walters. The minister's critique is explained by Methodism's shift away from ecstatic religious experience. Fawn Brodie is shown to have made innovative yet flawed arguments within the narrow scope allowed by her conclusion that Joseph was a charlatan—a conclusion that did not allow for alternative interpretations of new evidence. Walters is shown to make fallacious arguments of irrelevant proof and negative proof in his understandably determined effort to undermine Joseph Smith's credibility. Close-minded believers in Joseph's vision are similarly likely to make unfounded assumptions unless they become open to the rich historical record Joseph created. Belief in the vision should correspond to Christian empathy for and civility toward critics.

Numerous books and many more websites work to undermine faith in Joseph Smith's first vision. Historically this criticism has taken the form of just three main arguments that have been repeated by various critics and are even current today. The first argument arose when the minister to whom Joseph reported his vision announced that there were no such things as visions in modern times. More than a century later,

Fawn Brodie, writing with literary grace to mask historical deficiencies in her argument, claimed that Joseph concocted the vision in 1838, years after he said it happened. Then a generation later, the third argument emerged when Wesley Walters charged Joseph with inventing the story of a revival in western New York around 1820. Walters claimed that a lack of historical evidence "proved" there was no revival and hence no subsequent vision. For some it is a foregone conclusion that there are no such things as visions, that Joseph failed to mention his experience for years, and that he gave conflicting accounts that do not match historical facts.[1]

Each of the three arguments begins with the premise that Joseph's initial vision simply could not have happened, at least not as he described it. Philosophers call that kind of premise *a priori*, a Latin term that refers to knowledge that is, essentially, presumed or self-evident. In other words, a priori knowledge does not rely on firsthand experience for verification but, rather, is based on definitions, widely shared beliefs, and rational assumptions. By contrast, knowledge derived from experience is termed *a posteriori*. The epistemology in Joseph's first vision accounts is a posteriori. He testified that he actually experienced a divine revelation. The epistemology of his critics' counterclaims is generally a priori. They know that what Joseph said happened could not have happened because all reasonable people know that such things as heavenly visions do not happen.

The Methodist Minister

"Some few days after I had this vision," Joseph reported, "I happened to be in company with one of the Methodist preachers" who had contributed to the religious fervor. "I took occasion to give him an account of the vision. . . . I was greatly surprised at his behavior; he treated my communication not only

---

1. For example, Dan Vogel, *Joseph Smith: The Making of a Prophet* (Salt Lake City: Signature Books, 2004), xv.

lightly, but with great contempt, saying it was all of the devil, that there were no such things as visions or revelations in these days; that all such things had ceased with the apostles, and that there would never be any more of them" (Joseph Smith—History 1:21). The preacher's premises were all a priori, namely:

- Joseph's story was of the devil.
- There were no such things as revelations in what Dickens later called the "age of railways."
- Visions or revelations ceased with the apostles.
- There would never be any more visions.

This fellow was probably sincere in each of these beliefs and striving as best he knew to prevent Joseph from becoming prey to fanaticism. But he did not know from experience the validity of any of the four premises he set forth as positive facts. All he knew a posteriori is that he had not had a vision or a revelation. On what basis, then, could this minister evaluate Joseph's claims and make such sweeping statements?

An answer lies in understanding the pressures placed on a Methodist minister in Joseph's area in 1820. Joseph did not name the minister to whom he reported the vision. It is not clear that it was George Lane, whom Joseph's brother William and Oliver Cowdery credited with awakening Joseph spiritually. Joseph could have heard or visited with Reverend Lane more than once during his ministry that frequently took him from his home in Pennsylvania to Joseph's district between 1819 and the early 1820s.[2] There were local Methodist ministers to whom Joseph may have reported his experience. All of them were conscious that Methodism was tending away from the kind of spiritual experiences Joseph described and toward presumably more respectable, reasonable religion. John Wesley, the found-

---

2. *The Latter Day Saints' Messenger and Advocate* (Kirtland), October 1834, 42. William Smith, *William Smith on Mormonism* (Lamoni, Iowa, 1883), 6. *Deseret Evening News* (Salt Lake City), 20 January 1894, 11. Larry C. Porter, "Reverend George Lane—Good 'Gifts,' Much 'Grace,' and Marked 'Usefulness,'" *BYU Studies* 9/3 (Spring 1969): 336.

er of Methodism, had worried that Methodists would multiply exponentially in number only to become "a dead sect, having the form of religion without the power."[3] And Methodism indeed grew abundantly because it took the claims of people like Joseph so seriously. Its preachers encouraged personal conversions that included intimate experiences with God like visions and revelations. But then, as Wesley had worried, Methodism became less welcoming to such manifestations.[4] As Joseph was coming of age, Methodism was becoming embarrassed by what respectable people regarded as its emotional excesses. Methodism had risen to meet the needs of the many people who could not find a church that took their spiritual experiences seriously. But with Methodism's phenomenal growth came a shift from the margin to the mainstream.

Joseph was likely naive about that shift, which is easier to see from the perspective of history than it was for the people of Joseph's day. Probably all Joseph knew is that he had caught a spark of Methodism and wanted to feel the same spiritual power as the folks he saw and heard at the meetings. He finally experienced that power in his encounter with heavenly messengers in the woods, as so many Methodist converts, encouraged by their preachers, appeared to have done before him. So it was shocking to him when the minister reacted against what Joseph assumed would be welcome news.

---

3. John Wesley, "Thoughts upon Methodism," in *The Methodist Societies: History, Nature, and Design*, ed. Rupert E. Davies, vol. 9 of *The Bicentennial Edition of the Works of John Wesley*, ed. W. Reginald Ward and Richard P. Heitzenrater (Nashville: Abingdon, 1984–), 527.

4. Christopher C. Jones, "The Power and Form of Godliness: Methodist Conversion Narratives and Joseph Smith's First Vision," *Journal of Mormon History* 37/2 (Spring 2011): 88–114. Jon Butler, *Awash in a Sea of Faith: Christianizing the American People* (Cambridge: Harvard University Press, 1990), 241. John H. Wigger, "Methodism Transformed," in his *Taking Heaven by Storm: Methodism and the Rise of Popular Christianity in America* (Chicago: University of Illinois Press, 1998).

As for the minister, he may have heard messages in Joseph's story that led him to respond negatively, especially if Joseph told how he had learned that religious professors spoke well of God but denied his power. No Methodist minister wanted to hear that his founder's fear had been realized. Yet by 1820 many such ministers were concerned about what had for nearly two hundred years been termed "enthusiasm," a term "derived from Greek *en theos*, meaning to be filled with or inspired by a deity."[5] To be accused of enthusiasm in Joseph Smith's world was not a compliment. It meant that one was perceived as mentally unstable and irrational. Methodists had for several generations tried to walk a fine line that valued authentic spiritual experience yet stopped well short of enthusiasm. Young Joseph likely was not attuned to the sophisticated difference worked out by Methodist theologians. He reported to the minister what he thought would be a highly valued experience, one resembling that of other sincere Christians, but his account of his vision was received as an embarrassing example of enthusiasm and thus condemned.

Fawn Brodie

Fawn Brodie largely shaped the more recent skeptical interpretations of Joseph's first vision. She first articulated major criticisms that others have since adopted and published and that continue to circulate widely today. In the first edition of her biography of Joseph Smith (1945), Brodie cited his 1838 history, the one excerpted in the Pearl of Great Price. She reported that her efforts to research at the LDS Church's archives had been thwarted.[6] For example, she had sought but had been denied access to Joseph's 1832 diary. Though that document

---

5. Ann Taves, *Fits, Trances, & Visions: Experiencing Religion and Explaining Experience from Wesley to James* (Princeton: Princeton University Press, 1999), 17.

6. Newell G. Bringhurst, *Fawn McKay Brodie: A Biographer's Life* (Norman: University of Oklahoma Press, 1999), 84–85.

does not include an account of Joseph's first vision, both his 1832 letterbook and 1835 journal do. Discovery and publication of those accounts would wait until the 1960s, when Brodie would work them into her second edition. Not knowing of the evidence that Joseph had repeatedly reported the vision earlier than she recognized, Brodie concluded that no one had spoken of the vision between 1820 and about 1840. She interpreted the evidence she had to mean that Joseph concocted the vision in the wake of the 1837 banking crisis, "when the need arose for a magnificent tradition."[7]

She did not change her assumptions and conclusions when she revised her biography of Joseph after the 1832 and 1835 accounts had been discovered and published. She did not reconsider her interpretation in light of the evidence that showed Joseph had written and spoken openly of the vision on more than one occasion before 1838. Rather, with characteristic insinuation, she simply substituted *1830* for *1834* in this sentence about the vision: "It may have been sheer invention, created some time after 1830 when the need arose for a magnificent tradition."[8] She also noted in her second edition the differences in details between the accounts, suggesting that their inconsistencies evidenced Joseph's invention and embellishment of the story. So the second edition of Brodie's biography adjusted some sentences to accommodate new factual evidence without altering the fundamental, a priori premise that the vision did not occur as Joseph said it did.

Although Brodie persuaded her publisher by emphasizing her "attitude of complete objectivity," privately she and Dale Morgan, her closest adviser, knew of her psychological need to understand Joseph's life and escape his influence. Writing the book, Brodie reflected, enabled her to assert her indepen-

---

7. Fawn M. Brodie, *No Man Knows My History: The Life of Joseph Smith the Mormon Prophet* (New York: Alfred A. Knopf, 1945), 25.

8. Fawn M. Brodie, *No Man Knows My History: The Life of Joseph Smith the Mormon Prophet*, 2nd ed. (New York: Vintage, 1995), 25.

dence. She called it a "compulsion to liberate myself wholly from Mormonism." She decided in the process of preparing the biography to see in the historical facts evidence that Joseph consciously concocted the vision with intent to deceive. Having read an early draft of her biography, Morgan wrote that he was "particularly struck with the assumption your MS makes that Joseph was a self-conscious impostor." Though sympathetic to her work, Morgan worried about what he called her "bold judgments on the basis of assumptions." A later reviewer noted similarly that she regularly stated "as indisputable facts what can only be regarded as conjectures supported by doubtful evidence."[9]

It is not hard to empathize with Fawn Brodie. Having been raised as a Latter-day Saint, she chose to leave the faith and underwent a painful reorientation process that required her to account for the Book of Mormon and to reinterpret Joseph's first vision. None of us are so very different from her in the sense that our identities and psychologies are bound up in our various commitments. We cannot escape the import of Joseph's first vision any more than she could, and we work to make sense of the evidence for ourselves in ways that are satisfying to our intellects and to our souls. But whatever her motives and our efforts to empathize, it is Brodie's method that concerns us here. Similar critical interpretations of Joseph's vision often share a common hermeneutic (explanatory method) of skepticism. They presume to know how a person in Joseph's position, or how people in his neighborhood, must have acted if his story were true, and then they attempt to show that his accounts vary from the assumed scenarios. They usually postulate a hypothetical alternative to Joseph's own explanation.[10]

9. Bringhurst, *Fawn McKay Brodie*, 80, 87, 95, 105, 115.

10. Bringhurst, *Fawn McKay Brodie*, 106.

Reverend Wesley Walters

That is what Wesley Walters did. He originated the enduring argument that Joseph's canonized first vision account is anachronistic. In 1967, as pastor of the United Presbyterian Church in Marissa, Illinois, Walters published an innovative essay asserting that there is no evidence of a religious revival in Palmyra, New York, in the spring of 1820 and that, consequently, Joseph's claim to have been influenced by such religious fervor must be false.[11] Richard Bushman said that Walters "performed a very positive service to the cause of Mormon history because he was a delver. He went deep into the heart of the archives. And Mormons had accepted a lot of things as simple facts—for example, that there was a revival in Joseph Smith's neighborhood around the 1820 period."[12] Walters noted accurately that, prior to his work, Mormon scholars had "*assumed* that Joseph Smith's account must be correct."[13] According to Bushman, Reverend Walters "made us realize that we can't assume anything. Everything had to be demonstrated and proved."[14]

That realization led Truman G. Madsen and the Institute of Mormon Studies at Brigham Young University to sponsor a team of talented, well-educated young Mormon historians to research all the evidence they could find.[15] As a result of their research, it is clear that there are two main weaknesses in the Walters argument, namely, the fallacies of negative proof and of irrelevant proof. Historian David Hackett Fischer defined the fallacy of negative proof as "an attempt to sustain a factual

---

11   See, for example, Wesley P. Walters, "New Light on Mormon Origins from the Palmyra Revival," reprinted in *Dialogue* 4/1 (1969): 60–67.

12.   Richard L. Bushman, interview by Samuel Dodge, 31 July 2009, Provo, UT, transcription in possession of the author.

13.   Walters, "New Light on Mormon Origins," 61.

14.   Bushman, interview.

15.   Truman G. Madsen, "Guest Editor's Prologue," *BYU Studies* 9/3 (Spring 1969): 235–40.

proposition merely by negative evidence. It occurs whenever a historian declares that 'there is no evidence that X is the case,' and then proceeds to affirm or assume that not-X is the case."[16] Walters argued creatively that "a vision, by its inward, personal nature, does not lend itself to historical investigation," but "a revival is a different matter." He posited, therefore, that he could disprove Joseph's claim to a vision by showing "that in 1820 there was no revival in any of the churches in Palmyra and its vicinity."[17] In doing so, he disregarded the historical method by arguing that a lack of evidence for a Palmyra revival was proof that a revival, and hence the first vision, did not occur.

Reverend Walters also erred in arguing an irrelevant proof. Joseph's accounts do not claim that the revivalism centered in Palmyra itself, as Walters argues, or that the revivalism occurred in 1820. Rather, Joseph said the excitement began in the second year after his family moved to Manchester, New York, meaning in 1819, and he located the "unusual excitement on the subject of religion" around Manchester, not Palmyra. Joseph used a Methodist term to describe a wider geographical scope than Walters's emphasis on the village of Palmyra. Joseph said that "the whole *district* of country seemed affected" by the revivalism (Joseph Smith—History 1:5). To nineteenth-century Methodists, a district was somewhat akin to today's LDS stake or a Catholic diocese. Joseph claimed only that there was unusual religious excitement in the region or district around Manchester that began sometime in 1819, during the second year after his family's move there (JS—H 1:5).

There is evidence that an intense revival stirred Palmyra in 1816–17, when Joseph moved there with his family. It may have catalyzed his 1832 description of his mind becoming seriously concerned for the welfare of his soul "at about the age of

---

16. David Hackett Fischer, *Historians' Fallacies: Toward a Logic of Historical Thought* (New York: Harper, 1970), 47.

17. Walters, "New Light on Mormon Origins," 61.

twelve years."[18] About 1818 Joseph's family purchased a farm in Manchester, a few miles south of Palmyra. The next summer, Methodists of the Genesee Conference assembled at Vienna (now Phelps), New York, within walking distance of the Smith farm. The Reverend George Lane and dozens of other exhorters were present. One participant remembered the result as a "religious cyclone which swept over the whole region."[19] Joseph's contemporary and acquaintance Orsamus Turner remembered that Joseph caught a "spark of Methodism" at a meeting along the road to Vienna.[20] A Palmyra newspaper and the diary of a Methodist minister confirm a weekend camp meeting in Palmyra in June 1820 at which "about twenty were baptized and forty united with the [Methodist] Church."[21] Had Walters known about this evidence, given the way he consistently interpreted evidence in support of his conclusion, he may have objected that a June 1820 camp meeting would have been too late to have catalyzed Joseph's early spring vision. And he might have been quite right, but not necessarily. It snowed heavily on May 28 that year, and given his realities in that environment, Joseph's conception of "early spring" may have been quite different from our own. But Joseph's descriptions are not depen-

18. Quoted in John W. Welch and Erick B. Carlson, eds., *Opening the Heavens: Accounts of Divine Manifestations, 1820–1844*, 4.

19. Quoted in Milton V. Backman Jr., "Awakenings in the Burned-over District: New Light on the Historical Setting of the First Vision," *BYU Studies* 9/3 (Spring 1969): 308.

20. Orsamus Turner, *History of the Pioneer Settlement of Phelps and Gorham's Purchase, and Morris' Reserve . . .* (Rochester, NY: William Alling, 1851), 214. Richard L. Anderson evaluates Turner's credibility as a witness in "Circumstantial Confirmation of the First Vision through Reminiscences," *BYU Studies* 9/3 (Spring 1969): 373–404.

21. Aurora Seager wrote in his diary, "I attended a camp-meeting at Palmyra" in June 1818. He said that over the weekend about twenty people were baptized and forty became Methodists. See E. Latimer, *The Three Brothers: Sketches of the Lives of Rev. Aurora Seager, Rev. Micah Seager, Rev. Schuyler Seager, D.C.* (New York: Phillips & Hunt, 1880), 12, quoted in D. Michael Quinn, "Joseph Smith's Experience of a Methodist 'Camp Meeting' in 1820," *Dialogue* Paperless E-Paper 3, 20 December 2006, 3.

dent on external events in Palmyra or in 1820. The diaries of Methodist itinerant preacher Benajah Williams evidence that Methodists and others were hard at work in Joseph's district all the while. They combed the countryside and convened camp meetings to help unchurched souls like Joseph get religion. The response was phenomenal, especially in western New York, the home of nearly one-fourth of the six thousand Presbyterian converts in 1820. Baptist churches expanded similarly.[22] Methodism expanded most impressively as traveling preachers like Williams gathered anxious converts.[23]

Reverend Walters focused on the word *reformation*, used by Oliver Cowdery to describe the scope of the religious excitement, and on the Reverend George Lane, whom both Cowdery and William Smith, Joseph's brother, credited with being "the key figure in the Methodist awakening." Walters wrote that "there is no evidence" for these claims, which was an unwise thing to do.[24] Undiscovered evidence is not the same as nonexistent evidence, and when Walters made the bold claim that no evidence existed, researchers quickly set out to see for themselves. Among the several evidences discovered since are the Williams journals. They document much religious excitement in Joseph's district and region of country in 1819 and 1820. They report that Reverend Lane was indeed in that area in both of those years and that while there in July 1820 he "spoke on Gods method in bringing about Refformations."[25] Indeed, the Williams diaries attest that not only Lane but also many other Methodist preachers in Joseph's time and place catalyzed unusual religious excitement as Joseph described. Writers who have not studied this evidence continue to parrot Walters

---

22. Butler, *Christianizing the American People*, 268–69. Backman, "Awakenings in the Burned-over District."

23. Wigger, *Taking Heaven by Storm*, 3–6.

24. Walters, "New Light on Mormon Origins," 62, 76.

25. Diaries of Benajah Williams, in possession of Michael Brown, Philadelphia, Pennsylvania (original spelling maintained).

and claim that "there was no significant revival in or around Palmyra in 1820," but the evidence fits Joseph's description nicely.[26]

Although Walters consistently interpreted them otherwise, Joseph's accounts are consistent with the mounting evidence. Joseph said that the unusual religious excitement in his district or region "commenced with the Methodists" and that he became "somewhat partial" to Methodism (JS—H 1:5–8). The Walters thesis, though tenaciously defended by him and uncritically accepted and perpetuated by others, no longer seems tenable or defensible.[27] Walters succeeded in establishing the fact that "his [Joseph's] immediate neighborhood shows no evidence of an 1820 revival," but without showing that anything Joseph said was false.[28] Thin evidence for revivalism in Palmyra village in 1820 is not evidence that there was not a vision in the woods near Manchester in the wake of well-documented religious excitement "in that region of country" (v. 5).

Latter-day Saint historians of the first vision have credited Walters with awakening them to investigate the context of Joseph's accounts, but they fault him for forcing his thesis.[29] We can easily understand, however, the reasons behind his determined efforts and unwillingness to give up his point. Joseph's most definitive account of his vision relates how he told his mother, "I have learned for myself that Presbyterianism is not true." He also quoted the Savior saying that the Christian creeds "were an abomination" (JS—H 1:19–20). Latter-day Saints who

---

26. Robert D. Anderson, *Inside the Mind of Joseph Smith: Psychobiography and the Book of Mormon* (Salt Lake City: Signature Books, 1999).

27. Backman, "Awakenings in the Burned-over District," 309; Bushman "First Vision Story Revived," 85.

28. Walters, "New Light on Mormon Origins," 69.

29. Dean C. Jessee, James B. Allen (27 July 2009), Richard L. Anderson (29 July 1009), Larry Porter (30 July 2009), Richard L. Bushman (31 July 2009), Milton V. Backman Jr. (12 August 2009), interviews by Samuel Dodge, tape recording, transcriptions in possession of author.

feel defensive about the Reverend's efforts to discredit the vision should be able to empathize with his response to Joseph's testimony. In one sense, his determined and enduring devotion to his cause is admirable. Even so, his arguments are not as airtight as they may seem, and his evidence—or lack thereof—does not prove what he claimed it did.

A Hemeneutic of Suspicion

The critics' a priori certainty that the vision never happened as Joseph said it did is not a proven historical fact based on the testimony of witnesses or on textual evidence. Rather, those determined beliefs reflect each critic's heartfelt, reasoned belief about what was possible. Their commitment to skepticism about the kind of supernatural events Joseph described prevented them from believing in the possibilities that the historical accounts offer. In other words, all of the unbelieving explanations share a common hermeneutic—the hermeneutic of suspicion, which in this case simply means interpreting Joseph Smith's statements skeptically, with an unwillingness to trust that he might be telling the truth. One historian said that he could not trust the accounts of the first vision because they were "subjective" and that it was his job to figure out what really happened. But how will this skeptic discover the truth when he is unwilling to trust the only eyewitness or the process of personal revelation?

Such historians assume godlike abilities to discern the truth while denying both God's ability to impart truth and their own ability to receive it. They do not seem to grasp the profound irony that they are replacing the subjectivity of historical witnesses with their own. I call their method "subjectivity squared." They dismiss the historical documents and severely limit possible interpretations by predetermining that Joseph's story is not credible.

When Joseph's 1832 account was discovered in the 1960s, opening to Fawn Brodie new interpretive possibilities, she did not respond with willingness to consider that Joseph might be telling the truth; rather, she simply fit the new evidence into her previous conclusion. And because the evidence is now more abundant than ever, parts of Fawn Brodie's thesis are not as compelling as they once were. The evidence she analyzed in her second edition suggested to her that Joseph embellished each telling of the vision until it matured into the canonized 1838–39 account. But even the later accounts do not become longer, more detailed, or elaborate. Rather, these accounts return to sounding like Joseph's earlier, less-developed accounts.[30] This evidence can be interpreted as Joseph's intention to make his 1838 account definitive and developed for publication, whereas some of the less-developed accounts, including ones later than 1838, were created for other purposes. Some were delivered on the spur of the moment and captured by someone remembering and writing later.

The discovery of considerable evidence of camp meetings and revivals in both 1819 and 1820 in and around Palmyra, and especially in the broader region that Joseph described, did not alter the argument that Wesley Walters continued to make. No matter what evidence came to light, he interpreted it according to his original conclusion. He chose not to see the possibilities available to those who approach Joseph's accounts on a quest to discover if he could possibly be telling the truth.

For those who choose to read Joseph's accounts with the hermeneutic of suspicion, the interpretation of choice is likely to remain that Joseph elaborated "some half-remembered dream" or concocted the vision as "sheer invention."[31] Those are not historical facts. They are skeptical interpretations of the fact that Joseph reported he saw a vision. There are other ways

---

30. Quoted in Welch and Carson, *Opening the Heavens*, 17–29.
31. Brodie, *No Man Knows My History* (1995), 25.

to interpret that fact. Indeed, the several scholars who have
studied the accounts of the vision for decades and published
seminal findings share what one of them described as a "hermeneutic of trust."[32]

One will arrive at the same conclusions as the skeptics if one
shares their assumptions about what the facts mean. But if one
is open-minded, other meanings for the same facts are possible.
The danger of close-mindedness is as real for believers as for
skeptics. Many believers seem just as likely to begin with pre-
conceived notions rather than a willingness to go where Joseph's
accounts lead them. The reasoning process of many believers
is no different than Fawn Brodie's. Some *assume*, for instance,
that Joseph obviously would have told his family of the vision
immediately, that he would have written it down immediately,
that he understood all of its implications perfectly or consistently
through the years, that he would always remember or tell exactly
the same story, and that it would always be recorded and trans-
mitted the same. But none of those assumptions are supported
by the evidence. Unfortunately, some believers become skeptics
in short order when, upon learning of Joseph's various accounts
of his first vision, they find that their own assumptions of what
would have happened if Joseph were telling the truth are not supported by the historical record. Yet upon closer examination and
in light of the latest findings, the very difficulties that once could
be seen as posing challenges to the authenticity of Joseph's vi-
sionary experience turn out to be points in its favor.

Toward a Civil Dialogue

Richard Bushman had just won the historians' prestigious
Bancroft Prize when he responded with civility and grace to
Reverend Walters. When I asked him why he chose that meth-
od, Bushman replied, "Simply as a tactical matter in any kind

32. Bushman, interview.

of controversy, it never serves you well to show scorn towards your opponent. That may make the people who are on your side rejoice and say, 'Kick them again.' But for those who are in the middle who are trying to decide which truth is right, you just alienate them, you just drive them into the hands of your opponent."[33] Sometimes, in an effort to defend the faith, Latter-day Saints have reacted with hostility to the critics of Joseph's vision. If there ever was an appropriate time for such a response, it is now passed.

We are removed enough from the battlefront that we can respond less defensively and try instead to meet the needs of those who are undecided. Although I disagree with the a priori assumptions and historical interpretations of Fawn Brodie, Reverend Walters, and the Methodist minister who reproved Joseph, I empathize with these people. I may well have responded as they did if I were in different circumstances. Indeed, the minister's and the reverend's responses were not so different from many LDS defenses of Mormonism. Each of these critics is a vulnerable personality, like the rest of us. They worked hard to figure out how to relate to Joseph Smith's first vision. I wish to treat them as I would like to be treated by them—and as Joseph taught the Relief Society sisters in Nauvoo. To them he said, "The nearer we get to our heavenly Father, the more are we dispos'd to look with compassion on perishing souls—to take them upon our shoulders and cast their sins behind our back. . . . If you would have God have mercy on you, have mercy on one another."[34]

---

33. Bushman, interview.

34. Discourse, 9 June 1842, Nauvoo, Illinois. See "A Record of the Organization and Proceedings of the Female Relief Society of Nauvoo, 61–64, LDS Church Archives. Also in *History of the Church*, 5:23–25; and Andrew F. Ehat and Lyndon W. Cook, *The Words of Joseph Smith: The Contemporary Accounts of the Nauvoo Discourses of the Prophet Joseph* (Provo, UT: Religious Studies Center, Brigham Young University, 1980), 122–24.

Steven C. Harper is a historian for the Church of Jesus Christ of Latter-day Saints. He was professor of church history and doctrine at Brigham Young University from 2002–2012 and at BYU Hawaii from 2000–2002. Since 2002 he has served as an editor of the Joseph Smith Papers and as document editor of BYU Studies. He earned a PhD in early American history from Lehigh University in Bethlehem, Pennsylvania, and is the author of a book on colonial Pennsylvania titled Promised Land and of Making Sense of the Doctrine and Covenants, along with several articles. His book, Joseph Smith's First Vision: A Guide to the Historical Accounts, *is forthcoming from Deseret Book.*

CHRISTIAN FAITH IN CONTEMPORARY CHINA

Louis C. Midgley

Review of Lian Xi. *Redeemed by Fire: The Rise of Popular Christianity in Modern China*. New Haven: Yale University, 2010. 352 pp., with glossary, bibliography and index. $45.00 (hardcover).

On 30 August 2010 leaders of The Church of Jesus Christ of Latter-day Saints announced that "a series of high-level meetings" had taken place in Salt Lake City between representatives of the Church "and an official from the People's Republic of China" that are eventually "expected to lead to 'regularized' operations of the Church in China."[1] For me this announcement was news that rivaled those unanticipated and providentially dramatic events allowing the building of an LDS temple in what was then East Germany, and later the preaching of the gospel in Eastern Europe and Russia, and the series of events promoting the stunning growth of the Church in sub-Saharan Africa. For those curious, as I am, about Christianity in China, *Redeemed by Fire* is a fine resource, though it is not, however, the only solid account of the stunning growth in Christian religiosity following the dramatic events that changed the face of China after World War II.[2]

---

1. See http://newsroom.lds.org/article/church-in-talks-to-regularize-activities-in-china.

2. Some of the literature on the amazing growth in Christian faith in China has been produced by journalists. For example, recently a sympathetic non-Christian Chinese journalist, Liao Yiwu, published a wonderful collection of interviews with those whose faith survived brutal persecution, as well as testimonies of those who, in search of a moral anchor in the emptiness of the

Many years ago I suffered through a dreadfully dull survey course on Chinese history. It was only later when I encountered Chinese graduate students at Brigham Young University that my interest in their immense, diverse, and wonderful homeland was aroused. The climax of this experience was the reaction of some of those students (while we were reading together Alexis de Tocqueville's *Democracy in America*) to the series of events that took place in and around Tiananmen Square (beginning on 15 April and ending on 4 June 1989). Subsequently I was able to travel to China, where my wife and I saw some evidence of large congregations of thriving Christian communities in cities the name of which I could not even locate on a map. This was my first direct introduction to what was for me an entirely unexpected and quite amazing growth of Christianity in contemporary China.

In *Redeemed*, Lian Xi points out that Christianity first reached China in AD 635 when Alopen (A'huoben), a Syrian monk, reached what is now Xi'an, the capital of the Tang Dynasty (AD 618–907), with Nestorian (aka Dyophysite) Christian faith.[3] But the primary focus of Lian's account is

affluence found in contemporary China, have become Christians. This remarkable collection of interviews is now available in English under the title *God is Red: The Secret Story of How Christianity Survived and Flourished in Communist China*, trans. by Wenguang Huang (New York: HarperCollins, 2011). See also a solid scholarly study edited by Nikka Rukanen and Paulos Huang, entitled *Christianity and Chinese Culture* (Grand Rapids, MI: Eerdmans, 2010). This is a collection of nineteen essays on a range of topics, each followed by a valuable response from other scholars. See also David A. Palmer, Glen Shiva and Philip L Wickeri (eds.), *Chinese Religious Life* (New York: Oxford University Press, 2011). For a massive general survey of varieties of religious devotion in contemporary China, see Vincent Goossaert and David A. Palmer, *The Religious Question in Modern China* (Chicago: University of Chicago, 2011). (There is a brief mention of Latter-day Saints in China on pp. 349–50 of this study of the politics, cultural movements and dramatic events, beginning in 1989, that examines the way in which religion, broadly understood, has challenged secular Chinese ideology.

3.   See Daniel H. Bays, *A New History of Christianity in China* (Hoboken, NJ: Wiley-Blackwell, 2011), which is fine historical survey by a distinguished scholar, beginning with the initial arrival of Diophysite Christian faith to China.

the phenomenal growth of Christianity in China after Mao Zedong established the Peoples Republic of China in 1949, and especially when Chairman Mao launched the Cultural Revolution (1966–1976). When this massive effort to purge it began in 1966, "Christianity in China was facing a bleak, and uncertain future: having been abruptly weaned from Western missions, it now found itself in the hands of an enraged state" (p. 204). After having survived seasons of "warlordism, banditry, foreign invasion, civil war, and the attending miseries," Christians in China were faced with "the hostilities of an atheist government" (p. 204)–that is, a regime intent on clamping down on Christian missions and churches. But wide varieties of Christian faith not only survived, they prospered.

Lian estimates that currently there are 17 million Roman Catholics and 50 million Protestants in China (p. 3), while others place the number of Christians in China as high as 108 million.[4] Whatever the real numbers, since some have argued that conservative Protestants have overestimated their numbers,[5] the growth of Christianity, which is believed to have numbered less than a million in 1949, is unparalleled in history, even if we consider Constantine's transforming of Christianity into the official cult of the Roman Empire. The Christian faith's stunning growth in China has essentially taken place without foreign management and control, and in very difficult situa-

---

4. See especially the report entitled "Spotlight on China" prepared by the Pew Forum on Religion and Public Life, which is available at http://www.pewforum.org/Christian/Global-Christianity-china.aspx, with the estimates of Christians of various stripes found in "Appendix C: Methodology for China," http://www.pewforum.org/uploadedFiles/Topics/Religious_Affiliation/Christian/ChristianityAppendixC.pdf.

5. See Mark Ellis, "China Survey Reveals Fewer Christians than some Evangelicals Want to Believe," ASSIST News Service (ANS), 1 October 2007, available at http://www.assistnews.net/STORIES/2007/s07100011.htm, also Mark Ellis, "New China Survey reveals fewer Christians than most estimates," *Christian Examiner*, November 2007, available at http://www.christianexaminer.com/Articles/Articles%20Nov07/Art_Nov07_17.html

tions.[6] American tourists in China, if they are not looking for a place to eat a hamburger or souvenirs, may actually see in Chinese cities large churches probably affiliated with either the state-approved and regulated Protestant Three-Self Patriotic Movement or the Patriotic Catholic Association. And if they ask a few questions, they are likely to learn about the unregulated "house churches" as well.

Lian describes the "evangelistic fervor, biblical literalism, charismatic ecstasies, and fiery eschatology not infrequently tinged with nationalistic exuberance" (p. 3) that are currently found even among the officially recognized and regulated Chinese Christian churches and especially in the house churches. The recent growth of Christianity does not seem to have been the work of, or even managed by, foreigners. It seems to have been, instead, an essentially indigenous movement among the faithful. "Will popular Christianity," Lian asks at the end of his book, "inspire a violent uprising?" His conclusion: "Given the overwhelming power of the centralized state in contemporary China, there is little likelihood in the near future that a fragmented, however spirited, Christian movement will foment popular revolt" (p. 246). As interesting as his speculation about what he calls "the long run" might be, what interest me the most about his book are his accounts of some truly amazing and quite unanticipated events that have taken place in the last four decades in China.

I have longed to understand the peoples and their ways in that ancient land. I am confident that other Latter-day Saints are also concerned about the future of the covenant people of God in China. I believe that *Redeemed by Fire* provides some

---

6. See older studies by David Aikman, *Jesus in Beijing: How Christianity is Transforming China and Changing the Global Balance of Power*, rev. ed. (Washington, DC: Regnery, 2006), and see also Tony Lambert, *China's Christian Millions*, updated ed. (Oxford: Monarch Books, 2006). Lambert provides figures (in three appendices, see pp. 255–77) that chart the growth of Christian faith province by province beginning in 1900 through 2002–2005.

useful information on Christian faith in China and, hence, I recommend it to Latter-day Saints anxious, as I am, for a better understanding of the way the winds are blowing.

Louis Midgley (PhD, Brown University) is an emeritus professor of political science at Brigham Young University. Dr. Midgley has had an abiding interest in the history of Christian theology. He wrote his doctoral dissertation on Paul Tillich, the then-famous German-American Protestant theologian and political theorist/ religious-socialist activist. Midgley also studied the writings of other influential Protestant theologians such as Karl Barth. Eventually he took an interest in contemporary Roman Catholic theology, and was also impacted by the work of important Jewish philosophers, including especially Leo Strauss and his disciples.

Revisiting the Forgotten Voices of Weeping in Moses 7: A Comparison with Ancient Texts

Jeffrey M. Bradshaw, Jacob Rennaker, David J. Larsen

Abstract: The LDS Book of Moses is remarkable in its depiction of the suffering of the wicked at the time of the Flood. According to this text, there are three parties directly involved in the weeping: God (Moses 7:28; cf. v. 29), the heavens (Moses 7:28, 37), and Enoch (Moses 7:41, 49). In addition, a fourth party, the earth, mourns—though does not weep—for her children (Moses 7:48–49). The passages that speak of the weeping God and the mourning earth have received the greatest share of attention by scholars. The purpose of this article is to round out the previous discussion so as to include new insights and ancient parallels to the two voices of weeping that have been largely forgotten—that of Enoch and that of the heavens.[1]

One of the most moving passages in the "extracts from the Prophecy of Enoch"[2] included in the LDS Book of Moses describes weeping for the suffering of the wicked who were to perish in the Flood:

> 28 And it came to pass that the God of heaven looked upon the residue of the people, and he **wept**; and Enoch bore record of it, saying: How is it that the heavens

---

1. An expanded and revised version of material contained in this study will appear as part of Jeffrey M. Bradshaw and David J. Larsen, *Enoch, Noah, and the Tower of Babel* (Salt Lake City, UT: Eborn Publishing, forthcoming, 2014). All translations from non-English sources are by the first author unless otherwise specifically noted.

2. Joseph Smith, Jr., *History of the Church of Jesus Christ of Latter-day Saints (Documentary History)*, 7 vols. (Salt Lake City, UT: Deseret Book, 1978), December 1830, 1:133.

weep, and shed forth their tears as the rain upon the mountains?

29 And Enoch said unto the Lord: How is it that thou canst **weep**, seeing thou art holy, and from all eternity to all eternity? . . .

32 The Lord said unto Enoch: Behold these thy brethren; they are the workmanship of mine own hands, . . .

33 . . . but behold, they are without affection, and they hate their own blood; . . .

37 But behold, their sins shall be upon the heads of their fathers; Satan shall be their father, and misery shall be their doom; and the whole heavens shall **weep** over them, even all the workmanship of mine hands; wherefore should not the heavens **weep**, seeing these shall suffer? . . .

39 And That which I have chosen hath pled before my face. Wherefore, he suffereth for their sins; inasmuch as they will repent in the day that my Chosen shall return unto me, and until that day they shall be in torment.

40 Wherefore, for this shall the heavens **weep**, yea, and all the workmanship of mine hands.

41 And it came to pass that the Lord spake unto Enoch, and told Enoch all the doings of the children of men; wherefore Enoch knew, and looked upon their wickedness, and their misery, and **wept** and stretched forth his arms, and his heart swelled wide as eternity; and his bowels yearned; and all eternity shook. . . .

48 And it came to pass that Enoch looked upon the earth; and he heard a voice from the bowels thereof, saying: Wo, wo is me, the mother of men; I am pained, I am weary, because of the wickedness of my children . . .

49 And when Enoch heard the earth mourn, he **wept**, and cried unto the Lord, saying: O Lord, wilt thou not

have compassion upon the earth? Wilt thou not bless the children of Noah?

According to this text, there are three parties directly involved in the weeping: God (Moses 7:28; cf. v. 29), the heavens (Moses 7:28, 37), and Enoch (Moses 7:41, 49). In addition, a fourth party, the earth, mourns—though does not weep—for her children (Moses 7:48–49).

Daniel Peterson[3] has previously discussed the interplay among the members of this chorus of weeping voices, citing the arguments of non-LDS biblical scholar J.J.M. Roberts[4] that identify three similar voices within the laments of the book of Jeremiah: the feminine voice of the mother of the people (corresponding in the Book of Moses to the voice of the earth, the "mother of men"), the voice of the people (corresponding to Enoch), and the voice of God Himself.

Because of their eloquent rebuke of the idea of divine impassibility[5]—the notion that God does not suffer pain or distress—the passages in Moses 7 that speak of the voice of the weeping God have received the greatest share of attention in LDS scholarship, eliciting the pioneering notices of Hugh Nibley,[6] followed by lengthy articles by Eugene England[7] and Peterson.[8] Most recently, a book relating to the topic has been written by Terryl and

3. Daniel C. Peterson, "On the Motif of the Weeping God in Moses 7," in *Reason, Revelation, and Faith: Essays in Honor of Truman G. Madsen*, ed. Donald W. Parry, Daniel C. Peterson, and Stephen D. Ricks (Provo, UT: Foundation for Ancient Research and Mormon Studies, 2002).

4. J. J. M. Roberts, "The Motif of the Weeping God in Jeremiah and its Background in the Lament Tradition of the Ancient Near East," in *The Bible and the Ancient Near East: Collected Essays*, ed. J.J.M. Roberts (Winona Lake, IN: Eisenbrauns, 2002).

5. See, e.g, discussion in Peterson, "Weeping God," 285–98.

6. Hugh W. Nibley, *Enoch the Prophet*, The Collected Works of Hugh Nibley (Salt Lake City, UT: Deseret Book, 1986), 5–7, 42–44, 68–70, 189–91, 198–99.

7. Eugene England, "The Weeping God of Mormonism," *Dialogue* 35/1 (2002).

8. Peterson, "Weeping God."

Fiona Givens.[9] In addition, with regard to the complaints of the earth described in Moses 7:48–49, valuable articles by Andrew Skinner[10] and Peterson,[11] again following Nibley's lead,[12] discuss interesting parallels in ancient sources.

The purpose of this article is to round out the previous discussion so as to include two voices of weeping that have been largely forgotten by LDS scholarship—that of Enoch and that of the heavens.

The Weeping of Enoch

The tradition of a weeping prophet is perhaps best exemplified by Jeremiah who cried out in sorrow, "Oh that my head were waters, and mine eyes a fountain of tears, that I might **weep** day and night for the slain of the daughter of my people!" (Jeremiah 9:1).[13] In another place, he wrote, "Let mine eyes run down with tears night and day, and let them not cease: for the

---

9. Terryl L. Givens and Fiona Givens, *The God Who Weeps: How Mormonism Makes Sense of Life* (Salt Lake City, UT: Ensign Peak, 2012).

10. Andrew C. Skinner, "Joseph Smith Vindicated Again: Enoch, Moses 7:48, and Apocryphal Sources," in *Reason, Revelation, and Faith: Essays in Honor of Truman G. Madsen*, ed. Donald W. Parry, Daniel C. Peterson, and Stephen D. Ricks (Provo, UT: Foundation for Ancient Research and Mormon Studies, 2002), 373–80. In his discussion, Skinner cites ancient texts such as George W. E. Nickelsburg, ed. *1 Enoch 1: A Commentary on the Book of 1 Enoch, Chapters 1–36; 81–108* (Minneapolis, MN: Fortress Press, 2001), 7:6, 9:2, 87:1, pp. 182, 202, 364; Michael Wise, Martin Abegg, Jr, and Edward Cook, eds, *The Dead Sea Scrolls: A New Translation* (New York City, NY: Harper-Collins, 1996), 4Q203 Frag. 8:9, p. 294. See also Bakhayla Mika'el, "The Book of the Mysteries of the Heavens and the Earth," in *The Book of the Mysteries of the Heavens and the Earth and Other Works of Bakhayla Mika'el (Zosimas)*, ed. E. A. Wallis Budge (Oxford: Oxford University Press, 1934; repr., Berwick, ME: Ibis Press, 2004), p. 29: "[e]ven the earth complained and uttered lamentations."

11. In addition to discussing one of the *1 Enoch* passages mentioned by Skinner, Peterson follows J. J. M. Roberts in citing examples of Sumerian laments of the mother goddess ("Weeping God," 298–306).

12. Nibley, *Enoch*, 11–14, 74–75, 205–206.

13. Cf. Isaiah 22:4: "Therefore said I, Look away from me; I will weep bitterly, labour not to comfort me, because of the spoiling of the daughter of my people."

virgin daughter of my people is broken with a great breach, with a very grievous blow" (Jeremiah 14:17).

Less well-known is the story of Enoch as a weeping prophet. In the pseudepigraphal book of *1 Enoch*, his purported words are very near to those of Jeremiah, "O that my eyes were a [fountain][14] of water, that I might **weep** over you; I would pour out my tears as a cloud of water, and I would rest from the grief of my heart."[15]

We find the pseudepigraphal Enoch, like Enoch in the Book of Moses, weeping in response to visions of mankind's wickedness. Following the second of these visions, he is recorded as saying, "And after that I **wept** bitterly, and my tears did not cease until I could no longer endure it, but they were running down because of what I had seen . . . I **wept** because of it, and I was disturbed because I had seen the vision."[16]

In the *Apocalypse of Paul*, the apostle meets Enoch, "the scribe of righteousness," "within the gate of Paradise," and, after having been cheerfully embraced and kissed,[17] sees the

---

14. The text reads *dammana* [cloud], which Nickelsburg takes to be a corruption in the Aramaic (*1 Enoch 1*, 95:1, 463–64). Nibley plausibly takes motif of the "weeping" of clouds in this verse to be a parallel to Moses 7:28 (Nibley, *Enoch*, 199). On the other hand, Nibley's translation of *1 Enoch* 100:11–13 as describing a weeping of the heavens is surely a misreading (p. 198; cf. Nickelsburg, *1 Enoch 1*, 100:11–13, p. 503).

15. Nickelsburg, *1 Enoch 1*, 95:1, 460.

16. Nickelsburg, *1 Enoch 1*, 90:41–42, p. 402.

17. Following this encounter and embrace, Paul is told by an angel: "'Whatever I now show you here, and whatever you shall hear, tell no one on earth.' And he led me and showed me; and there I heard words which it is not lawful for a man to speak [2 Corinthians 12:4]." See J. K. Elliott, "The Apocalypse of Paul (Visio Pauli)," in *The Apocryphal New Testament: A Collection of Apocryphal Christian Literature in an English Translation*, ed. J. K. Elliott (Oxford, England: Oxford University Press, 2005), 20:628. In the version of the *Apocalypse of Paul* found at Nag Hammadi, Paul's encounter at the entrance to the seventh heaven is told differently, see George W. MacRae, William R. Murdock, and Douglas M. Parrott, "The Apocalypse of Paul (V, 2)," in *The Nag Hammadi Library*, ed. James M. Robinson (San Francisco, CA: HarperSanFrancisco, 1990), 22:23–23:30, p. 259. At that entrance, Paul is challenged with a series of questions from Enoch. In answer to Enoch's final question, Paul is instructed: "'Give him [the]

prophet weep, and says to him, "'Brother, why do you weep?' And again sighing and lamenting he said, 'We are hurt by men, and they grieve us greatly; for many are the good things which the Lord has prepared, and great is his promise, but many do not perceive them.'"[18] A similar motif of Enoch weeping over the generations of mankind can be found in the pseudepigraphal book of 2 Enoch.[19] "There is, to say the least," writes Nibley "no gloating in heaven over the fate of the wicked world. [And it] is Enoch who leads the weeping."[20]

Another instance of Enoch as a righteous and compassionate scribe appears in the Testament of Abraham. The archangel Michael opens to Abraham a vivid view of the heavenly judgment scene, whereupon Abraham asks:[21]

"Lord, who is this judge? And who is the other one who brings the charges of sins?" And Michael said to Abraham, "Do you see the judge? This is Abel, who first bore witness, and God brought him here to judge. And the one who produces (the evidence) is the teacher of heaven and earth and the scribe of righteousness, Enoch. For the Lord sent them here in order that they might record the sins and the righteous deeds of each person." And Abraham said, "And how can Enoch bear the weight of the souls, since he has not seen death? Or how can he give the sentence of all the souls?" And Michael said, "If he were to give sentence concerning

---

sign that you have, and [he will] open for you.' And then I gave [him] the sign." Whereupon "the [seventh] heaven opened."

18. Elliott, "Apocalypse of Paul," 20, p. 628.

19. F. I. Andersen, "2 (Slavonic Apocalypse of) Enoch," in The Old Testament Pseudepigrapha, ed. James H. Charlesworth (Garden City, NY: Doubleday and Company, 1983), 41:1 [J], p. 166: "[And] I saw all those from the age of my ancestors, with Adam and Eve. And I sighed and burst into tears."

20. Nibley, Enoch, 5.

21. E. P. Sanders, "Testament of Abraham," in Old Testament Pseudepigrapha, ed. Charlesworth 11:1–10 [Recension B], p. 900.

them, it would not be accepted. But it is not Enoch's business to give sentence; rather, the Lord is the one who gives sentence, and it is this one's (Enoch's) task only to write. For Enoch prayed to the Lord saying, 'Lord, I do not want to give the sentence of the souls, lest I become oppressive to someone.' And the Lord said to Enoch, 'I shall command you to write the sins of a soul that makes atonement, and it will enter into life. And if the soul has not made atonement and repented, you will find its sins (already) written, and it will be cast into punishment.'"

Here, Abraham voices the concern that a relatively mortal Enoch (one who "has not seen death") would not have the capacity to "bear the weight of the souls" who were being judged. However, Enoch exhibits his capacity for compassion and sympathy by taking into account the feelings of those being judged, fearing that he might "become oppressive to someone" should he judge amiss.

It is surprising that, so far as we have been able to ascertain, a thorough comparison of modern revelation with ancient sources bearing on the weeping of Enoch has never been undertaken.[22] Mere coincidence is an insufficient explanation for Joseph Smith's association of weeping with Enoch, as it is an attribute of this patriarch that occurs nowhere in scripture or other sources where the Prophet might have seen it,[23] and

---

22.   Sanders, "Testament of Abraham," 5–7, 14, 68, 189, 192, 205 addresses this topic, citing a handful of ancient parallels. Peterson, "Weeping God," 296 cites part of the passage from *Midrash Rabbah* included later in this article, but his focus is on the weeping of God rather than that of Enoch.

23.   Richard Laurence first translated the book of Enoch into English in 1821, but it is very unlikely that Joseph Smith would have encountered this work. Revised editions were published in 1833, 1838, and 1842, but these appeared subsequent to the Book of Moses account, which was received in 1830.

similar accounts of weeping are not associated with comparable figures in his translations and revelations.[24]

Besides Moses 7:41 and 49, we find two additional descriptions of Enoch's weeping in early LDS sources. The first instance is to be found in the words of a divinely-given song, recorded in Joseph Smith's *Revelation Book 2*,[25] where Enoch is said to have "gazed upon nature and the corruption of man, and mourned their sad fate, and wept." The second instance is in *Old Testament Manuscript 2* of the Joseph Smith Translation, where the revelatory account was corrected to say that it was Enoch rather than God who wept (see figure 1).

Moses 7:28 follows the description of *Old Testament Manuscript 1* where it is God who weeps, "And it came to pass that the *God of heaven* looked upon the residue of the people, and he **wept**; and *Enoch bore record of it, saying: How is it that*

---

24. An exception is, of course, Jesus Christ, who is recorded as having wept both in the New Testament (John 11:35) and in the Book of Mormon (3 Nephi 17:21–22; cf. Jacob 5:41). In 2 Nephi 4:26, Nephi once asks "why should my heart weep and my soul linger in the valley of sorrow?"

25. Joseph Smith, Jr. et al., *Manuscript Revelation Books, Facsimile Edition*, ed. Dean C. Jessee, Ronald K. Esplin, and Richard Lyman Bushman, *The Joseph Smith Papers, Revelations and Translations* (Salt Lake City, UT: The Church Historian's Press, 2009), Revelation Book 2, 48 [verso], 27 February 1833, 508–509, spelling and punctuation modernized. The preface to the entry in the revelation book says that it was "sung by the gift of tongues and translated." An expanded and versified version of this song that omits the weeping of Enoch was published in *Evening and Morning Star*, (Independence, MO and Kirtland, OH: 1832–1834; repr., Basel Switzerland: Eugene Wagner, 2 vols., 1969), 1:12, May 1833.

It has been argued by Frederick G. Williams that both the original and versified version of this song should be attributed to his ancestor of the same name. See Frederick Granger Williams, "Singing the Word of God: Five Hymns by President Frederick G. Williams," *BYU Studies* 48/1 (2009). On the other hand, the editors of the relevant volume of the Joseph Smith Papers note: "An undated broadside of the hymn states that it was 'sung in tongues' by David W. Patten and 'interpreted' by Sidney Rigdon. ("Mysteries of God." Church History Library.) This item was never canonized" (Smith et al., *Manuscript Revelation Books*, 377 n.65).

*the heavens **weep**,* and shed forth [*her*][26] tears as the rain upon the mountains?"

By way of contrast, version 2 of the manuscript is amended to say that it was Enoch who wept instead of God, "And it came to pass, that *Enoch* looked upon the residue of the people and **wept**; and *he beheld and lo! the heavens **wept** also,* and shed forth *their* tears as the rain upon the mountains."[27]

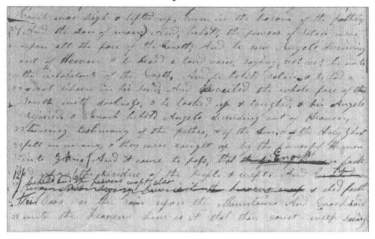

Figure 1. Old Testament Manuscript #2, page 21 (Moses 7:24–29); handwriting of John Whitmer, corrections in the hand of Sidney Rigdon[28]

Within the theme of the weeping Enoch, there are several specific subthemes that are common in both the Book of Moses and ancient literature:

26. OT1 says "her"; Moses 7:28 says "their." See Scott H. Faulring, Kent P. Jackson, and Robert J. Matthews, eds., *Joseph Smith's New Translation of the Bible: Original Manuscripts* (Provo, UT: BYU Religious Studies Center, 2004), 618; Jackson, *Book of Moses*, 124.

27. Faulring, et al., *Original Manuscripts*, 618; Jackson, *Book of Moses*, 123–24.

28. From Kent P. Jackson, *The Book of Moses and the Joseph Smith Translation Manuscripts* (Provo, UT: BYU Religious Studies Center, 2005), 122 . Image courtesy Church of Christ.

- Weeping in similitude of God
- Weeping because of divine withdrawal from the earth
- Weeping because of the insulting words of the wicked
- Weeping followed by heavenly vision

We will discuss each of these in turn.

Weeping in similitude of God.
In the *Midrash Rabbah* on Lamentations, Enoch is portrayed as weeping in likeness of God when the Israelite temple was destroyed:[29]

> At that time the Holy One, blessed be He, wept and said, "Woe is Me! What have I done? I caused my *Shekhinah* to dwell below on earth for the sake of Israel; but now that they have sinned, I have returned to My former habitation. . . ." At that time Metatron [who is Enoch in his glorified state] came, fell upon his face, and spake before the Holy One, blessed be He: "Sovereign of the Universe, let me **weep**, but do Thou not **weep**." He replied to him: "if thou lettest Me not **weep** now, I will repair to a place which thou hast not permission to enter,[30] and will **weep** there," as it is said, "But if ye will not hear it, My soul shall **weep** in secret for pride" (Jeremiah 13:17).

The dialogue between God and Enoch in this passage is reminiscent of the one in Moses 7:28–41:

> 28 And it came to pass that the God of heaven looked upon the residue of the people, and he **wept**; and Enoch

---

29. H. Freedman and Maurice Simon, eds., *Midrash Rabbah*, 3rd ed., 10 vols. (London: Soncino Press, 1983), 41 (Lamentations 24).

30. I.e, the inner chambers of the heavenly temple. See also Babylonian Talmud *Hagigah 5b*, cited in Herbert W. Basser, "A Love for All Seasons: Weeping in Jewish Sources," in *Holy Tears: Weeping in the Religious Imagination*, ed. Kimberley Christine Patton and John Stratton Hawley (Princeton, NJ: Princeton University Press, 2005), 184–85.

bore record of it, saying: How is it that the heavens **weep**, and shed forth their tears as the rain upon the mountains?

29 And Enoch said unto the Lord: How is it that thou canst **weep**, seeing thou art holy, and from all eternity to all eternity?

Enoch, seeing God weeping, judges this emotional display to be inappropriate for the holy, eternal God. In the Book of Moses account, God, in response, proceeds to show Enoch the wickedness of the people of the Earth and how much they will suffer in consequence. After seeing this vision of the misery that would come upon God's children, Enoch commiserates with God and begins to weep inconsolably.[31]

Speaking of Old Testament prophets in general, Abraham Heschel explains that "what convulsed the prophet's whole being was God. His condition was a state of suffering in sympathy with the divine pathos."[32] This view of prophets stands in stark contrast to Philo of Alexandria's parallel description of the relationship between the high priest and God in *De Specialibus Legibus*. In this passage, Philo is commenting upon the law in Leviticus 21:10–12 which prohibits the high priest from mourning for (or even approaching) the bodies of deceased parents. In a statement reflective of Philo's thoroughly Greek philosophical thought, he writes:[33]

---

31. Cf. Noah's expression of grief in John J. Collins, "Sibylline Oracles," in *Old Testament Pseudepigrapha*, ed. Charlesworth, 1:190–191, p. 339: "how much will I lament, how much will I weep in my wooden house, how many tears will I mingle with the waves?"

32. Abraham Joshua Heschel, *The Prophets*, Two Volumes in One ed. (Peabody, MA: Hendrickson, 2007), 1:118, cf. 1:80–85, 91–92, 105–27; 2:101–103.

33. Philo, "On the Special Laws (De Specialibus Legibus)." Translated by F. H. Colson. In *Philo*, ed. F. H. Colson. 12 vols. *The Loeb Classical Library 320*, 7:97–607, 17–43. (Cambridge, MA: Harvard University Press, 1937), 1:113–16, pp. 165, 167, emphasis added.

[T]he high priest is precluded from all outward mourn-ing and surely with good reason. For the services of the other priests can be performed by deputy, so that if some are in mourning none of the customary rites need suffer. But no one else is allowed to perform the functions of a high priest and therefore he must always continue undefiled, never coming in contact with a corpse, so that he may be ready to offer his prayers and sacrifices at the proper time without hindrance on be-half of the nation.

Further, since he is dedicated to God and has been made captain of the sacred regiment, *he ought to be es-tranged from all the ties of birth and not be so overcome by affection* to parents or children or brothers as to ne-glect or postpone any one of the religious duties which it were well to perform without any delay. He forbids him also either to rend his garments for his dead, even the nearest and dearest, or to take from his head the in-signia of the priesthood, or on any account to leave the sacred precincts under the pretext of mourning. *Thus, showing reverence both to the place and to the personal ornaments with which he is decked, he will have his feel-ing of pity under control and continue throughout free from sorrow.*

For the law desires him to be endued with a nature higher than the merely human and to approximate to the Divine, on the border-line, we may truly say, between the two, that men may have a mediator through whom they may propitiate God and God a servitor to employ in extending the abundance of His boons to men.

Philo's view of a dispassionate yet mediating high priest is not only at odds with the portrayal of Jesus as high priest pre-sented in Hebrews 4:15 ("For we have not an high priest which cannot be touched with the feeling of our infirmities"), but certainly also with Heschel's perspective of mediating prophets as those who have entered into "a fellowship with the feelings of God."[34] As in the case of Enoch, a model of divine sympathy calls into question teachings regarding divine apathy.

The *Mishnah* describes weeping as part of the rituals of the high priest on *Yom Kippur*:[35]

1:4 A.   All seven days they did not hold back food or drink from him.

B.   [But] on the eve of the Day of Atonement at dusk they did not let him eat much,

C.   for food brings on sleep.

1:5 A.   The elders of the court handed him over to the elders of the priesthood,

B.   who brought him up to the upper chamber of Abtinas.

C.   And they imposed an oath on him and took their leave and went along.

D.   [This is what] they said to him, "My lord, high priest: We are agents of the court, and you are our agent and agent of the court.

E.   "We abjure you by Him who caused his name

---

34. Heschel, *Prophets*, 31. More generally, this attitude opposes Alma's description of the distinctive traits of any who are desirous to be called God's covenant people in Mosiah 18:8–9 ("willing to bear one another's burdens, that they may be light; . . . willing to mourn with those that mourn; yea, and comfort those that stand in need of comfort"; cf. D&C 42:45). This covenantal sympathy turns out later to be a sort of *imitatio dei*, as God states, "I know of the covenant which ye have made unto me; and I will covenant with my people and deliver them out of bondage. And *I will also ease the burdens which are put upon your shoulders, that even you cannot feel them upon your backs,* even while you are in bondage; and this will I do that ye may stand as witnesses for me hereafter, and that ye may know of a surety that I, the Lord God, do visit my people in their afflictions" (Mosiah 24:13–14, emphasis added). Note also the emphasis in both Mosiah 18:9 and 24:14 on standing "as witnesses" of God through this sympathetic interaction.

35. Jacob Neusner, ed. *The Mishnah: A New Translation* (London: Yale University Press, 1988), 1:4–1:6, p. 266.

to rest upon this house, that you will not vary in any way from all which we have instructed you."

F.   He turns aside and **weeps**.

G.   And they turn aside and **weep**.

1:6   A.   If he was a sage, he expounds [the relevant Scriptures].

B.   And if not, disciples of sages expound for him.

The explanation for the weeping of the high priest and the people is given as follows in the *Gemara*:[36]

"He turns aside and **weeps** and they turn aside and **weep**." He turned aside and **wept** because he was suspected of being a Sadducee, and they turned aside and **wept**, for as Rabbi Joshua ben Levi said—When someone suspects another who is guiltless, he will be punished bodily. What was all this about?—so that he would not arrange the incense outside and then bring it into the Holy of Holies, as the Sadducees were apt to do. The Rabbis taught: There was once a Sadducee who arranged the incense outside and then brought it in. As he was departing he was very joyous. His father met him and said: Though we are Sadducees, we are afraid of the Pharisees.

Moses Maimonides, the great 13th century Jewish scholar, elaborated on this interpretation as follows:[37]

Halacha 7. In the days of the second temple a free-thinking spirit flourished in Israel; and the Sadducees arose — may they soon disappear! — who do not believe oral teaching. They said that, on the day of atonement, the incense was to be lighted in the temple

---

36.   Leo Auerbach, *The Babylonian Talmud in Selection* (New York City, NY: Philosophical Library, 1944), 58.

37.   Moses Maimonides, "The ritual of the Day of Atonement," http://www.edwardfudge.com/written/app5.html.

outside the veil, and that when the smoke ascended therefrom it was to be carried inside into the holiest of holiest[.] The reason for this is, that they explain the words of Scripture (Leviticus 16:2, "For I will appear in the cloud on the mercy-seat") as referring to the clouds proceeding from the incense[.] But sages have learnt by tradition that the frankincense was first lighted in the holy of holies facing the ark, as it is written (Leviticus 16:13), "And he shall put the incense upon the fire before Jehovah." Now, because in the second temple they entertained the apprehension that the then existing high priest might incline to the free-thinking party, they therefore, on the preparation day for the day of atonement, conjured him, saying: "My lord! high priest! We are delegates of the high court, but thou art delegate both for us and the high court; we conjure thee by Him who causes His name to rest upon this house, we conjure thee to make no change in anything that we have said to thee." Thereupon he goes away and **weeps** because they had suspected him of free-thinking, and they go away and **weep** because they had entertained a suspicion against a person whose conduct was unknown to them; for perhaps he had nothing of the kind in his thoughts.

To us, the explanations of the *Gemara* and of Maimonides seem like a late post hoc explanation of the practice, and other directions for its origins ought to be explored. As one possible avenue into related practices in the ancient Near East, Kenton L. Sparks has noted that certain aspects of the Israelite Day of Atonement rite "seem to mimic" events of the Babylonian *akītu* festival.[38] The Babylonian king, as part of the ceremonies of the

---

38. Kenton L. Sparks, *Ancient Texts for the Study of the Hebrew Bible: A Guide to the Background Literature* (Peabody, MA: Hendrickson Publishers, 2005), 167. Cf. Roy E. Gane, "Schedules for Deities: Macrostructure of Israelite,

akītu festival, was required to submit to a royal ordeal involving an initial period of suffering and ritual death. Once this phase was complete, the king washed his hands and entered the temple for the rites of (re)investiture, as described in Black's reconstruction of events. Note the importance of the weeping of the king at the end of the ceremony:

> The šešgallu, who is in the sanctuary, comes out and divests the king of his staff of office, ring, mace, and crown. These insignia he takes into the sanctuary and places on a seat. Coming out again, he strikes the king across the face. He now leads him into the sanctuary and pulling him by the ears, forces him to kneel before the god. The king utters the formula:
>
> > *I have not sinned, Lord of the lands,*
> > *I have not been negligent of your godhead.*
> > *I have not destroyed Babylon,*
> > *I have not ordered her to be dispersed.*
> > *I have not made Esagil quake,*
> > *I have not forgotten its rites.*
> > *I have not struck the privileged citizens in the faces,*
> > *I have not humiliated them.*
> > *I have paid attention to Babylon,*
> > *I have not destroyed her walls . . . .*
>
> He leaves the sanctuary. The šešgallu replies to this with an assurance of Bel's favor and indulgence towards the king: "He will destroy your enemies, defeat your adversaries," and the king regains the customary composure of his expression and is reinvested with his insignia, fetched by the šešgallu from within the sanctuary. Once more he strikes the king across the face,

for an omen: if the king's tears flow, Bel is favorably disposed; if not, he is angry.[39]

Gane notes a difference in theology between Babylon and Israel that is consistent with the fact that the Day of Atonement ritual included the people in weeping, whereas the *akītu* rite of atonement involved only the king:[40] "The king of Babylon, whose relation with the gods affected the Babylonian people, affirmed his innocence before Marduk, . . . but he admitted no need of forgiveness. In Israel, on the other hand, impurity came from the people themselves, and it was cleansed from the sanctuary along with moral faults which they had committed (Leviticus 16:16; cf. verse 21)."[41]

The theme of shared sorrow between God and prophet is explored at length by theologian Terence Fretheim.[42] According to Fretheim, "The prophet's life was reflective of the divine life. This became increasingly apparent to Israel. God is seen to be present not only in what the prophet has to say, but in the word as embodied in the prophet's life. To hear and see the prophet was to hear and see God, a God who was suffering on behalf of the people."[43] So close was the association between God and prophet that the prophet's very presence could serve as a sort of

---

39. Jeremy A. Black, "The New Year Ceremonies in Ancient Babylon: 'Taking Bel By the Hand' and a Cultic Picnic," *Religion* 11/1 (1981), 44–45.

40. Gane, "Schedules," 243.

41. See Benjamin D. Sommer, "The Babylonian Akitu Festival: Rectifying the King or Renewing the Cosmos?" *Journal of the Ancient Near Eastern Society* 27 (2000) for a refutation of J.Z. Smith's argument that the purpose of the ritual humiliation of the king was to assert "the legitimacy of the foreigners who ruled Babylon during the Hellenistic age." Instead, Sommer argues for "a revised version of the older consensus" that "the festival was intended to destroy and subsequently renew the cosmos," which required both a rite of atonement for the king and the renewal of kingship, "Babylonian Akitu Festival," 81.

42. Terence Fretheim, *The Suffering of God: An Old Testament Perspective* (Philadelphia, PA: Fortress Press, 1984), 149. See especially chapter 10, "Prophet, Theophany, and the Suffering of God," 149–66.

43. Fretheim, *Suffering*, 149.

"ongoing theophany,"[44] providing Israel with a very visible and tangible representation of God's concern.[45]

Fretheim argues that the prophet's "sympathy with the divine pathos" was not the result of contemplating the divine, but rather a result of the prophet's participation in the divine council. He writes:[46]

> [T]he fact that the prophets are said to be a part of this council indicates something of the intimate relationship they had with God. The prophet was somehow drawn up into the very presence of God; even more, the prophet was in some sense admitted into the history of God. The prophet becomes a party to the divine story; the heart and mind of God pass over into that of the prophet to such an extent that the prophet becomes a veritable embodiment of God.

In the case of Enoch, the prophet enters into the presence of God (Moses 7:20) and witnesses the weeping of God and a heavenly host over the wickedness of humanity (vv. 28–31, 37, 40). As a result of this participation in the heavenly council, Enoch becomes divinely sensitized to the plight of the human race and begins to weep himself (vv. 41, 44).

---

44. Fretheim, *Suffering*, 151.

45. Some of Israel's neighbors also held this view. Humanity's capacity to weep as the gods did is alluded to in the *Middle Egyptian Coffin Text 1130*. It reads, "I have created the gods from my sweat, and the people from the tears of my eye," Miriam Lichtheim, ed. *Ancient Egyptian Literature: A Book of Readings*, 3 vols. (Berkeley, CA: The University of California Press, 2006), 132. In making this association between the creation of humanity and the tears of the god, the author is playing on the Egyptian words for "people" (*rmt*) and "tears" (*rmyt*), suggesting a link between the two terms (Miriam Lichtheim, ed. *Ancient Egyptian Literature*, 133 n. 3; cf. Nibley, *Enoch*, 43, citing Hornung). Nibley cites a very close association with our Book of Moses text in a manuscript, where, in a mention of the Ugaritic Enoch, it is asked: "Who is Krt that he should weep? Or shed tears, the Good one, the Lad of El?" (*Enoch*, 42; cf. Moses 6:31).

46. Fretheim, *Suffering*, 150.

Weeping because of divine withdrawal from the earth.
A full chorus of weeping that begins with the Messiah and expands to include the heavens and its angelic hosts is eloquently described in a Jewish mystical text called the *Zohar*:

> Then the Messiah lifts up his voice and **weeps**, and the whole Garden of Eden quakes, and all the righteous and saints who are there break out in crying and lamentation with him. When the crying and **weeping** resound for the second time, the whole firmament above the Garden begins to shake, and the cry echoes from five hundred myriads of supernal hosts until it reaches the highest Throne.[47]

The reason for this weeping "of all the workmanship of [God's] hands" (Moses 7:40) is the loss of the temple—the withdrawal of the divine presence from the earth. One might see here some degree of affinity with the requirement for the weeping of the king on the fifth day of the Babylonian *akītu* festival, following the symbolic razing of the temple on the festival's second day.[48] In Jewish tradition, the withdrawal of the divine presence is portrayed as having occurred in a series of poignant stages. This is vividly illustrated in Ezekiel 9–11. Because of the priests' wickedness within the temple precincts, the "glory of the God of Israel" moves from its resting place within the temple compound to the threshold of the temple (Ezekiel 9:3), where it remains for a time. Finally, after surveying the extent of the wicked priests' actions within the temple, Ezekiel sees the "glory of Yahweh" leave the temple, continue east through the city of Jerusalem, and finally come to rest upon the Mount of Olives (Ezekiel 11:23). This departure of the God of Israel from

---

47. Harry Sperling, Maurice Simon, and Paul P. Levertoff, eds., *The Zohar: An English Translation*, 5 vols. (London: Soncino Press, 1984), Shemoth 8a, 3:22. See also the mention of the "two tears of the Holy One, . . . namely two measures of chastisement, which comes from both of those tears" (Shemoth 19b, 3:62).

48. See Philo, "On the Special Laws (De Specialibus Legibus)," above note 33.

the great city of Jerusalem was especially significant from the perspectives of the nations who surrounded Israel. According to the Hebrew Bible scholar Margaret Odell, "In ancient Near Eastern thought, a city could not be destroyed unless its god had abandoned it."[49] With the presence of God removed from the city, it now lay exposed and vulnerable to attack, a condition that was exploited by the Babylonians.

The withdrawal of the divine presence from the temple is a fitting analogue to the taking up of Enoch's Zion from the earth. Whereas in the above passages, where God withdraws His presence, or His glory, due to the wickedness of the people, Moses 7 (vv. 21, 23, 27, 31) has God removing the righteous city of Zion in its entirety from among the wicked nations that surround it. The differences in the two pericopes may actually have more in common than is immediately apparent. In Jewish literature there is a significant correspondence between Zion and the *Shekhinah* (Divine Presence). Zion is often personified as the Bride of God (Revelation 21:2). *Shekhinah* is a feminine noun in Hebrew and often associated with the female personified Wisdom. It is likewise described in later Jewish writings as the Bride of God. The idea of Zion being taken up and the *Shekhinah* being withdrawn are parallel motifs.

Weeping because of the insulting words of the wicked.
Pheme Perkins has rightly argued that:

> Speech is much more carefully controlled and monitored in a traditional, hierarchical society than it is in modern democracies. We can hardly recapture the sense of horror at blasphemy that ancient society felt because for us words do not have the same power that they do in traditional societies. Words appear to have

---

49. Margaret Odell, *Ezekiel* (Macon, GA: Smyth and Helwys, 2005), 119.

considerably less consequences than actions. In traditional societies, the word is a form of action. [50]

Consistent with this idea, a Manichaean text describes an Enoch who weeps because of the harsh words of the wicked, "I am Enoch the righteous. My sorrow was great, and a torrent of tears [streamed] from my eyes because I heard the insult which the wicked ones uttered." [51] Elsewhere, Enoch is said to have prophesied a future judgment upon such "ungodly sinners" who have "uttered hard speeches . . . against [the Lord]." [52] Rabbi Eliezer gives examples of such insults, "We don't need Your drops of rain, neither do we need to walk in Your ways." [53] Having been told by Noah that all mankind would be destroyed by the Flood if they did not repent, these same "sons of God" are said to have defiantly replied, "If this is the case, we will stop human reproduction and multiplying, and thus put an end to the lineage of the sons of men ourselves." [54]

Likewise, in Moses 8:21, we find these examples of truculent boasting in the mouths of the antediluvians, "Behold, we are the sons of God; have we not taken unto ourselves the daughters of men? And are we not eating and drinking, and marrying and giving in marriage? And our wives bear unto us

---

50. Pheme Perkins, *First and Second Peter, James, and Jude* (Louisville, KY: John Knox, 1995), 154, cited in Ben Witherington, III, *Letters and Homilies for Jewish Christians: A Socio-Rhetorical Commentary on Hebrews, James and Jude* (Downers Grove, IL: IVP Academic, 2007), Jude 14–16, p. 624.

51. John C. Reeves, *Heralds of that Good Realm: Syro-Mesopotamian Gnosis and Jewish Traditions*, ed. James M. Robinson and Hans-Joachim Klimkeit (Leiden: E. J. Brill, 1996), 183. Cf. Ron Cameron and Arthur J. Dewey, eds., *The Cologne Mani Codex (P. Colon. inv. nr. 4780) 'Concerning the Origin of His Body,'* (Missoula, MN: Scholars Press, 1979), 58:6–20, p. 45.

52. Jude 1:15, citing Nickelsburg, *1 Enoch 1*, 1:9, p. 142. See also 1 Enoch 5:4, 27:2, 101:3. 2 Peter 2:5 labels this same generation as "ungodly."

53. Marc-Alain Ouaknin and Éric Smilévitch, eds., *Chapitres de Rabbi Éliézer (Pirqé de Rabbi Éliézer): Midrach sur Genèse, Exode, Nombres, Esther*, Les Dix Paroles (Lagrasse: Éditions Verdier, 1992), 22:134.

54. Ouaknin et al., ed., *Chapitres de Rabbi Éliézer*, 22:136.

children, and the same are mighty men, which are like unto men of old, men of great renown."

An ancient exegetical tradition cited by John Reeves associates the speech of Job in 21:7–15 "to events transpiring during the final years of the antediluvian era,"[55] rather than to the time of Job. Likewise, in *3 Enoch* these verses are directly linked, not to Job, but to Enoch himself.[56] In defiance of the Lord's entreaty to "love one another, and . . . choose me, their Father" (Moses 7:33),[57] the wicked are depicted as "say[ing] unto God, . . . Depart from us: for we desire not the knowledge of thy ways.What is the Almighty, that we should serve him? And what profit should we have if we pray unto him?" (Job 21:14–15)[58] Reeves characterizes these words as "a blasphemous rejection of divine governance and guidance . . . wherein the wicked members of the Flood generation verbally reject God."[59]

Weeping followed by heavenly vision.

In the *Cologne Mani Codex*, Enoch's tearful sorrow is directly followed by an angelophany: "While the tears were still in my eyes and the prayer was yet on my lips, I beheld approaching me s[even] angels descending from heaven. [Upon seeing] them I was so moved by fear that my knees began knocking."[60]

A description of a similar set of events is found in *2 Enoch*,[61] which Moshe Idel called "the earliest evidence for mystical

55. Reeves, *Heralds*, 187. For a list of ancient sources, see pp. 183, 200 n.17.

56. P. Alexander, "3 (Hebrew Apocalypse of) Enoch," in *Old Testament Pseudepigrapha*, ed. Charlesworth, 4:3, p. 258: "When the generation of the Flood sinned and turned to evil deeds, and said to God, 'Go away! We do not choose to learn your ways' [cf. Job 21:14], the Holy One, blessed be he, took me [Enoch] from their midst to be a witness against them in the heavenly height to all who should come into the world, so that they should not say, 'The Merciful One is cruel!'"

57. Cf. Isaiah 1:2–3, where Isaiah "pleads with us to understand the plight of a father whom his children have abandoned" (Heschel, *Prophets*, 1:80).

58. Cf. Exodus 5:2; Malachi 3:13–15; Mosiah 11:27; Moses 5:16.

59. Reeves, *Heralds*, 188.

60. Reeves, *Heralds*, 183.

61. Andersen, "2 Enoch," A (short version), 1:2–4, pp. 105, 107.

weeping": "In the first month, on the assigned day of the first month, I was in my house alone, **weeping** and grieving with my eyes. When I had lain down on my bed, I fell asleep. And two huge men appeared to me, the like of which I had never seen on earth."[62]

The same sequence of events, Enoch's weeping and grieving followed by a heavenly vision, can be found in modern revelation within the song of *Revelation Book 2* mentioned earlier: "Enoch... gazed upon nature and the corruption of man, and mourned their sad fate, and **wept**, and cried out with a loud voice, and heaved forth his sighs: 'Omnipotence! Omnipotence! O may I see Thee!' And with His finger He touched his eyes[63]

---

62. Moshe Idel, *Kabbalah: New Perspectives* (New Haven, CN: Yale University Press, 1988), 76. Later adepts of mystical Judaism emulated the example of Enoch in a deliberate effort to obtain a vision by weeping, see pp. 75–88.

63. See also Moses 6:35–36, where Enoch is asked to anoint his eyes with clay prior to receiving a vision (cf. John 9:6–7). When the Lord spoke with Abraham, He first put His hand upon the latter's eyes to prepare him for his vision of the universe (see Abraham 3:11–12). Joseph Smith was reportedly so touched at the beginning of the First Vision, and perhaps prior to receiving D&C 76 (see D&C 76:19–20 and J. Smith, Jr. (or W. W. Phelps), *A Vision*, 1 February 1843, stanzas 15–16, p. 82, reprinted in Larry E. Dahl, "The Vision of the Glories," in *The Doctrine and Covenants*, ed. Robert L. Millet and Kent P. Jackson (Salt Lake City: Deseret Book, 1989), 297. (Thanks to Bryce Haymond for pointing out the latter reference.)

With respect to the First Vision, Charles Lowell Walker recorded the following "Br. John Alger said while speaking of the Prophet Joseph, that when he, John, was a small boy he heard the Prophet Joseph relate his vision of seeing the Father and the Son. [He said t]hat God touched his eyes with his finger and said 'Joseph, this is my beloved Son hear him.' As soon as the Lord had touched his eyes with his finger, he immediately saw the Savior. . . . [Br. Alger said] that Joseph while speaking of it put his finger to his right eye, suiting the action with the words so as to illustrate and at the same time impress the occurrence on the minds of those unto whom he was speaking," Charles Lowell Walker, *Diary of Charles Lowell Walker*, ed. A. Karl Larson and Katharine Miles Larson, 2 vols. (Logan, UT: Utah State University Press, 1980), 2 February 1893, 2:755–756, punctuation and capitalization modernized.

The two accounts of Enoch mentioned previously can be profitably compared to the experience of Lehi who, "because of the things which he saw and heard he did quake and tremble exceedingly," and "he cast himself upon his bed, being overcome with the Spirit" (1 Nephi 1:6–7). Whereupon the heavens were the opened to him (see 1 Nephi 1:8). See also, e.g, Baruch's weeping for the loss of

and he saw heaven. He gazed on eternity and sang an angelic song."[64]

Noting that this pattern is not confined to Enoch, Reeves writes: "Prayer coordinated with weeping that leads to an angelophany is also a sequence prominent in [other] apocalyptic traditions."[65]

The Weeping of the Heavens

Providing a plausible echo of the imagery of the weeping of the heavens in Enoch's account is an ancient Jewish theme that is always associated with the second day of Creation, when the heavenly and earthly waters were separated by the firmament. According to David Lieber: "The *Midrash* pictures the lower waters weeping at being separated from the upper waters, suggesting that there is something poignant in the creative process when things once united are separated."[66]

So painful was the command of God for the waters to separate that they actually rebelled, as Heschel recounts:

> On the second day of creation, the Holy and Blessed One said: "Let there be an expanse (*raki'a*) in the midst of the water, that it may separate water from water. God made the expanse, and it separated the water that was below the expanse from the water which was above the expanse" (Genesis 1:6–7). "God said to the waters:

the temple, A. F. J. Klijn, "2 (Syriac Apocalypse of) Baruch," in *Old Testament Pseudepigrapha*, ed. Charlesworth, 35:2, p. 632, quoting Jeremiah 9:1, which was also followed by a vision.

64. Smith et al., *Manuscript Revelation Books, Facsimile Edition*, Revelation Book 2, 48 [verso], 27 February 1833, 508–509, spelling and punctuation modernized.

65. Reeves, *Heralds*, 189, citing 4 Ezra 5:13, 20; 6:35; 2 Apoc. Bar. 6:2–8:3; 9:2–10:1; 3 Apoc. Bar. 1:1–3; and Daniel 10:2–5. Reeves also observes that weeping is a component of ritual mourning (see Deuteronomy 21:13).

66. David L. Lieber, ed. *Etz Hayim: Torah and Commentary* (New York City, NY: Jewish Publication Society, 2001), 5.

divide yourselves into two halves; one half shall go up, and the other half shall go down; but the waters presumptuously all went upward. Said to them the Holy and Blessed One: I told you that only half should go upward, and all of you went upward?! Said the waters: We shall not descend! Thus did they brazenly confront their Creator. . . . What did the Holy and Blessed One do? God extended His little finger, and they tore into two parts, and God took half of them down against their will. Thus it is written: 'God Said, let there be an expanse (*raki'a*)' (Genesis 1:6)—do not read 'expanse' (*raki'a*) but 'tear' (*keri'a*).[67]

Heschel makes it clear "that the waters rebelled against their Creator not out of competitiveness or jealousy but rather out of protest against the partition made by the Holy and Blessed One between the upper and lower realms."[68] Avivah Zornberg has the lower waters complaining: "We want to be in the presence of the King."[69] This statement is made meaningful by the understanding that the partition that divided the upper and lower divisions of the waters was an allusion to the veil that divided off the Holy of Holies in the temple. Because of their separation, the lower waters no longer enjoyed the glory of the direct presence of God. Note Louis Ginzberg's reconstruction of Jewish tradition about the days of Creation, "God told the angels: On the first day of Creation, I shall make the heavens and stretch them out; so will Israel raise up the Tabernacle as the dwelling place of my Glory (Exodus 40:17–19). On the second day I shall put a division between the terrestrial waters

---

67. Abraham Joshua Heschel, *Heavenly Torah as Refracted Through the Generations*, trans. Gordon Tucker, 3 in 1 vols. (New York City, NY: Continuum International, 2007), 124, citing Midrash Konen, *Otzar Midrashim*, 254.

68. Heschel, *Heavenly Torah*, 125.

69. Avivah Gottlieb Zornberg, *Genesis: The Beginning of Desire* (Philadelphia, PA: Jewish Publication Society, 1995), 5–6.

and the heavenly waters, so will [Moses] hang up a veil in the Tabernacle to divide the Holy Place and the Most Holy (Exodus 40:20–21)."[70]

Even though the heavens may seem far above the earth, Jewish sages knew them as being very near at hand. In one story, Ben Zoma is recorded as having said:

> I was pondering the creation of the universe and I have concluded that there was scarcely a handbreadth's division between the upper and lower waters. For we read in Scripture, "The spirit of God hovered over the waters" (Genesis 1:2). Now Scripture also says: "Like an eagle who rouses his nestlings, hovering over his young" (Deuteronomy 32:11). Just as an eagle, when it flies over its nest, barely touches the nest, so there is barely a handbreadth's distance separating the upper and lower waters."[71]

Given the creation setting of this motif, it should not be surprising for those who regard the Book of Moses as an ancient account that it associates the weeping of the heavens with the story of the Flood,[72] which, in essence, recounts the destruction

---

70. Louis Ginzberg, ed. *The Legends of the Jews*, 7 vols. (Philadelphia, PA: Jewish Publication Society, 1909–1938; repr., Baltimore, MD: Johns Hopkins University Press, 1998), 1:51.

71. Heschel, *Heavenly Torah*, 125, citing Tosefta Hagigah 2:6; PT Hagigah 2:1 (77a-b); BT Hagigah 15a; Genesis Rabbah 2:4.

72. Other accounts from the ancient Near East also describe the weeping of the heavens (or the heavenly host) in response to a cataclysmic flood. In the *Epic of Gilgamesh*, the goddess Ishtar laments her support for the destruction of humanity by means of a flood; see Andrew George, ed. *The Epic of Gilgamesh* (London,: Penguin Group, 2003), 11:117–24, p. 92:

> The goddess cried out like a woman in childbirth,
> Belet-ili wailed, whose voice is so sweet:
> "The olden times have turned to clay,
> > because I spoke evil in the gods' assembly,
> How could I speak evil in the gods' assembly,
> > And declare a war to destroy my people?
> "It is I who give birth, these people are mine!

and the *re*-creation of the earth.[73] On the other hand, for those who do not accept the divine provenance of the book, it is a puzzling anomaly indeed that the theme of the weeping of the heavens, which Joseph Smith could not have encountered in scripture or in Jewish lore, has reappeared in modern revelation in such a fitting context.

To fully appreciate the complex symbology in the stories of the Creation and the Flood with respect to the separation and uniting of the waters, an explanation of the imagery of the Ark as it would have been seen through ancient eyes must be made.[74] As in the moment immediately preceding the Creation, when God descended and "his pavilion round about him were dark waters and thick clouds of the skies" (Psalm 18:11), so scripture would have told the observant reader from a previous time that Noah was to ride in his glorious Ark over the stormy deep as a prelude to the remaking of the world.[75] Nibley notes

And now, like fish, they fill the ocean!"
In response, the heavenly host join in a chorus of weeping over the dire situation, 11:125–27, p. 92:

The Anunnaki gods were weeping with her,
    wet-faced with sorrow, they were weeping [with her,]
their lips were parched and stricken with fever.

73. See Jeffrey M. Bradshaw, "The Ark and the Tent: Temple Symbolism in the Story of Noah" (paper presented at the Symposium on "The Temple on Mount Zion," Provo, UT, 22 September 2012) for more on this theme. See also http:www.templethemes.net.

74. See Bradshaw, "The Ark and the Tent."

75. Cf. Marvin Meyer, "The Secret Book of John (The Apocryphon of John)," in *The Nag Hammadi Scriptures: The International Edition*, ed. Marvin Meyer (New York City, NY: HarperOne, 2007), 29:135–136, p. 130:

It did not happen the way that Moses said, "They hid in an ark" [Genesis 7:7]. Rather, they hid in a particular place, not only Noah, but also many other people from the unshakable generation. They entered that place and hid in a bright cloud. Noah knew about his supremacy ["he (Noah) recognized his authority" (Frederik Wisse, "The Apocryphon of John (II, 1, III, 1, IV, 1, and BG 8502,2)," in *The Nag Hammadi Library in English*, ed. James M. Robinson (San Francisco, CA: HarperSanFrancisco, 1990), 29:12, p. 121); "Noah was aware of his divine calling" (Nibley, *Enoch*, p. 268)]. With him was the enlightened one who had enlightened them, since the first ruler had brought darkness upon the whole earth.

that in such accounts, where torrential waters and thick darkness above and beneath occlude the horizon, "the distinction between earth-travel and sky-travel often disappears."[76]

In the story of the Ark's motions upon the waters, however, we witness something more grave than a blurring of the distinction between earth-travel and sky-travel. Rather, we are made to understand that, figuratively speaking, the very sky has fallen and the "habitable and culture-orientated world lying between the heavens above and the underworld below, and separating them"[77] by "a handbreadth's distance,"[78] has utterly disappeared.[79] The waters above and the waters below had become one again, as at the beginning. In the words of *1 Enoch*, "heaven . . . fell down upon the earth. And when it fell upon the earth, . . . the earth was swallowed up in the great abyss."[80]

---

76. Hugh Nibley, "Tenting, Toll, and Taxing," in *The Ancient State*, ed. Donald W. Parry and Stephen D. Ricks (Salt Lake City, UT: Deseret Book, 1991), 41. Cf. William Shakespeare, "The Winter's Tale," in *The Riverside Shakespeare*, ed. G. Blakemore Evans (Boston, MA: Houghton-Mifflin Company, 1974), 3:3:84–86: "I am not to say it is a sea, for it is now the sky, betwixt the firmament and it you cannot thrust a bodkin's point."

A hymn of self-praise by the Sumerian king Šulgi of the Ur III Dynasty speaks of sky-travel via the royal *magur*-boat, e.g.: "The king, the [pure] *magur*-boat, [which traverses the sky]," Jacob Klein, *Three Sulgi Hymns: Sumerian Royal Hymns Glorifying King Sulgi of Ur* (Ramat-Gan, Israel: Bar-Ilan University Press, 1981), Sulgi D, 48, p. 75; "His shining royal magur-boat . . . Which . . . was shining in the midst of the sky," Sulgi D, 355–56, p. 87. *Magur*-boats were also used for divine travel (e.g, the *magur*-boat of Enki, p. 118 n. 354–61). See also Pinhas Artzi, Jacob Klein, and Aaron Jacob Skaist, eds., *Bar-Ilan Studies in Assyriology: Dedicated to Pinhas Artzi* (Ramat Gan: Bar-Ilan University Press, 1990), 65–136, esp. 96, 105–107.

77. Nicolas Wyatt, "The Darkness of Genesis 1:2," in *The Mythic Mind: Essays on Religion and Cosmology in Ugaritic and Old Testament Literature*, ed. Nicholas Wyatt (London: Equinox, 2005), 93.

78. Heschel, *Heavenly Torah*, 125, citing Tosefta Hagigah 2:6; PT Hagigah 2:1 (77a-b); BT Hagigah 15a; Genesis Rabbah 2:4.

79. Cf. 2 Peter 3:6: "the world that then was, being overflowed with water, perished."

80. Nickelsburg, *1 Enoch 1*, 83:3–4, p. 345. Compare with Nickelsburg's paraphrase of this reversion to "primordial chaos": "Heaven's canopy—stretched out at creation to separate the waters above from the deep—is torn off and hurled onto the earth, which collapses and sinks back into the abyss," 349 nn. 3–4).

After that violent crash, all that remained was a jumbled watery confusion—with one exception.

The motion of the Ark "upon the face of the waters" (Genesis 7:18), like the Spirit of God "upon the face of the waters" at Creation (Genesis 1:2), was a portent of light and life. However, new life cannot come into being without some measure of pain and destruction, as Enoch's account reminds us when it compares the elements of mortal birth to those involved in spiritual rebirth.[81] Like human birth, the re-breaking of the waters when the earth was created anew involved pain—and the action of tearing:[82] "The tear in the waters was necessary to create space in which life could develop, and the tear of birth is necessary for the baby to begin an independent life." The weeping of the heavens witnessed by Enoch was an inevitable accompaniment to the pain of the birthing of a new heaven and a new earth.

Conclusion

Ancient and modern Saints know that all mortal sorrow will be done away at the end time when God shall "gather

---

81. See Moses 6:59–60: "That by reason of transgression cometh the fall, which fall bringeth death, and inasmuch as ye were born into the world by water, and blood, and the spirit, which I have made, and so became of dust a living soul, even so ye must be born again into the kingdom of heaven, of water, and of the Spirit, and be cleansed by blood, even the blood of mine Only Begotten; that ye might be sanctified from all sin, and enjoy the words of eternal life in this world, and eternal life in the world to come, even immortal glory; For by the water ye keep the commandment; by the Spirit ye are justified, and by the blood ye are sanctified." The Old Testament #1 manuscript of the Joseph Smith Translation of Moses 6:59 reads "that inasmuch as *they* were born into the world by *the fall, which bringeth death,* by water, and blood, and the spirit which I have made, and so became of dust a living soul, even so ye must be born again [*into the kingdom of heaven* is omitted here] of water, and the Spirit, and cleansed by blood, even the blood of mine Only Begotten, *into the mysteries of the kingdom of heaven*; that ye might be sanctified from all sin, and enjoy the words of eternal life in this world, and eternal life in the world to come, even immortal glory," Faulring, Jackson, and Matthews, *Original Manuscripts*, 102.

82. Heschel, *Heavenly Torah*, 124 n.46.

together in one all things in Christ, both which are in heaven, and which are on earth" (Ephesians 1:10). God said to Noah that in that day: "thy posterity shall embrace the truth, and look upward, then shall Zion look downward, and all the heavens shall shake with gladness, and the earth shall tremble with joy" (JST Genesis 9:22). Describing the human dimension of the great at-one-ment of the heavenly and earthly Zion, when tears of joy shall replace tears of mourning, is the account of Enoch himself where we read, "Then shalt thou and all thy city meet them there, and we will receive them into our bosom, and they shall see us; and we will fall upon their necks, and they shall fall upon our necks, and we will kiss each other" (Moses 7:63).

Jeffrey M. Bradshaw (Ph.D., University of Washington) is a Senior Research Scientist at the Florida Institute for Human and Machine Cognition (IHMC) in Pensacola, Florida (www.ihmc. us/groups/jbradshaw/). His professional writings have explored a wide range of topics in human and machine intelligence. Jeff has written a detailed commentary on the first five chapters of the Book of Moses (In God's Image and Likeness, Eborn, 2010), and is currently preparing a second volume on the stories of Enoch, Noah, and the Tower of Babel (www.templethemes.net). He has also authored Temple Themes in the Book of Moses, Temple Themes in the Oath and Covenant of the Priesthood, *and articles on temple studies and the ancient Near East for* Studies in the Bible and Antiquity, Element: A Journal of Mormon Philosophy and Theology, *and* BYU Studies.

Jacob Rennaker is a PhD Candidate in Hebrew Bible at Claremont Graduate University, holding a Master's degree in Comparative Religion from the University of Washington and a Bachelor's degree in Ancient Near Eastern Studies from Brigham Young University. He has presented papers at regional and national conferences of the Society for Biblical Literature on the subject of temples in ancient Mesopotamia, the Hebrew Bible, and in Jewish and Christian interpretation. His dissertation will deal with these themes, and is titled "Her Sacred Shades: A Comparative Approach to Temples in the Enuma Elish, Genesis 1-3, and Paradise Lost."

David J. Larsen is currently finishing his dissertation for his doctoral degree from the University of St Andrews in Scotland. He holds an undergraduate degree in Near Eastern Studies from BYU and a Master's degree in Biblical Theology from Marquette University. His research focuses on the use of the Royal Psalms in the Dead Sea Scrolls. He currently lives in Springville, UT with his wife, Marluce, and their four children.

Variants in the Stories of the First Vision of Joseph Smith and the Apostle Paul

John A. Tvedtnes

Abstract: Some critics of The Church of Jesus Christ of Latter-day Saints have noted that the different accounts of Joseph Smith's first vision, though written by the prophet himself, vary in some details. They see this as evidence that the event did not take place and was merely invented to establish divine authority for his work. They fail to realize that the versions of Paul's vision on the road to Damascus, in which the risen Christ appeared to him, also differ from one another. Indeed, they vary more than Joseph Smith's accounts of his experience. This article examines those variants.

Some critics have suggested that Joseph Smith contradicted himself in different accounts of his first vision. In one, for example, he says that the Lord told him that all the churches were wrong, while in another he says that he had already come to this conclusion before going out in the woods to pray. I see no real contradiction between Joseph Smith believing, when he went to pray, that he should join none of the churches, and the Lord confirming that thought by revelation. After all, he went into the woods to get an answer. If his mind was already made up and he merely needed confirmation, this fits the pattern described in D&C 9:8 where the Lord said, "you must study it out in your mind; then you must ask me if it be right." The point of the official published version of Joseph Smith's story is that he received a revelation on the issue. But even that version does not preclude the idea that he had already determined the answer and needed confirmation.

In one account, Joseph says that he saw "the Lord," while in another he notes that he saw "two personages." Similarly, one account mentions that he saw "angels," a fact omitted in the others. Rather than viewing this as contradictory, I see it as merely a matter of emphasis. I have done the same thing when recounting events in my life, sometimes omitting details that are irrelevant to the point I am trying to make or that do not suit the audience or the medium of expression. But this does not mean that I am inventing the story. As for the variants "the Lord," "two personages," and "angels," we can note that, in the Bible, the Lord is often said to be an angel (which merely means messenger).[1] As late as 1880, John Taylor used verbiage similar to that of Joseph Smith, speaking of the Prophet's first vision. When mentioning the Father and the Son, like Joseph, Taylor also used the term *Lord*: "as a commencement the Lord appeared unto Joseph Smith, both the Father and the Son, the Father pointing to the Son said 'this is my beloved Son in whom I am well pleased, hear ye him.'"[2]

Other LDS scholars have already effectively dealt with the variants in the different accounts of Joseph Smith's first vision, and while I recommend them to the reader, I shall not rehearse their words here.[3]

---

1   E.g., Genesis 22:15–16; Exodus 3:2–7.

2   John Taylor. 1880. "Discourse by President John Taylor. Delivered in the Salt Lake Assembly Hall, at the Quarterly Conference, Sunday Afternoon, January 4, 1880," *Journal of Discourses* 21:61–71.

3   For a book-length treatment, see Milton V. Backman Jr., *Joseph Smith's First Vision: Confirming Evidences and Contemporary Accounts* (2nd ed., Salt Lake City: Bookcraft, 1980). The following articles also deal with the subject: Richard L. Anderson, "Circumstantial Confirmation of the First Vision," *BYU Studies* 9/3 (Spring 1969): 373–404; Milton V. Backman Jr., "Awakenings in the Burnt-over District: New Light on the Historical Setting of the First Vision," *BYU Studies* 9/3 (Spring 1969): 301–20; Richard L. Bushman, "The First Vision Story Revived," *Dialogue: A Journal of Mormon Thought* 4/1 (Spring 1969): 82–93. See also Steven C. Harper, "Evaluating Three Arguments

The real subject of the present paper is another "first vision," the one experienced by the apostle Paul while en route to Damascus. As with Joseph Smith's first vision, we have several accounts of what happened to Paul in three books of the New Testament (Acts 9:1–30; 22:5–21; 26:12–20; Galatians 1:11–24; and 2 Corinthians 11:32–33). Not surprisingly, these accounts are at variance one with another. Indeed, there are fewer differences between the various accounts of Joseph Smith's first vision than between the five different accounts of Paul's first vision and his trip to Damascus.[4]

We begin with a chart that compares the different accounts of Paul's experience, in order that the reader may better visualize the gaps and variants.

---

against Joseph Smith's First Vision" at http://www.mormoninterpreter.com/evaluating-three-arguments-against-joseph-smiths-first-vision/.

    4   One can also truthfully say that there are greater differences in the various accounts of Christ's resurrection found in the four gospels (Matthew, Mark, Luke, John) than in Joseph Smith's accounts of his first vision, but it is not our purpose to delve into that subject in this paper.

Acts 9:	Acts 22:	Acts 26:	Galatians 1:
			11 But I certify you, brethren, that the gospel which was preached of me is not after man.
			12 For I neither received it of man, neither was I taught it, but by the revelation of Jesus Christ.
	5 As also the high priest doth bear me witness, and all the estate of the elders: from whom also I received letters unto the brethren, and went to Damascus, to bring them which were there bound unto Jerusalem, for to be punished.		13 For ye have heard of my conversation in time past in the Jews' religion, how that beyond measure I persecuted the church of God, and wasted it:
			14 And profited in the Jews' religion above many my equals in mine own nation, being more exceedingly zealous of the traditions of my fathers.
1 And Saul, yet breathing out threatenings and slaughter against the disciples of the Lord, went unto the high priest,	12 Whereupon as I went to Damascus with authority and commission from the chief priests,		15 But when it pleased God, who separated me from my mother's womb, and called me by his grace,
2 And desired of him letters to Damascus to the synagogues, that if he found any of this way, whether they were men or women, he might bring them bound unto Jerusalem.			
3 And as he journeyed, he came near Damascus: and suddenly there shined round about him a light from heaven:	6 And it came to pass, that, as I made my journey, and was come nigh unto Damascus about noon, suddenly there shone from heaven a great light round about me.	13 At midday, O king, I saw in the way a light from heaven, above the brightness of the sun, shining round about me and them which journeyed with me.	

Acts 9:

4 And he fell to the earth, and heard a voice saying unto him, Saul, Saul, why persecutest thou me?
5 And he said, Who art thou, Lord? And the Lord said, I am Jesus whom thou persecutest: it is hard for thee to kick against the pricks.
6 And he trembling and astonished said, Lord, what wilt thou have me to do? And the Lord said unto him, Arise, and go into the city, and it shall be told thee what thou must do.

Acts 26:

14 And when we were all fallen to the earth, I heard a voice speaking unto me, and saying in the Hebrew tongue, Saul, Saul, why persecutest thou me? it is hard for thee to kick against the pricks.
15 And I said, Who art thou, Lord? And he said, I am Jesus whom thou persecutest.
16 But rise, and stand upon thy feet: for I have appeared unto thee for this purpose, to make thee a minister and a witness both of these things which thou hast seen, and of those things in the which I will appear unto thee;
17 Delivering thee from the people, and from the Gentiles, unto whom now I send thee,

Acts 22:

7 And I fell unto the ground, and heard a voice saying unto me, Saul, Saul, why persecutest thou me?
8 And I answered, Who art thou, Lord? And he said unto me, I am Jesus of Nazareth, whom thou persecutest

Galatians 1:

16 To reveal his Son in me, that I might preach him among the heathen; immediately I conferred not with flesh and blood:
[continued below]

Acts 9:

7 And the men which journeyed with him stood speechless, hearing a voice, but seeing no man.

8 And Saul arose from the earth; and when his eyes were opened, he saw no man: but they led him by the hand, and brought him into Damascus.

9 And he was three days without sight, and neither did eat nor drink.

Acts 26:

18 To open their eyes, and to turn them from darkness to light, and from the power of Satan unto God, that they may receive forgiveness of sins, and inheritance among them which are sanctified by faith that is in me.

19 Whereupon, O king Agrippa, I was not disobedient unto the heavenly vision:

Acts 22:

9 And they that were with me saw indeed the light, and were afraid; but they heard not the voice of him that spake to me.

10 And I said, What shall I do, Lord? And the Lord said unto me, Arise, and go into Damascus; and there it shall be told thee of all things which are appointed for thee to do.

11 And when I could not see for the glory of that light, being led by the hand of them that were with me, I came into Damascus

Galatians 1:

Acts 9:

10 And there was a certain disciple at Damascus, named Ananias; and to him said the Lord in a vision, Ananias. And he said, Behold, I am here, Lord.

11 And the Lord said unto him, Arise, and go into the street which is called Straight, and enquire in the house of Judas for one called Saul, of Tarsus: for, behold, he prayeth,

12 And hath seen in a vision a man named Ananias coming in, and putting his hand on him, that he might receive his sight.

13 Then Ananias answered, Lord, I have heard by many of this man, how much evil he hath done to thy saints at Jerusalem:

14 And here he hath authority from the chief priests to bind all that call on thy name.

Acts 26:

Acts 22:

12 And one Ananias, a devout man according to the law, having a good report of all the Jews which dwelt there.

Galatians 1:

Acts 22:

13 Came unto me, and stood, and said unto me, Brother Saul, receive thy sight. And the same hour I looked up upon him.

14 And he said, The God of our fathers hath chosen thee, that thou shouldest know his will, and see that Just One, and shouldest hear the voice of his mouth.

15 For thou shalt be his witness unto all men of what thou hast seen and heard.

16 And now why tarriest thou? arise, and be baptized, and wash away thy sins, calling on the name of the Lord

Acts 26:

Acts 9:

15 But the Lord said unto him, Go thy way: for he is a chosen vessel unto me, to bear my name before the Gentiles, and kings, and the children of Israel:

16 For I will shew him how great things he must suffer for my name's sake.

17 And Ananias went his way, and entered into the house; and putting his hands on him said, Brother Saul, the Lord, even Jesus, that appeared unto thee in the way as thou camest, hath sent me, that thou mightest receive thy sight, and be filled with the Holy Ghost.

18 And immediately there fell from his eyes as it had been scales: and he received sight forthwith, and arose, and was baptized.

19 And when he had received meat, he was strengthened. Then was Saul certain days with the disciples which were at Damascus.

Acts 9:

Acts 26:

Acts 22:

Galatians 1:

20 And straightway he preached Christ in the synagogues, that he is the Son of God.

21 But all that heard him were amazed, and said; Is not this he that destroyed them which called on this name in Jerusalem, and came hither for that intent, that he might bring them bound unto the chief priests?

20 But shewed first unto them of Damascus, and at Jerusalem, and throughout all the coasts of Judaea, and then to the Gentiles, that they should repent and turn to God, and do works meet for repentance.

22 But Saul increased the more in strength, and confounded the Jews which dwelt at Damascus, proving that this is very Christ.

Acts 9:

23 And after that many days were fulfilled, the Jews took counsel to kill him:

24 But their laying await was known of Saul. And they watched the gates day and night to kill him.

25 Then the disciples took him by night, and let him down by the wall in a basket.

26 And when Saul was come to Jerusalem, he assayed to join himself to the disciples: but they were all afraid of him, and believed not that he was a disciple.

27 But Barnabas took him, and brought him to the apostles, and declared unto them how he had seen the Lord in the way, and that he had spoken to him, and how he had preached boldly at Damascus in the name of Jesus.

Acts 26:

Acts 22:

17 And it came to pass, that, when I was come again to Jerusalem, even while I prayed in the temple, I was in a trance;

18 And saw him saying unto me, Make haste, and get thee quickly out of Jerusalem: for they will not receive thy testimony concerning me.

19 And I said, Lord, they know that I imprisoned and beat in every synagogue them that believed on thee:

20 And when the blood of thy martyr Stephen was shed, I also was standing by, and consenting unto his death, and kept the raiment of them that slew him.

2 Corinthians 11:

32 In Damascus the governor under Aretas the king kept the city of the Damascenes with a garrison, desirous to apprehend me:

33 And through a window in a basket was I let down by the wall, and escaped his hands.

Galatians 1:[continued]

17 Neither went I up to Jerusalem to them which were apostles before me; but I went into Arabia, and returned again unto Damascus.

18 Then after three years I went up to Jerusalem to see Peter, and abode with him fifteen days.

19 But other of the apostles saw I none, save James the Lord's brother.

20 Now the things which I write unto you, behold, before God, I lie not.

21 Afterwards I came into the regions of Syria and Cilicia;

22 And was unknown by face unto the churches of Judaea which were in Christ:

Acts 9:

28 And he was with them coming in and going out at Jerusalem.

29 And he spake boldly in the name of the Lord Jesus, and disputed against the Grecians: but they went about to slay him.

30 Which when the brethren knew, they brought him down to Caesarea, and sent him forth to Tarsus.

Acts 26:

Acts 22:

21 And he said unto me, Depart: for I will send thee far hence unto the Gentiles.

Galatians 1:

23 But they had heard only, That he which persecuted us in times past now preacheth the faith which once he destroyed

In most cases, as in Joseph Smith's different accounts of his first vision, there are no outright contradictions in the different versions of Paul's first vision, but some information given in one account is often left out of others. For example, while Acts 22:6 and 26:13 indicate that the vision occurred about noon, Acts 9:3 does not give the time of day. Acts 9:1–2 says that Paul got letters from "the high priest," Acts 26:12 says it was "from the chief priests," and Acts 22:5 says it was "the high priest . . . and all the estate of the elders." This is the very same kind of supposed "contradiction" in Joseph Smith's account of whom he saw in his vision. And yet neither Joseph's nor Paul's accounts are really contradictory.

Also significant is the fact that the words of Jesus to Paul, as recorded in Acts 26:15–18, are much more extensive than the words attributed to him in Acts 9:5–6 and 22:7. Indeed, if these are intended to be verbatim accounts, then there are clear contradictions. Note the following comparisons:

Acts 9:4–5	Acts 26:14–16	Acts 22:7–8
Jesus: "Saul, Saul, why persecutest thou me?"	Jesus: "Saul, Saul, why persecutest thou me? it is hard for thee to kick against the pricks."	Jesus: "Saul, Saul, why persecutest thou me?"
Saul: "Who art thou, Lord?"	Saul: "Who art thou, Lord?"	Saul: "Who art thou, Lord?"
Jesus: "I am Jesus whom thou persecutest: it is hard for thee to kick against the pricks"	Jesus: "I am Jesus whom thou persecutest."	Jesus: "I am Jesus of Nazareth, whom thou persecutest"
Saul: "Lord, what wilt thou have me to do?"	Saul: [no response]	[conversation ends here]
Jesus: "Arise, and go into the city, and it shall be told thee what thou must do."	Jesus: "But rise, and stand upon thy feet:" [Here Christ details Paul's mission, with no indication that he should go "into the city."]	

The words of Ananias reported in Acts 9:17 are also at great variance with those found in Acts 22:13–16.

Acts 9:26–30 has Paul coming from Damascus to Jerusalem, where Barnabas introduced him to the apostles, after which he went to Caesarea, then Tarsus. But Paul later wrote to the Galatians (Galatians 1:17–21) that he went first to Arabia, then returned to Damascus and went to see Peter and James three years later before going on to Syria and Cilicia (where Tarsus was located). The much abridged account in Acts 26:20 has him coming from Damascus to Jerusalem and throughout Judaea, with no mention of seeing the apostles. In Acts 22:17–21, we read that Paul came to Jerusalem, where he was praying in the temple when the Lord warned him to flee. Elsewhere, in 2 Corinthians 11:32–33, Paul adds a detail missing from all the other stories, telling how he escaped from Damascus by being let down in a basket through a window.

The point I wish to make is that if we are to allow the Bible to give different versions of Paul's first vision and his reaction thereto (including different versions of the conversations that took place), it seems unreasonable for anyone to criticize Joseph Smith for similar variants in the different accounts of his first vision.

John A. Tvedtnes earned degrees in anthropology, Middle East area studies, linguistics, and Hebrew, and studied Egyptian and Semitic languages at the Hebrew University in Jerusalem. He taught at the University of Utah and the BYU Salt Lake and Jerusalem centers before joining the Foundation for Ancient Research and Mormon Studies, which became BYU's Neal A. Maxwell Institute for Religious Scholarship. John has lectured at several other universities and has presented dozens of symposium papers in Israel and the USA. Though most of his ten books and more than 300 articles address LDS subjects, his writings have been published by four universities and several professional societies. John retired in 2007 as senior resident scholar for BYU's Neal A. Maxwell Institute for Religious Scholarship.

Rethinking the Apostle Peter's Role in the Early Church

Noel B. Reynolds

Review of Martin Hengel, *Saint Peter: The Underestimated Apostle*. English translation by Thomas H. Trapp. Grand Rapids: William B. Eerdmans, 2010. 161 pp., with indices. $18.00.

This posthumously published translation of Martin Hengel's last work brings together his pet project on the apostle Peter and a study of the role apostles' families played in providing homes for the establishment and growth of the early Christian movement.

In retrospect, Martin Hengel can be appreciated as one of the most influential scholars of early Christianity over the last half century. He will be remembered for his passionate commitment to both the critical historical approach to scholarly work and to the Christian gospel, a combination that has been seen to be contradictory by so many scholars and laymen, but which now inspires a growing cadre of Bible scholars.

Hengel wrote in German, but arranged for most of his work to be quickly translated into English, a strategy which many believe contributed to his rapid emergence as an internationally recognized scholar. His emphasis from the beginning was on Hellenic Judaism. While today many of his strongest supporters take somewhat softer positions that those that made Hengel famous, his basic insight about the importance of recognizing the deep inroads made by Hellenistic culture into pre-Christian Judaism, and subsequently into Judaic Christianity, has become the standard assumption of scholars who work in those periods.

Hengel's main contributions include: (1) his rigorous use of chronology to demonstrate the remarkably rapid flowering of the Christian movement with its claims for Christ's divine mission and its focus on meetings of the faithful for joint worship, (2) the realization that Greek-speaking Christians assembled first at Jerusalem, (3) the possibility that Q—the hypothetical collection of Jesus's sayings in Greek that may have been used by the authors of the gospels—was also produced in the Jerusalem community, (4) that early Christian accounts of the atonement were drawn from Greek culture, and (5) that early Christianity can only be understood properly in the context of the Judaism of its day.

These themes return in various ways in this new study of Peter, the apostle that Hengel finds to be underestimated, in spite of the reverence given to him by both Catholics and Protestants. Hengel relies on a comprehensive assemblage of all early references to Peter, and his own interpretations of what these do and do not say, to paint a stronger picture of this first leader among the apostles. In the process, he develops a richer and in many ways a more convincing account of the relationships of Peter to James and to Paul, the two early Christians most often seen as his competitors.

While Hengel does not believe that Peter ever became a skilled writer, and especially not in Greek, he does believe that he was one of the most powerful and widely respected *witnesses* of Jesus Christ. Although he did not have Richard Bauckham's path-breaking study of the eyewitnesses behind the New Testament gospels[1] available when he wrote this little book on Peter, he would agree strongly with Bauckham's conclusion

---

1. Richard Bauckham, *Jesus and the Eyewitnesses: The Gospels as Eyewitness Testimony* (Grand Rapids, MI: Eerdmans, 2006). See my review in *Mormon Studies Review* 23/1 (2011): 155–56.

that Mark was the first gospel, that it was based on Peter's accounts, and that this was a principal reason why Matthew and Luke relied so heavily on Mark and respected Peter so highly.

Hengel begins his study with a recognition of the authoritative position assigned to Peter in Matthew 16:17–19 as first among the disciples. However, the traditional Catholic argument that sees the Roman bishop as inheritor of this authority seems to him to be without basis, though this is only implied and not spelled out, because the Christian community in Rome was organized decades before Peter's visit there, and derived originally from the Christian congregations in Jerusalem itself, and not from missionary efforts. Virtually all historians today recognize that Rome only came to pre-eminence in the fourth century after the emperor Constantine took a leadership role in Christian affairs.

Hengel also offers a powerful linguistic analysis to show that the nickname of Kepha was given to Peter by Jesus himself and that it should be best translated as "rock" or "rock fragment" rather than as "stone"—the translation that has been widely favored of late. On Hengel's account, Peter served as the foundation or rock for the church for thirty-five years before his martyrdom in Rome.

Hengel finds in Peter the effective organizer, theological thinker, and effective proclaimer of the faith that made the first decades of successful establishment and propagation possible. He even sees Peter as a superior missionary to the Gentiles in comparison to Paul. He finds much of the perceived conflict between Peter and Paul on the one hand, and Peter and James on the other, to be overblown. James is described as head of the church in Jerusalem—the largest and most important Christian congregation in Peter's lifetime—and as the first of the monarchical bishops, who established an organizational pattern that was then imitated in other large urban settings where the Christian movement had taken hold and had outgrown a few house churches.

The situation with Paul is more complex. Hengel believes Paul was deeply hurt when Peter, who had been living with Gentiles in Antioch, went over to eat with the Jerusalem delegation that continued to observe ritual purity laws. But in Peter's defense, Hengel points out that the Jerusalem Christians were wisely continuing this adherence to traditional Judaism as a policy matter—to protect themselves from persecution from zealous Jewish parties that ruled in Jerusalem in those decades. By showing support for them, Peter was protecting Palestinian Christians from persecution, and not deserting the theological acceptance of Gentiles that he had already endorsed. Paul's troubles with Petrine delegates in Corinth are seen by Hengel as disputes arising between their respective disciples that would not necessarily have occurred between the principals in person. Hengel further hypothesizes that Luke lets Peter drop out of his account after the 48/49 council in Jerusalem, even though he continues to be the principal figure in the church in those years—to avoid featuring the ongoing dispute between these two church leaders. Hengel further agrees with those interpreters who find some bits of evidence that Peter and Paul did eventually reconcile themselves, including that they were in Rome at the same time when they were martyred.

These conflicts between the disciples are treated with great care and detail in Hengel's analysis, but the nuances are far too complex for summary here. LDS readers will be forcibly reminded of the revelation received by Joseph Smith which confirmed that Jesus's "disciples, in days of old, sought occasion against one another and forgave not one another in their hearts; and for this evil they were afflicted and sorely chastened" (Doctrine and Covenants 64:8).

Referring to the witness of Christ provided in the writings of Paul and the four evangelists, Hengel concludes his analysis with the following:

This *common "apostolic witness,"* in spite of the apparent tensions that are preserved therein, is *unique* for the church and—in the full sense of the word—*foundational.* Appropriate explication of it is the central task for all Christian confessions. Ecumenical discussion can go forward in a meaningful way only on the basis of this foundation, which is held in common by all. This original witness does not continue to develop ad infinitum in terms of content, but it seeks rather *to call back to itself* each generation anew. Through such turning back and returning, Christ, according to Matthew, builds his community upon the "rock," Peter.[2]

The second part of the book is a study entitled "The Family of Peter and Other Apostolic Families." I will not review this in any detail here, but I merely point out that Hengel has assembled considerable evidence to show that the families and homes of the early apostles and other disciples played a key role in the way the Christian movement was organized and propagated. Two interesting conclusions he reaches are (1) that apostolic families and missionary couples played an essential role in establishing the new church throughout the empire, and (2) that later Christian demotion of marriage was a rejection of first-century belief and practice.

Noel Reynolds (PhD, Harvard University) is an emeritus professor of political science at Brigham Young University, where he taught a broad range of courses in legal and political philosophy, American Heritage, and the Book of Mormon. His research and publications are based in these fields and several others, including authorship studies, Mormon history, Christian history and theology, and the Dead Sea Scrolls.

---

2   Hengel, *Saint Peter,* 102.

WHY WAS ONE SIXTH
OF THE 1830 BOOK OF MORMON SET
FROM THE ORIGINAL MANUSCRIPT?

Royal Skousen

Abstract: *Evidence from the manuscripts of the Book of Mormon (as well as internal evidence within the Book of Mormon itself) shows that for one sixth of the text, from Helaman 13:17 to the end of Mormon, the 1830 edition of the Book of Mormon was set from the original (dictated) manuscript rather than from the printer's manuscript. For five-sixths of the text, the 1830 edition was set from the printer's manuscript, the copy prepared specifically for the 1830 typesetter to use as his copytext. In 1990, when the use of the original manuscript as copytext was first discovered, it was assumed that the scribes for the printer's manuscript had fallen behind in their copywork, which had then forced them to take in the original manuscript to the 1830 typesetter. Historical evidence now argues, to the contrary, that the reason for the switch was the need to take the printer's manuscript to Canada in February 1830 in order to secure the copyright of the Book of Mormon within the British realm. During the month or so that Oliver Cowdery and others were on their trip to nearby Canada with the printer's manuscript, the 1830 typesetter used the original manuscript to set the type, although he himself was unaware that there had been a temporary switch in the manuscripts.*

Physical evidence from the Book of Mormon manuscripts shows that the compositor (that is, the typesetter) for the 1830 edition normally used the printer's manuscript to set the type for the first edition of the Book of Mormon. The printer's manuscript (P) was the copy of the dictated or original manuscript (O) that the scribes made and took to E. B. Grandin's print shop in Palmyra, New York. But for one sixth of the text, from Helaman 13:17 to the end of Mormon (that is, through Mormon 9:37), the 1830 compositor actually used O to set the type. The question is: Why was O used and not P for that part of the text?

In 1990, I first discovered that the original manuscript had been used to set the type for this part of the text when I noticed that a good-sized fragment of O, from 3 Nephi 26–27 (owned by the LDS Church and housed in the Church's Historical Department) was full of the penciled-in punctuation marks that John Gilbert, the 1830 compositor, frequently added to his copy-text before setting the type. For 3 Nephi 26–27, it appeared that Gilbert had used O to set the type for the 1830 edition. I remember asking Glenn Rowe of the Historical Department if this fragment might have come from P rather than O, but in going home I examined my photographic copy of P and noted that the corresponding leaf in P was fully intact and completely unmarked. The Church's fragment definitely came from O, not P.

When I did my initial transcription of P from the photographic copy, I noticed that the 1830 edition consistently misspelled *Cumorah* as *Camorah* (9 times in Mormon 6–8) while P virtually always read as either *Cumorah* (6 times) or *Comorah* (2 times). For this part of the text, the scribe in P was the unknown scribe 2 (perhaps Martin Harris). It was clear that if P had been used to set the type, then the misspelling *Camorah* shouldn't have occurred in the 1830 edition. On the other hand, we know that Oliver Cowdery frequently mixed up his *u*'s and *a*'s, so for this 1830 misspelling it looked like the compositor set the type from a text written in Oliver's hand, namely O.[1] Interestingly, in P scribe 2 wrote the first *Cumorah* as *Camorah*,

---

1. On Oliver Cowdery mixing up his *u*'s and *a*'s, see Royal Skousen, ed., *The Printer's Manuscript of the Book of Mormon: Typographical Facsimile of the*

as it would have been in O, but Oliver Cowdery corrected that misspelling in P to *Cumorah* when he later proofed P against O. Oliver knew the correct spelling, even though he tended to write it as if it had been *Camorah*. On the other hand, the 1830 compositor had no idea that what he read as *Camorah* in O was wrong and thus he set *Camorah*.[2]

In April 1991, I spent two weeks in Independence, Missouri, at the RLDS Church Archives working directly with the printer's manuscript and discovered that for 72 pages of P, from Helaman 13:18 through Mormon, there were no physical signs that those pages had been seen, much less used, by the 1830 compositor. The 72 pages were found in four gatherings of folded sheets, from the 16th through the 19th gathering. In fact, these four gatherings had never been cut up or marked with the compositor's punctuation marks, unlike surrounding gatherings of P. In fact, for these four gatherings the threads holding the folded sheets together had been removed only in the early years of the 20th century. Heavy stains from those threads are found in the center gutter for only these four gatherings. For any gathering of P that the compositor worked on, the threads had been removed upon delivery of the bound gathering to the print shop, in order, it would appear, to facilitate the typesetting from individual leaves of the gathering.

In the summer of 1991, fragments from about two percent of the original manuscript were discovered, and in the fall of that year these fragments of O were conserved by Robert Espinosa and his fellow conservators in BYU's Harold B. Lee Library. These fragments of O are owned by the Wilford Wood family. Some of these fragments come from the last part of

---

Entire Text in Two Parts (Provo, Utah: Foundation for Ancient Research and Mormon Studies , 2001), 22.

2.   For a complete discussion of this manuscript evidence, see under Mormon 6:2 in volume 4 of the critical text, Royal Skousen, *Analysis of Textual Variants of the Book of Mormon*, part 6 (Provo, Utah: Foundation for Ancient Research and Mormon Studies, 2009), 3636–3638.

Helaman and the first part of 3 Nephi and show the 1830 compositor's penciled-in punctuation marks, just like the fragment from 3 Nephi 26–27.

At that point in the critical text project, I tentatively proposed the following reason for why O was being used by the 1830 compositor for this part of the text: namely, the copyists had fallen behind in their copywork and they had instead decided to bring in O to the print shop. Originally, they had been assigned the task of copying the text of O into a second copy, the printer's manuscript (P), and to take only the latter manuscript to Grandin's Palmyra shop for typesetting. This they had faithfully done until they got to Helaman 13, but at that point, I conjectured, they had been unable to produce copytext fast enough for the compositor, so they decided to take in O itself but to still continue copying and producing P. Eventually, in order to catch up with the compositor, the copyists doubled their efforts by having Oliver Cowdery jump ahead to the book of Ether and stop copying from where he had gotten to (3 Nephi 19:21) and letting scribe 2 of P continue from that place in 3 Nephi and finish that part of the text, from 3 Nephi 19:21 to the end of Mormon. I proposed that by the time Oliver and scribe 2 got caught up, the compositor was ready to begin the book of Ether, so they resumed taking in P to the print shop, thus having the compositor set the remainder of the Book of Mormon from P, from the beginning of Ether on to the end of Moroni.

One important question for this scenario is why did the copyists do that part of P that they supposedly fell behind in producing? If they had fallen behind and O was being used by the compositor, why not just skip over what was being typeset from O and work on producing P a few pages further on and thus catch up virtually immediately? In fact, they could have gone back later on to make the copy for that skipped portion of the text. Further, it seems rather strange that it would take them one sixth of the text to catch up. Of course, one could conjecture that they didn't want Joseph Smith to know they were taking in O to the print shop rather than P (which was apparently against their earlier instructions). The whole point of making P was to have a backup for the text, just in case part of O was lost or stolen. But once some part of the text had been set from O, why worry about making a superfluous copy of the skipped portion? All of this conjecturing adds a conspiratorial aspect to this catch-up process. And one final conundrum: why did Oliver Cowdery proof scribe 2's work in P against O (from 3 Nephi 19:21 to the end of Mormon) if all they needed to do was make Joseph Smith think they had made the copy as instructed?

Another question is whether there is actually any evidence that the copyists ever had a problem in keeping up in their copywork. We only have one point of reference for this question, but that clearly shows that the copyists were at the time over one month ahead in their copywork. Originally, at the beginning of August 1829, there was only the original manuscript. Sometime in August, Oliver Cowdery copied out the first gathering of P, 24 pages of text covering the first 14 chapters of 1 Nephi. Some time later, when Oliver got to Mosiah 25, he was relieved by the unknown scribe 2 of P. And several times this scribe 2 was momentarily relieved by Hyrum Smith. This relief work by scribe 2 and Hyrum went on until scribe 2 got into Alma 13, at which point Oliver took over once more as the main copyist. By 6 November 1829, the copywork had advanced at least up to Alma 36 because on that date Oliver Cowdery wrote a letter to Joseph Smith stating that they had reached that point in the copywork: "I have just got to Alma's commandment to his son in copying the manuscript".[3]

Here I will construct a time-line for the 1829–30 typesetting of the first edition and assume that the typesetting

---

3. Printed in Dan Vogel, comp. and ed., *Early Mormon Documents*, volume 2 (Salt Lake City, Utah: Signature Books, 1998), 406, spelling and punctuation standardized.

proceeded fairly steadily up to about a week before the bound book was actually available, on 26 March 1830. We get the following approximate time-line for the end of each month:

Time-line for the 1829–30 Typesetting

Month	Number of Working Days	Running Total	Percent of Text Printed (averaged)	Place in Text (averaged)
August	4	4	2.3	1 Nephi 4:28
September	26	30	17.2	2 Nephi 24:22
October	27	57	32.8	Mosiah 18:30
November	25	82	47.1	Alma 19:35
December	26	108	62.1	Alma 51:6
January	24	132	75.9	Helaman 15:12
February	24	156	89.7	Mormon 6:21
March	18	174	100.0	<end of book>

I would guess that after all 37 signatures had been printed, a few dozen copies could be bound from the printed sheets within a week's time or so. The typesetting began on about 27 August 1829 and continued through, then, to 20 March 1830. I assume here that the printers worked six days a week and took off maybe a couple days (at least for Christmas Day and maybe for New Year's Day). This gives a total of 174 days for typesetting and printing the 37 signatures in the 1830 edition (this analysis is based on the actual 1829–30 calendar). Within these parameters, the printers are therefore averaging about 4.7 days to set and print each signature.

On 6 November 1829, the date of Oliver Cowdery's letter to Joseph Smith, the printers would have been on their 62nd day and setting the text somewhere near Mosiah 26:28. They would have reached Alma 36 on the 95th day, about 15 December 1829, over a month later. So there is no evidence, at least by November 1829, that the copyists were falling behind in their work in producing P.

In January of 1830, Abner Cole illegally published three excerpts from the Book of Mormon, printed in three issues of *The Palmyra Reflector*, including a section from Alma 43, published on 22 January 1830. This last excerpt conclusively shows that the printing of the 22nd signature, covering Alma 41–46, had already been completed by Grandin. The above time-line argues that this 22nd signature would have been completed on about 24 December 1829, right before Christmas.

A recent article by Stephen Ehat discusses the attempts of Joseph Smith in early 1830 to get the copyright of the Book of Mormon secured in Canada. Ehat's article discusses the trip of Oliver Cowdery and Hiram Page (and apparently two others) to Ontario, Canada, sometime from January to March 1830, in order to protect the Book of Mormon's copyright in the British realm.[4] Perhaps Joseph was concerned that in Canada either Cole or someone else could print purloined excerpts from the already printed signatures in Palmyra—and with impunity if there were no copyright protection in Canada. Ehat's article provides evidence from an 1879 interview with David Whitmer that the trip took place in early 1830 when the ice on Lake Ontario was frozen over, allowing Cowdery and Page and the others to walk over the ice, at least part of the way.[5] Later, in an 1886 interview published in various newspapers, David Whitmer said that Hyrum Smith had suggested that the brethren "take the manuscript to Canada".[6] They could not have taken a printed copy of the 1830 edition since that first edition was not yet finished, yet it appears that they felt they needed to have a complete text of the Book of Mormon in their possession.

---

4.   Stephen Kent Ehat, "'Securing' the Prophet's Copyright in the Book of Mormon: Historical and Legal Context for the So-called Canadian Copyright Revelation," *BYU Studies* 50/2 (2011): 4–70.

5.   Ehat, "Securing the Copyright," 15. From an interview by John Traughber.

6.   See Ehat, "Securing the Copyright," 16, 24 for the citation.

Thus one possibility is that the Abner Cole affair in January 1830 awakened Joseph Smith to the possible threat of a pirated edition or of unauthorized excerpts being published in Canada. The problem with taking a copy of the Book of Mormon to Canada was that in January 1830 there was still only one complete copy of the text, namely, the original manuscript. And the Palmyra printer needed to have access to a completed copy in order to keep the printing going. It appears that by about the middle of January 1830 Oliver Cowdery, in his normal copy work producing P from O, had gotten up to 3 Nephi 19, the point where scribe 2 of P took over once more for him. According to the above time-line, on 22 January 1830 (the publishing date of Cole's last printed excerpt) the Palmyra printer would have been on the 130th day of printing and up to about Helaman 13:17. But this is precisely where the printer started using O to set the type, although the compositor himself, John Gilbert, seems to have been unaware of the switch in manuscripts. (According to Gilbert's 10 February 1879 letter to James Cobb, "But one copy of the manuscript was furnished the printer. I never heard of but one".[7]) Probably a little before January 22, Joseph Smith had decided to have the printer's manuscript completed as soon as possible and then taken to Canada, just in case it was needed to secure the copyright there. I would conjecture that scribe 2 of P took over the copywork from 3 Nephi 19:21 on and worked to complete P up through Mormon while simultaneously Oliver Cowdery jumped ahead in his copywork to make the copy for the books of Ether and Moroni. In other words, these two copyists seem to have split up the remaining copywork in order to quickly finish the printer's manuscript, the second complete copy of the text. Scribe 2 of P ended up doing the equivalent copywork for 44 pages in the 1830 edition, while Oliver did the equivalent of 54 pages.

---

7.   Vogel, *Early Mormon Documents*, 2:522, underlining in the original.

In the meantime, the compositor was working from O, namely, that portion from Helaman 13:17 through 3 Nephi 19:21, from the part that Oliver had already copied from O into P.

This physical as well as internal evidence from the manuscripts helps to determine, I think, when Oliver Cowdery and the others went to Canada, namely during the month of February, when it was sufficiently cold for the lake to freeze. They had a complete manuscript in their possession (that is, the printer's manuscript), just in case that was needed as evidence of the book's existence. The time period agrees with the time when Lake Ontario would have been frozen over, and gives four to five weeks for the round-trip.

At the end of February or beginning of March, Oliver Cowdery, Hiram Page, and the others returned from Canada with the printer's manuscript. They had not been able to get a Canadian publisher for the Book of Mormon.[8] Soon thereafter the 1830 Palmyra compositor started to set type once more from P, beginning with the book of Ether, which would have occurred on about the 158th day of printing (around 2 March 1830). This means that overall O was used by the 1830 compositor from about January 22 through March 2. Perhaps Oliver Cowdery, Hiram Page, and the others left a week or so after January 22, after Oliver and scribe 2 of P had completed P. Most importantly, it appears that all this work of quickly finishing up P was done under the instigation and approval of Joseph Smith.

From a textual point of view, the decision to have the compositor set this part of the text from O means that for Helaman 13:17 through the end of Mormon (for one sixth of the text) we have two firsthand copies of the original manuscript, namely, the printer's manuscript and the 1830 edition. For that part of the text, then, we can usually determine the reading of O (even though it is mostly missing here) since there are two

---

8.   See Ehat, "Securing the Copyright," for what was actually accomplished by this trip to Canada.

independent copies. Where both P and the 1830 edition agree, we can be pretty sure that O read that way. When they disagree, the reading in O is probably one of the two, although determining which one it is in any given case is not automatic and may involve considerable analysis, as can be seen for numerous readings from Helaman 13:17 through Mormon 9:37 in volume 4 of the critical text.[9] Despite some textual difficulties, having two sources for determining O is very helpful in recovering the original text of the Book of Mormon for this part of the text. Indeed, it would have been better if Joseph Smith had always had the 1830 compositor set the type from O. But at least now we have a better understanding of why O was used to set the type for one sixth of the text. It is very unlikely that it had anything to do with the scribes falling behind in their copywork. Instead, I would argue that in January 1830 Joseph Smith decided, probably at the suggestion of his brother Hyrum, that they needed to have a second complete copy of the text in hand when they went to secure the copyright in Canada. During this time period, John Gilbert continued to set the type, but now from the only other complete copy of the text, the original manuscript of the Book of Mormon.

---

9.   See Royal Skousen *Analysis of Textual Variants*, part five (Provo, Utah: Foundation for Ancient Research and Mormon Studies, 2008), 3084–3434 and Skousen, *Analysis of Textual Variants*, part six, 3435–3711.

Notes

This write-up is preliminary and subject to revision. A complete version of this proposed explanation for why the 1830 compositor used the original manuscript for this part of the text will appear in volume 3 of the critical text, *The History of the Text of the Book of Mormon* (to be published by the Foundation for Ancient Research and Mormon Studies).

Here I wish to acknowledge Stephen Ehat's helpful review of this preliminary write-up. His *BYU Studies* article has done much to provide important evidence for this episode in the history of the Book of Mormon text, although I must add here that the historical evidence argues only for the possibility of what I propose here. Without additional historical evidence, it will be difficult to conclusively demonstrate what actually happened in the printing of the Book of Mormon during the early months of 1830.

For further information on the printing of the 1830 edition of the Book of Mormon, see my article "John Gilbert's 1892 Account of the 1830 Printing of the Book of Mormon," *The Disciple as Witness: Essays on Latter-day Saint History and Doctrine in Honor of Richard Lloyd Anderson,* edited by Stephen D. Ricks, Donald W. Parry, and Andrew H. Hedges (Provo, Utah: Foundation for Ancient Research and Mormon Studies, 2000), 383–405.

Royal Skousen, professor of linguistics and English language at Brigham Young University, has been the editor of the Book of Mormon critical text project since 1988. In 2009, Skousen published with Yale University Press the culmination of his critical text work, The Book of Mormon: The Earliest Text. *He is also known for his work on exemplar-based theories of language and quantum computing of analogical modeling.*

Shaken Faith Syndrome and the Case for Faith

Stephen O. Smoot

Abstract: *Michael R. Ash is a Mormon apologist who has written two thoughtful books and a number of insightful articles exploring a wide range of controversial issues within Mormonism. His recent book* Shaken Faith Syndrome: Strengthening One's Testimony in the Face of Criticism and Doubt *is an outstanding apologetic resource for individuals searching for faith-promoting answers that directly confront anti-Mormon allegations and criticisms. Ash does an excellent job in both succinctly explaining many of the criticisms leveled against The Church of Jesus Christ of Latter-day Saints and articulating compelling answers to these criticisms.*

Review of Michael R. Ash. *Shaken Faith Syndrome: Strengthening One's Testimony in the Face of Criticism and Doubt*. Redding, CA: Foundation for Apologetic Information and Research, 2008. x + 301 pp., with index. $19.95 (paperback).

> "Wherefore Didst Thou Doubt?"
>
> (Matthew 14:31)

A favorite scripture of Latter-day Saint scholars is Doctrine and Covenants 88:118: "And as all have not faith, seek ye diligently and teach one another words of wisdom; yea, seek ye out of the best books words of wisdom; seek learning, even by study and also by faith." While it is usually the last phrase ("seek learning, even by study and also by faith") of this scripture that resonates with LDS scholars, the first part of this passage is equally profound. As "all have not faith," or, one might say, have had their faith challenged or shaken, we are to teach each other words of wisdom from the best books. This scripture is a mandate to bolster each other's faith as much as it is an invitation to pursue truth.

Additional scriptures from the Doctrine and Covenants invite Latter-day Saints to engage with the Gospel intellectually as well as spiritually. "Seek not for riches but for wisdom," admonishes D&C 6:7. "Study and learn and become acquainted with all good books, and with languages, tongues and people," we are instructed in D&C 90:15. "Obtain a knowledge of history, and of countries, and of kingdoms, of laws of God and man," dictates D&C 93:53. The Latter-day Saints, accordingly, have long been keen students of history and cultures. As Elder Marlin K. Jensen, the previous Church Historian and Recorder, summarized:

> Several latter-day revelations speak to the subject of church history. In them the Lord clearly says He wants "a record kept" (D&C 21:1), and the record is to be kept "continually" (D&C 47:3). The record is to include "all things that transpire in Zion" (D&C 85:1) and is to chronicle the "manner of life" and the faith and works of the Latter-day Saints (D&C 85:2). It is to be written "for the good of the church, and for the rising generations that shall grow up on the land of Zion" (D&C 69:8). Those who keep the record—provided they are faithful—are promised "it shall be given [them] . . . by the Comforter, to write these things" (D&C 47:4).[1]

---

1. Marlin K. Jensen, "Making a Case for Church History," in *Preserving the History of the Latter-day Saints*, ed. Richard E. Turley and Steven C. Harper (Provo, UT: BYU Religious Studies Center, 2010), 4.

The need to buttress faith in the restored Gospel through study and prayer is necessitated by a sustained history of both sectarian and secular attacks on LDS beliefs and practices. Those bent on destroying the faith of the Saints, or at least trying to morph their faith into something totally alien to the-foundational tenets of Mormonism, have long been engaged in a crusade against Mormonism from both the pulpit and the press. Others have been subtler in their subterfuge, and have, like wolves in sheep's clothing (Matthew 7:15), attempted to undermine the faith of the Saints "from within."[2] Their goal has been, and remains, to prove that the ground and content of LDS faith is untenable, outrageous, or even a dangerous deception.[3] The goal of these critics is frequently to convince Church members to totally abandon Mormonism, or to radically re-mold Mormonism into a meaningless pastiche of moral relativism and benign atheism that denies the existence of God, divine nature and Atonement of Christ, and the historicity of the

---

2. Andreas Ross, writing for the *Frankfurter Allgemeine Zeitung*, perceived this tactic being used by a popular contemporary commentator on Mormonism. See Andreas Ross, "Alltag der Mormonen in Utah," *Frankfurter Allgemeine Zeitung*, at http://www.faz.net/aktuell/politik/ausland/alltag-der-mormonen-in-utah-fuer-alle-ewigkeit-11775372.html. The pertinent quote reads: "Der ehemalige Microsoft-Berate Dehlin hat seinen Job in Seattle aufgegeben, um Zeit für seine zweite, seine selbstgegebene Mission zu haben: die Kirche Jesu Christi der Heiligen der Letzten Tage mit ihren Widersprüchen zu konfrontieren. Von innen."

3. For some important chronicles on both past and contemporary anti-Mormonism, see J. Spencer Fluhman, *"A Peculiar People": Anti-Mormonism and the Making of Religion in Nineteenth-Century America* (Chapel Hill, N.C.: University of North Carolina, 2012); Terryl Givens, *The Viper on the Hearth: Mormons, Myths, and the Construction of Heresy* (New York: Oxford University Press, 1997); Craig L. Foster, *Penny Tracts and Polemics: A Critical Analysis of Anti-Mormon Pamphleteering in Great Britain, 1837–1860* (Salt Lake City: Kofford, 2002); Patrick Mason, *The Mormon Menace: Violence and Anti-Mormonism in the Postbellum South* (New York: Oxford University Press, 2011); Massimo Introvigne, "The Devil Makers: Evangelical Fundamentalist Anti-Mormonism," *Dialogue* 27/1 (Spring 1994): 165–81; Louis Midgley, "The Signature Books Saga," *FARMS Review* 16/1 (2004): 361–406.

founding claims of Joseph Smith, including the First Vision, the coming forth of the Book of Mormon, and the restoration of priesthood.

Even before the Book of Mormon came off the press, critics of Joseph Smith's "Gold Bible" scoffed at any claims of authenticity, and it was only a short time after the founding of The Church of Jesus Christ of Latter-day Saints that enemies began to vilify, mock, and otherwise denounce Joseph Smith's revelations as the vilest of frauds.[4] The entire affair surrounding Joseph Smith's account of the coming forth of the Book of Mormon seemed like nothing more than another sad example of religious fanaticism and imposition duping a credulous populace.[5]

The response to these attacks has led to a vigorous tradition of apologetics within the Church of Jesus Christ—although, as Richard Bushman has rightly observed, "proponents of the Book of Mormon face an uphill battle in resisting this onslaught" of critical arguments.[6] In the early to mid-nineteenth century, such luminaries as Oliver Cowdery,[7] Parley P. and Orson Pratt,[8] and President John Taylor[9] all took up the

---

4. Richard L. Bushman, *Joseph Smith: Rough Stone Rolling* (New York: Knopf, 2005), 80–83, 85, 88–94. As Bushman shows, some of Joseph Smith's earliest enemies were not even below breaking the law to hinder or prevent the publication of the Book of Mormon.

5. See Fluhman, *"A Peculiar People,"* 21–77.

6. Bushman, *Joseph Smith: Rough Stone Rolling*, 92.

7. See John W. Welch, "Oliver Cowdery's 1385 Response to Alexander Campbell's 1831 'Delusions,'" in *Oliver Cowdery: Scribe, Elder, Witness*, ed. John W. Welch and Larry E. Morris (Provo, UT: FARMS, 2006), 221–39.

8. Peter Crawley, "Parley P. Pratt: Father of Mormon Pamphleteering," *Dialogue* 15/3 (Autumn 1982): 15–28; David J. Whittaker, "Orson Pratt: Prolific Pamphleteer," *Dialogue* (Autumn 1982): 29–43; E. Robert Paul, "Early Mormon Intellectuals: Parley P. and Orson Pratt, a Response," *Dialogue* (Autumn 1982): 44–50.

9. James Williams, "Defending Plural Marriage to Vice President Colfax," in *John Taylor: Champion of Liberty*, ed. Mary Jane Woodger (Provo, UT: BYU Religious Studies Center, 2009), 219–31.

pen in defense of the faith. At the turn of the century, Elder B. H. Roberts,[10] Elder John A. Widtsoe,[11] and others offered responses to increasingly sophisticated attacks. And from the mid-twentieth century to the present, Hugh Nibley and other scholars have written extensively in response to contemporary assaults on the faith of the Saints.[12]

With the recent advent of easy access to the Internet, criticisms of the Church of Jesus Christ have been made widely available—though most remain retreads of the same tired, well-worn attacks that often date to the 1830s. So ubiquitous are these frequently half-baked and regurgitated criticisms, that in 2008 Elder M. Russell Ballard of the Quorum of the Twelve Apostles counseled the Saints to be more involved online to correct misinformation about the Church.[13] In response to Elder Ballard's counsel, and to combat this tidal wave of anti-Mormon websites, blogs, and message boards, numerous amateur LDS apologists have begun to defend the faith on the web. "Internet apologetics," as one might call it, has opened up a new realm of action that resembles something akin to the American "Wild West" of popular Hollywood depiction. Without the control of publication standards or peer review, and with the ability to hide in anonymity behind a computer screen, posters on blogs and message boards can get away with saying pretty much anything they please without repercussion, no matter how false, scurrilous, detestable, or putrid the claim may be.

---

10. B. H. Roberts, *New Witnesses for God*, 3 vols. (Salt Lake City: Deseret News, 1895–1909); B. H. Roberts, *In Defense of the Faith and the Saints*, 2 vols. (Salt Lake City: Deseret News, 1907–1912).

11. John A. Widtsoe, *Evidences and Reconciliations*, 3 vols. (Salt Lake City: Bookcraft, 1943–1951). Although published between 1943 and 1951, much of the material discussed by Elder Widtsoe in these volumes comes from earlier writings published in church periodicals and correspondences.

12. Hugh Nibley, *The Collected Works of Hugh Nibley*, 19 vols. (Provo, UT: FARMS, 1986–2011).

13. M. Russell Ballard, "Sharing the Gospel Using the Internet", *Ensign*, July 2008, 58–63.

On one particularly unpleasant message board dedicated to allowing apostates and critics to rant against the Church unfettered, breathtaking examples of (often highly vulgar) personal character assaults against LDS Church leaders and members can frequently be seen with nauseating consistency. While some Internet websites do foster civil and engaging discussion of Mormonism, many more seem to exist only to function as nothing more than intellectual gutter-holes.

Shaken Faith Syndrome: An Overview

Michael R. Ash has taken to heart the directive given in D&C 88:118. His passion for clarifying, expounding, and defending the restored gospel has produced two thoughtful books,[14] besides numerous articles both online and in print.[15] Ash typifies Hugh Nibley's "amateur" who, despite no formal academic degrees, has nevertheless offered respectable and substantive contributions to the current discussion.[16] With an impressive knowledge of the controversies being debated within Mormonism and a keen ability to distill complex issues into manageable discussions, Ash is a valuable asset to the Mormon community.

One of Ash's more recent offerings is the book *Shaken Faith Syndrome: Strengthening One's Testimony in the Face of Criticism and Doubt*. Published in 2008 by the Foundation for Apologetic Information and Research (FAIR), this book, according to the back cover, attempts to explain how Latter-day Saints "can be both critical thinkers and devout believers." This book is overtly

---

14. Michael R. Ash, *Of Faith and Reason: 80 Evidences Supporting the Prophet Joseph Smith* (Springville, UT: Cedar Fort, 2008); *Shaken Faith Syndrome: Strengthening One's Testimony in the Face of Criticism and Doubt* (Redding, CA: Foundation for Apologetic Information and Research, 2008).

15. For my own review of one of Ash's previous works, as well as a brief overview of his other contributions to Mormon apologetics, see Stephen O. Smoot, "The Faith and Reason of Michael R. Ash," *FARMS Review* 21/2 (2009): 225–37.

16. Hugh Nibley, "The Day of the Amateur," *New Era* (January 1971): 42–44.

apologetic in nature. But why is another book such as this necessary? In the foreword to *Shaken Faith Syndrome*, Ash explains
that current anti-Mormon arguments, especially those found on
the Internet, have led him to write with the hope that he can
(1) give readers unaware of LDS apologetic material an overview
and summary of this valuable information; (2) introduce readers
to the controversial material typically brought up by critics from
a faithful perspective, thus "inoculating" them against hostile efforts to use such issues against them; and (3) strengthen the faith
of Church members (vii–x).

The book is divided into two parts, "Misplaced Testimony
and Anti-Mormon Vulnerability" (1–108) and "Responses to
Specific Anti-Mormon Claims" (109–251). A list of sources
for further study is given at the end of each chapter in part 2.
Endnotes are provided (256–96), followed by an index (297–
301). Overall, the type, layout, and format of the book are aes-
thetically pleasing, although the use of endnotes instead of
footnotes is disappointing.

Part 1: Doubt, Cognitive Dissonance, and Paradigms

Part 1 of *Shaken Faith Syndrome* is devoted to establishing
the methodology that Ash will use to address specific topics
in part 2. Ash's examples of real people who have voiced their
concerns, thoughts, and opinions on message boards and in
other venues are commendable. Many of these narratives are
eye opening, taken directly from ex-Mormon message boards
that paint a vivid picture of what can happen to those who lose
confidence in the Church.

Ash explores important subjects such as the nature of paradigms, cognitive dissonance, and coping with doubt. He notes
that shaken faith may result from unrealistic expectations of
prophets or science (or both), and he goes on to describe the
danger of "fundamentalist, dogmatic, or closed-minded ideol-
ogies about certain facets of the gospel or early LDS historical

events" that can make believers "more likely to apostatize when they encounter challenging issues" (3; emphasis removed). An engaging chapter also responds to the common accusations leveled against Mormon scholars associated with the Maxwell Institute (83–102).

Most appropriately, the first chapter of *Shaken Faith Syndrome* (3–10) details how to handle doubt, with reference to the theory of cognitive dissonance. Ash explains that cognitive dissonance is "a psychological phenomenon that describes the discomfort felt when confronted with conflicting items of equally weighted information" (5).[17] In chapter 2 (11–17) Ash insightfully demonstrates that ex-Mormons also suffer from cognitive dissonance when confronted with faith-affirming information. Contrary to the façade fabricated by self-assured and insulated critics, cognitive dissonance is a two-edged sword that cuts both ways. No human can, or should, be free from its effects—it is part of how we learn, grow, and assimilate new information.

The two chapters of *Shaken Faith Syndrome* that many Latter-day Saints may find the most difficult to grasp are chapter 3 ("Unrealistic Expectations of Prophets," 19–30) and chapter 4 ("Confusing Tradition with Doctrine," 31–34). In these two chapters Ash admonishes his LDS readers not to set prophets on a pedestal of perfection and inerrancy nor to confuse folk traditions (even popular traditions) with established doctrine. Doing so, according to Ash, can lead to dissonance when one discovers the unsurprising (but to some still shocking) reality that prophets are human beings too, and that at times they have

---

17. The theory of cognitive dissonance was first developed by social psychologist Leon Festinger, who used the case study of a failed prophecy within a UFO religion to formulate his theory. See Leon Festinger, Henry Riecken, and Stanley Schachter, *When Prophecy Fails: A Social and Psychological Study of a Modern Group That Predicted the Destruction of the World* (New York: Harper-Torchbooks, 1956). Until recently it has been the standard theory in social psychology.

offered speculation or personal opinion on various matters or have not always been in full agreement with each other. Some members of the Church assume (if only implicitly and unconsciously) that every single word spoken by a prophet or an apostle constitutes a divine special revelation or official Church doctrine. Elder D. Todd Christofferson of the Quorum of the Twelve Apostles recently disapproved of this mentality during his address given at the 182nd Annual General Conference of the Church:

> At the same time it should be remembered that not every statement made by a Church leader, past or present, necessarily constitutes doctrine. It is commonly understood in the Church that a statement made by one leader on a single occasion often represents a personal, though well-considered, opinion, not meant to be official or binding for the whole Church. The Prophet Joseph Smith taught that "a prophet [is] a prophet only when he [is] acting as such."[18]

Or, if asked further, these members would agree that prophets are certainly not inerrant—and yet would still be extraordinarily troubled if any example of error came to their attention. This tendency, as documented by Ash, has led members to question their testimonies when confronted with information that contradicts their false assumptions. The prophets do not claim infallibility, but some members unwittingly act as if that is the case and are then disturbed if the prophets do not measure up to that unrealistic standard.

Likewise, Ash warns against confusing tradition with established doctrine. An example is how Latter-day Saints have viewed the geography of the Book of Mormon in the past. He notes: "It was the traditional view of a hemispheric geography,

---

18. D. Todd Christofferson, "The Doctrine of Christ," *Ensign*, May 2012, 88.

however, that was passed from generation to generation of Latter-day Saints as an unarguable truth. This 'truth' was spoken from the pulpit, integrated into manuals, taught in classes, and casually implied as LDS doctrine for nearly two hundred years among most Church members" (32). But even though a hemispheric model of the geography of the Book of Mormon has been taught in the past, it has never been official doctrine. Those who conclude that it is may experience cognitive dissonance and the accompanying negative effects on their faith.[19]

Chapters 7, 8, and 9 were perhaps my favorite in part 1 of *Shaken Faith Syndrome*. Chapter 7 ("Betrayal and Church 'Cover-Up,'" 71–75) addresses the common complaint that the church has undertaken to cover up damning or controversial aspects of Mormon history. In tackling this claim, Ash explains that the Church has actually been remarkably transparent in publishing controversial aspects of its history. "As we examine other challenging issues in LDS publications we find that many, if not all, of the [controversial] issues have been noted, examined, or discussed by believing LDS historians in a variety of LDS-targeted publications, conferences, and programs" (74). Official church publications such as the *Ensign* and the *Improvement Era*, and quasi-official publications such as *BYU Studies* and the *Encyclopedia of Mormonism*, have explored many controversial topics.[20] Ash himself provides a list of "examples of issues tackled by these official publications" (74), which should serve as solid evidence that the Church is not censoring its history. Although it could be argued that the Church could do more to foster a better cultural environment

---

19. For more on the history of different geographical theories of the Book of Mormon, see Matthew Roper, "Limited Geography and the Book of Mormon: Historical Antecedents and Early Interpretations," *FARMS Review* 16/2 (2004): 225–75.

20. See "Mormonism and history/Censorship and revision/Hiding the facts," at http://en.fairmormon.org/Mormonism_and_history/ Censorship_and_revision/Hiding_the_facts.

where Church members feel more safe asking about controversial issues, this is a far cry from the constant refrain of critics that the Church is deliberately suppressing its history.

Chapters 8 and 9 focus on the work done by scholars associated with the Neal A. Maxwell Institute for Religious Scholarship (formerly FARMS). Ash provides something of an overview of this work in chapter 8 ("Adding Cognitions [Beliefs]," 77–82) and counters arguments against the quality of work done by the Maxwell Institute in chapter 9 ("Anti-Mormon Disdain for LDS Scholarship and Apologetics," 83–102). The most common arguments put forth by critics that are answered by Ash include the following:

- LDS scholars are not real scholars (84–91).
- LDS apologists engage in ad hominem (91–93).
- LDS scholars are too biased to be objective (93–94).
- LDS scholars are really just paid apologists (94–95).
- FARMS articles are not peer-reviewed (95–97).
- Non-LDS scholars reject the arguments of FARMS and other LDS apologists (97–100).
- LDS scholars have changed, and are continuing to change, the Church and Church doctrine (100–102).

Ash ably answers these accusations, which, unfortunately, are routinely advanced by critics of Mormonism.

Part 2: Specific Responses to Anti-Mormon Arguments

Part 2 of *Shaken Faith Syndrome* is dedicated to answering specific criticisms of the Book of Abraham, the Book of Mormon, Joseph Smith, LDS Church history, and LDS doctrine. Just a few of the subjects discussed by Ash in part 2 of *Shaken Faith Syndrome* include the Book of Abraham and the Joseph Smith Papyri (113–28); Book of Mormon geography, archaeology, anachronisms, and historicity (129–200); the Kinderhook Plates (209–14), plural marriage (215–28); and the First Vision (237–43). As noted earlier, in part 2 Ash does not offer any new contributions to the arguments already put forth by LDS scholars. Rather, he provides a handy summary and overview of these issues with some of his own commentary added in.

The Book of Abraham and the Joseph Smith Papyri

Some Latter-day Saints with weakened faith cite the controversy surrounding the Book of Abraham and the Joseph Smith Papyri as a significant contributing factor. After all, the arguments against the Book of Abraham often create the impression that it is established beyond any reasonable doubt that the book is a patent fraud.[21] The evidence for Joseph Smith's deception, the critics claim, is so straightforward that nobody would be able to honestly continue to believe in the Book of Abraham after seeing the truth of the matter. However, there is much that has been said in favor of the Book of Abraham's authenticity, and the controversy is by no means settled.[22] Latter-

---

21. The most recent book-length attack on the Book of Abraham is found in Robert K. Ritner, *The Joseph Smith Egyptian Papyri: A Complete Edition* (Salt Lake City: Smith-Pettit Foundation, 2012). Besides the supplemental essays, and Ritner's own translation of the copies of the Book of the Dead found amongst the Joseph Smith Papyri, much of the material found in this volume is an updated expansion on Ritner's earlier polemical work on the Book of Abraham. See Robert K. Ritner, "'The Breathing Permit Of Hôr' Among the Joseph Smith Papyri," *Journal of Near Eastern Studies* 62/3 (2003): 161-180. For a review of Ritner's earlier problematic work, see Larry E. Morris, "The Book of Abraham: Ask the Right Questions and Keep on Looking," *FARMS Review* 16/2 (2004): 355-80; Kerry Muhlestein, "The Book of Breathings in Its Place," *FARMS Review* 17/2 (2005): 471-486. Another popular attack piece on the Book of Abraham is Charles M. Larson, *By His Own Hand Upon Papyrus: A New Look at the Joseph Smith Papyri* (Grand Rapids, MI: Institute for Religious Research, 1992). For two reviews of this work, see John Gee, "A Tragedy of Errors," *FARMS Review of Books on the Book of Mormon* 4/1 (1992): 93–119; and Michael D. Rhodes, "The Book of Abraham: Divinely Inspired Scripture," *FARMS Review of Books on the Book of Mormon* 4/1 (1992): 120–26.

22. Four recent offerings from John Gee, Kerry Muhlestein, and Kevin Barney demonstrate that, despite the *ex cathedra* pronouncements of some recent critics, the discussion around the Book of Abraham is still very much alive, and defenders of the book have not backed down from offering examples of

day Saint scholars have devoted much effort to defending the
Book of Abraham. To insist that the matter has been effective-
ly put to rest because, for example, a few scraps of the Joseph
Smith Papyri surfaced in 1967 is a gross oversimplification.[23]

Ash's discussion of the controversy surrounding the Book
of Abraham and the Joseph Smith Papyri primarily utilizes the
research of John Gee, who is perhaps the foremost expert on the
subject.[24] Ash also references work done by Michael D. Rhodes,
Brian M. Hauglid, and Hugh Nibley (128, 281–83). Ash's material in *Shaken Faith Syndrome* on the Book of Abraham is very
close to his work done elsewhere on this subject.[25] Considering
how complex the issues surrounding the Book of Abraham and
the Joseph Smith Papyri are, Ash does a fine job of bringing

---

evidence of its ancient authenticity. See Kevin Barney, "On Elkenah as Canaanite
El," *Journal of the Book of Mormon and Other Restoration Scripture* 19/1 (2010):
22–35; John Gee, "An Egyptian View of Abraham," in *Bountiful Harvest: Essays
in Honor of S. Kent Brown*, ed. Andrew C. Skinner, D. Morgan Davis, and Carl
Griffin (Provo, UT: Neal A. Maxwell Institute for Religious Scholarship, 2011),
137–56; John Gee and Kerry Muhlestein, "An Egyptian Context for the Sacrifice
of Abraham," *Journal of the Book of Mormon and Other Restoration Scripture* 20/2
(2011): 70–77; John Gee, "Formulas and Faith," *Journal of the Book of Mormon
and Other Restoration Scriptures* 21/1 (2012): 60–65. For my own overview of
this new research, see "The Book of Abraham and Continuing Scholarship: Ask
the Right Questions and Keep Looking," at http://www.fairblog.org/2012/08/21/
the-book-of-abraham-and-continuing-scholarship-ask-the-right-questions-
and-keep-looking/.

23. My somewhat haphazard bibliography of apologetic material on the Book of Abraham is available online, see "'A Most
Remarkable Book': Supplementary Reading" at http://www.fairblog.
org/2011/10/07/a-most-remarkable-book-supplementary-reading/.

24. Much of Gee's research can be accessed online at http://maxwellinsti-
tute.byu.edu/authors/?authorID=24.

25. Michael R. Ash and Kevin Barney, "The ABCs of the Book of Abraham,"
at http://www.fairlds.org/FAIR_Conferences/2004-Michael-Ash-and-Kevin-
Barney.pdf; and Ash, "Book of Abraham 201: Papyri, Revelation, and Modern
Egyptology," at http://www.fairlds.org/FAIR_Conferences/2006_Book_of_
Abraham_201.html.

together the work of LDS scholars into a manageable chapter that should be comprehensible to most lay readers.[26]

Book of Mormon Geography and Archaeology

In his discussion of the issues surrounding the historicity of the Book of Mormon, Ash follows the geographical model proposed by John L. Sorenson. This model, sometimes known as the Limited Geography Theory, posits that the events described in the Book of Mormon occurred primarily in southern Mexico and northern Guatemala.[27] Although competing theories exist, including those that place Book of Mormon events around the Great Lakes or in Peru in South America or elsewhere, it seems to me that Sorenson's model has the strongest backing from textual details in the Book of Mormon and physical evidence from archaeological investigation.[28] At the very least, the use of this geographical model; (1) demonstrates

---

26.   Recently Ash has appeared alongside Gee, Rhodes, and other LDS scholars in a DVD produced by FAIR discussing the Book of Abraham controversy from a faithful perspective. Much of the material presented by Ash in *Shaken Faith Syndrome* overlaps with his remarks on the DVD. See Tyler Livingston and J. D. Judlander, *A Most Remarkable Book: Evidence for the Divine Authenticity of the Book of Abraham* (Redding, CA: Foundation for Apologetic Information and Research, 2011). Of special note are two very recent articles on the Book of Abraham controversy by LDS Egyptologist Kerry M. Muhlestein and LDS scholar Brian M. Hauglid. See Kerry M. Muhlestein, "Egyptian Papyri and the Book of Abraham: A Faithful, Egyptological Point of View," in *No Weapon Shall Prosper: New Light on Sensitive Issues*, ed. Robert L. Millet (Provo, UT: BYU Religious Studies Center, 2011), 217–43; and Brain M. Hauglid, "Thoughts on the Book of Abraham," in Millet, *No Weapon Shall Prosper*, 244–58.

27.   John L. Sorenson, *An Ancient American Setting for the Book of Mormon* (Provo, UT: FARMS, 1985); Sorenson, "Viva Zapato! Hurray for the Shoe!," *Review of Books on the Book of Mormon* 6/1 (1994): 297–361; Sorenson, *Images of Ancient America: Visualizing Book of Mormon Life* (Provo, UT: FARMS, 1997); Sorenson, *Mormon's Map* (Provo, UT: FARMS, 2000).

28.   At about the time of the publication of *Shaken Faith Syndrome*, Brant Gardner offered a monumental commentary on the Book of Mormon that converges on many points with the scholarship of Sorenson: Brant Gardner, *Second Witness: Analytical and Contextual Commentary on the Book of Mormon*, 6 vols. (Salt Lake City: Kofford, 2007). Gardner's commentary is essential reading for those wishing to remain current on Book of Mormon scholarship.

that a hemispheric model is not the only viable option; and (2) introduces members new to the subject to an alternative view that they may not yet have encountered.

Besides giving an overview of the geography of the Book of Mormon, Ash gives detailed reviews of criticisms of the Book of Mormon including, but not limited to, alleged anachronisms (131–42), textual changes (149–56),[29] DNA (157–62),[30] and the allegedly questionable nature of the witnesses of the Book of Mormon (193–200).[31]

The Kinderhook Plates

The so-called Kinderhook Plates have often been touted by critics of Mormonism as evidence of Joseph Smith's deceptiveness or ineptitude as a translator. The Kinderhook Plates were a set of small, bell-shaped brass plates that were reportedly unearthed in Kinderhook, Illinois, in April 1843. The following month, the plates were brought to Joseph Smith, who, according to William Clayton, attempted a translation.[32] Later, in 1879, one of the eyewitnesses to the "recovery" of the plates, named Wilbur Fugate, confessed that the entire scheme was a joke perpetuated to lampoon the credulity of the Mormons.

29. Unquestionably the foremost authority on this subject is Royal Skousen, who has produced an exhaustive commentary on this subject. See Royal Skousen, *Analysis of Textual Variants of the Book of Mormon*, 6 vols. (Provo, UT: FARMS, 2004–2009).

30. See *The Book of Mormon and DNA Research*, ed. Daniel C. Peterson (Provo, UT: Maxwell Institute, 2008); Ugo A. Perego, "The Book of Mormon and the Origin of Native Americans from a Maternally Inherited DNA Standpoint," in Millet, *No Weapon Shall Prosper*, 171–216.

31. On the testimony of the witnesses of the Book of Mormon, see Richard L. Anderson, *Investigating the Book of Mormon Witnesses* (Salt Lake City: Deseret Book, 1981); Richard L. Anderson, "Attempts to Redefine the Experience of the Eight Witnesses," *Journal of Book of Mormon Studies* 14/1 (2005): 18–31; Steven C. Harper, "Evaluating the Book of Mormon Witnesses," *Religious Educator* 11/2 (2010): 37–49; Gale Yancey Anderson, "Eleven Witnesses Behold the Plates," *The Journal of Mormon History* 38/2 (Spring 2012): 145–62.

32. *An Intimate Chronicle: The Journals of William Clayton*, ed. George D. Smith (Salt Lake City: Signature Books, 1995), 100.

When in the early 1980s the plates were determined to be a forgery,[33] critics of Joseph Smith quickly used this as evidence of the Prophet's duplicity. Jerald and Sandra Tanner pronounced that

> it is obvious that Joseph Smith fell for the bait, hook, line, and sinker. Since Joseph Smith did not know the difference between ancient and modern brass plates, as the evidence clearly shows, and was oblivious to the fact that the hieroglyphics were forged, we cannot have any confidence in his work. While the Mormon leaders are supposed to have special powers of discernment, Joseph Smith certainly did not demonstrate a capability to discern when he was being tricked.[34]

However, careful research by Ash and others leads to a different conclusion: the historical evidence is not as cut-and-dried as the Tanners would like us to think. Although it is tempting to jump to conclusions from a surface-deep analysis of the evidence, further investigation sheds more light on this perplexing episode. As Ash explains: "It seems, instead, that after some initial excitement and interest in the plates, the matter was simply forgotten or dropped. It is logical and reasonable to surmise that the reason we don't have a translation of the Kinderhook Plates is because no translation ever took place. If it had, the pranksters would have crowed about duping the prophet immediately and not waited to discuss their scheme years or decades later (214)."[35]

33. Stanley B. Kimball, "Kinderhook Plates Brought to Joseph Smith Appear to Be a Nineteenth-Century Hoax," *Ensign*, August 1981, 66–74.

34. Jerald and Sandra Tanner, *Answering Mormon Scholars: A Response to Criticism Raised by Mormon Defenders* (Salt Lake City: Utah Lighthouse Ministry, 1996), 2:123.

35. A similar conclusion to Ash's has also been reached by Brian M. Hauglid, "Did Joseph Smith Translate the Kinderhook Plates?" in Millet, *No Weapon Shall Prosper*, 93–103. See also Richard L. Bushman, *Joseph Smith: Rough Stone*

Plural Marriage

The practice of plural marriage by early Latter-day Saints has been a point of heated controversy. So outraged were nineteenth-century Americans at this practice that the federal government enacted legislation (of highly questionable constitutionality) aimed at obliterating the Church as an institution solely for its acceptance of this practice. Today many people, both within and outside the Church, are understandably troubled by the history of Mormon polygamy. Ash discusses many criticisms such as Joseph Smith was a sexual predator because he married young women, Joseph Smith and other early Mormons were liars in denying that they practiced plural marriage, and sexual relations within polygamous marriages are indicative of Joseph Smith's lecherous nature.[36]

Besides responding to various criticisms of plural marriage, Ash speculates on the purpose of polygamy:

> Plural marriage, I believe, was the earthly restoration and manifestation of the key to this eternal unity—a unity that we can't completely appreciate until we arrive in the celestial kingdom and become fully one with God. In polygamous relationships (also known as

---

Rolling, 489–90: "Joseph seemed to be stepping into the trap, but then he pulled back. . . . After the first meeting, no further mention was made of translation, and the Kinderhook Plates dropped out of sight. Joseph may not have detected fraud, but he did not swing into a full-fledged translation as he had with the Egyptian scrolls. The trap did not spring shut, which foiled the conspirators' original plan."

36. These and other topics are addressed in an excellent recent volume: *The Persistence of Polygamy: Joseph Smith and the Origins of Mormon Polygamy*, ed. Newell G. Bringhurst and Craig L. Foster (Independence, MO: John Whitmer Books, 2010). Brian C. Hales has also very recently offered a thorough look at Joseph Smith's practice of plural marriage, and besides offering many helpful insights into the historical and doctrinal context of early Mormon plural marriage, has also challenged many of the negative conclusions reached by previous hostile authors. See Brian C. Hales, "Joseph Smith's Personal Polygamy," *The Journal of Mormon History* 38/2 (Spring 2012): 163–228.

"Celestial Marriage")—sealed by the binding powers of the priesthood—we get a glimpse of that heavenly family unit being practiced in mortality. In this limited earthly practice we primarily see the aggregation of multiple women to one man, but evidence suggests that Joseph foresaw more than this and practiced limited sealings that crossed marital bounds. In an at-one-ment with God we can appreciate the need for all potentially divine beings to be sealed together (p. 226).

The First Vision

Throughout his life Joseph Smith either wrote or dictated a number of different accounts of his 1820 theophany. The earliest recorded account dates to 1832, the latest to 1842. Besides Joseph Smith's firsthand testimony concerning the First Vision, a number of secondhand accounts are also extant.[37] Because of alleged discrepancies or contradictions between these accounts, Joseph Smith's detractors often make the following allegation, with various manifestations: "The conflicts and contradictions brought to light by the preceding historical evidence demonstrate that the First Vision story, as presented by the Mormon church today, must be regarded as the invention of Joseph Smith's highly imaginative mind. The historical facts and Joseph's own words discredit it."[38]

With the First Vision lying at the heart of Mormonism,[39] this is indeed a crucial and sensitive subject. It has long been

---

37. See Dean C. Jessee, "The Earliest Documented Accounts of Joseph Smith's First Vision," in *Opening the Heavens: Accounts of Divine Manifestation, 1820–1844*, ed. John W. Welch and Eric B. Carlson (Provo, UT: BYU Press and Deseret Book, 2005), 1–33.

38. Wesley P. Walters, "New Light on Joseph Smith's First Vision," accessed 15 November 2011, http://www.irr.org/mit//first-vision.html.

39. Gordon B. Hinckley, "The Marvelous Foundation of Our Faith," *Ensign* (November 2002): 80. "It [the first vision] either occurred or it did not occur. If it did not, then this work is a fraud. If it did, then it is the most important and wonderful work under the heavens."

debated. If doubt can be thrown upon the veracity of Joseph's initial revelation, this would cast a long and dark shadow over the rest of his prophetic career. Accordingly, critics have been relentless in attempting to undermine the validity of the First Vision. Notwithstanding, Latter-day Saints have not been silent in their defense of Joseph Smith.[40] Nor has Ash, who rebuts criticisms of supposed chronological inconsistencies and problematic content in the differing accounts and includes a chart showing the harmony among those accounts (243). Ash provides this cautionary note to sectarian critics of Joseph Smith who, in their zeal to discredit the Prophet, employ a double standard:

> Many of the criticisms leveled against Joseph Smith's vision apply equally well to Paul's vision. For instance the critics attack Joseph Smith because the earliest known record of his vision wasn't given until a dozen years after it happened. The first record of Paul's vision, however, which is found in 1 Corinthians 9:1, wasn't recorded until two dozen years after it happened. And just as the most detailed description of Joseph's vision

---

40. For a sampling of the LDS response to criticisms of the first vision, see the following: Richard L. Anderson, "Circumstantial Confirmation of the First Vision Through Reminiscences," *BYU Studies* 9/3 (1969): 373–404; Milton V. Backman, *Joseph Smith's First Vision: Confirming Evidences and Contemporary Accounts* (Salt Lake City: Bookcraft, 1980); Hugh Nibley, "Censoring the Joseph Smith Story," in *Tinkling Cymbals and Sounding Brass*, ed. David J. Whittaker (Provo, UT: FARMS, 1991), 53–96; James B. Allen and John W. Welch, "The Appearance of the Father and the Son to Joseph Smith in 1820," in *Opening the Heavens*, 35–75; Matthew B. Brown, *A Pillar of Light: The History and Message of the First Vision* (American Fork, UT: Covenant Book, 2009); Steven C. Harper, "A Seeker's Guide to the Historical Accounts of Joseph Smith's First Vision," in *The Religious Educator* 12/1 (2011): 165–76; Samuel Alonzo Dodge and Steven C. Harper, ed., *Exploring the First Vision* (Provo: BYU Religious Studies Center, 2012); Steven C. Harper, "Evaluating Three Arguments Against Joseph Smith's First Vision," *Interpreter: A Journal of Mormon Scripture* 2 (2012): 18–32, at http://www.mormoninterpreter.com/evaluating-three-arguments-against-joseph-smiths-first-vision/.

was one of his later accounts, so likewise, Paul's most detailed account of his vision was the last of several recorded. The details in both accounts are expanded because they are geared to different audiences. (242)[41]

As Ash demonstrates in this chapter, contrary to what Walters and other critics allege, the differing accounts of the vision "actually harmonize very well" (242) and together provide a fuller glimpse of this remarkable event.

Reservations and Critiques

Although I greatly enjoyed *Shaken Faith Syndrome*, there are a few aspects of the book that I found lacking. First, Ash uses a lot of Internet citations from message boards and other websites with long URLs that are either no longer active or difficult to access, making source-checking and further reading inconvenient. Second, some significant issues are either untouched by Ash or inadequately covered. These include the pre-1978 priesthood ban, the Church's stance on same-sex marriage, and the charge of institutionalized sexism within the Church. Of course, it is unreasonable to expect every single argument that has been raised against the Church to be covered in a single work, but in my judgment these three issues are raised often enough by detractors to have justified a response.

Finally, some aspects of Ash's book are now outdated, having been superseded by more recent and robust scholarship. Since the publication of *Shaken Faith Syndrome* in 2008, newer research has outdone some of Ash's own analysis.

---

41. Ash provides a citation to Richard Lloyd Anderson, "Parallel Prophets: Paul and Joseph Smith," *Ensign*, April 1985, 12–13. Anderson keenly perceives parallels between the "first visions" of Paul and Joseph Smith, and he deftly counters the questionable arguments of sectarian critics. For a parallel analysis of the first visions of Paul and Joseph Smith, see John A. Tvedtnes, "Variants in the Stories of the First Vision of Joseph Smith and the Apostle Paul," *Interpreter: A Journal of Mormon Scripture* 2 (2012): 73–86, at http://www.mormoninterpreter.com/journal/volume-2-2012/.

Conclusion

In the 1990s a popular television show called The X-Files made famous the catchphrase "The truth is out there." This is the main theme raised repeatedly by Ash throughout *Shaken Faith Syndrome* (especially 103–6). Sound answers to anti-Mormon criticisms are available. Those who are confronted with criticisms of Mormonism need not be overwhelmed by what may appear at first glance to be sophisticated attacks. The reality is that most criticisms leveled against Joseph Smith and his revelations rest on dubious allegations, rank fallacies, specious reasoning, or unwarranted assumptions. That is not to say there are no valid criticisms, for some controversies raised by the claims of Mormonism are, from an intellectual point of view, still debatable. In a few instances, fully satisfactory answers remain elusive.

Contrary to the caricature perpetuated by antagonists of the Church, Latter-day Saints have not planted their heads in the sand or thrown their hands in the air and sighed with resignation. There is yet a manifest spirit of apologetic fervor within the ranks of the Church of Jesus Christ, and there is no sign of that spirit abating anytime soon. As long as detractors continue to bring forth their strong reasons against the restored church, learned believers will be there to refute them (D&C 71:7–10).[42]

Despite its few shortcomings, *Shaken Faith Syndrome* is an excellent book. I highly recommend it for those who struggle with doubt or uncertainty stemming from weakened faith or a lack of knowledge regarding the issues that impinge on their faith. I also recommend it as a helpful resource to share with friends or loved ones in and out of the Church who merely have questions about the aforementioned criticisms of Mormonism. Ash should be commended for his ability to frame complex

---

42. See Daniel C. Peterson, "An Unapologetic Apology for Apologetics," *FARMS Review* 22/2 (2010): ix–xlviii.

issues and to engage in fruitful discussion and analysis of the salient facts pertaining to the controversies he explores. Although *Shaken Faith Syndrome* does not offer much new to the discussion, it does an admirable job of dispelling misconceptions and modeling a faithful approach to dealing with LDS-critical arguments. Its scope and depth of coverage make a compelling case for faith that stands to greatly benefit those experiencing any degree of shaken faith syndrome.

Stephen O. Smoot is an undergraduate student at Brigham Young University pursuing bachelor's degrees in Ancient Near Eastern studies, with an emphasis in biblical Hebrew and German studies. He is a writer for the Student Review, *an independent BYU student newspaper, a volunteer with the Foundation for Apologetic Information and Research, and an Editorial Consultant for* Interpreter: A Journal of Mormon Scripture.

Defending the King and His Kingdom

Louis C. Midgley

Again, if the trumpet does not sound a clear call, who will get ready for battle?

1 Corinthians 14:8 NIV

Abstract: *Some vocal cultural Mormons, busy asking themselves "why stay," claim that it is not at all probable that there is a God, or that there even was a Jesus of Nazareth. They also ridicule the Atonement. In the language of our scriptures they are antichrists—that is, they deny that there was or is a Christ. Being thus against the King and His Kingdom, their trumpet does not give a clear sound; they are clearly against the one whom they made a solemn covenant to defend and sustain. Instead of seeking diligently to become genuine Holy Ones or Saints, they worship an idol—they have turned from the Way by fashioning an idol. They preach and practice a petty idolatry. Genuine Saints, including disciple-scholars, have a duty to defend the King and His Kingdom.*

I must confess, while still flush with an idealism common to at least some naive young people, I was once an ardent supporter of *Dialogue: A Journal of Mormon Thought*. The reason is that I was pleased at the prospect of what I hoped would be a genuine Latter-day Saint academic journal—a venue in which those whom Elder Neal A. Maxwell would later call disciple-scholars[1] would use whatever gifts they might have to defend

---

1. For an essay by Elder Maxwell, see his essay entitled "The Disciple-Scholar," *Learning in the Light of Faith: The Compatibility of Scholarship and*

the King and build His Kingdom. I must also admit that, alas, I was soon disillusioned by this and some other similar publishing ventures. I began searching for appropriate venues. I had reasons for doing this. I believe that for the Saints not to defend and sustain the King and His Kingdom would be a serious violation of a sacred covenant, and hence offensive in the sight of God. In addition, Elder Maxwell earnestly appealed for true devotion to the Lord, which he insisted must be coupled with genuine humility, especially for those who aspire to become Latter-day Saint scholars. He made discipleship (and not quirky criticism or chronic complaining) qualify the word *scholar*. He was clearly calling for consecrated discipleship from those seeking to be sanctified scholar-Saints.

Being a Saint or . . .

When not busy describing ourselves as Mormons, we identify ourselves as Saints. Being known as a Latter-day Saint closely follows the pattern set down among those who in the primitive church chose to follow Jesus of Nazareth. They were originally part of what was called the "way" (see Acts 9:2; 19:9, 23; 22:4; 24:14).[2] Those who followed the *way* set out by the Lord (YHWH) during his ministry—the straight and narrow *way*— were known as Saints. (The Greek word *hagioi*, translated as "saints" in KJV English, means "holy ones"—that is, those who both seek and manifest in word and deed some measure of sanctification that sets them apart from the ordinary, profane world.) The first Saints were those in the primitive church who chose to *remember* and *keep* the covenant they had made with God. Following the restoration of priesthood keys to and then through Joseph Smith, the same has been true in this dispensa-

---

Discipleship, ed. Henry B. Eyring (Salt Lake City: Bookcraft, 1999), 1–18.
    2. This usage fits nicely with Christ's own wording in John 14:6.

tion. Those who now have made and strive to *remember*[3] their covenants are those for whom Jesus is the real King–that is, both Lord and merciful Redeemer from both temporal and spiritual death.

The apostle Paul insisted that even or especially those Gentiles who may have previously been without God (*atheos*) "are no longer strangers and aliens, but . . . are citizens with the saints and also members of the household of God" (Ephesians 2:19 NRSV). The Saints are also urged to "Sanctify Christ as Lord in your hearts, always being ready to make a *defense* to everyone who asks you to give an account for the hope that is in you" (1 Peter 3:15 NASB). Please note that the English word *defense*, which I have emphasized in this famous passage, is the Greek word *apologia*, meaning "to vindicate or defend"—that is, to give reasons or evidence (as in giving testimony before a court of law). In this case it means giving reasons for one's faith in the King in whom one has placed one's trust (or faith). Hence all genuine Saints are (or should be) apologists for their faith. Peter properly admonishes that this should be done "with gentleness and reserve," thereby keeping "a good conscience, so that in the thing in which you are slandered, those who revile your good behavior in Christ may be put to shame" (3 Peter 3:15–16 NASB). Please note that this necessary restraint does not absolve the Latter-day Saint from the necessity of defending the King and His Kingdom. There is nothing in our scriptures that calls for scholar-Saints to merely seek to promote mutual respect and goodwill among people of all faiths, as worthy as that goal might be. Instead, sustaining and defending the

---

3. On the crucial link between remembering and keeping, see Louis Midgley, "Preserving and Enlarging the Memory of the Saints," *FARMS Review* 19/2 (2007): 21-24, especially nn.1, 2. For some of the additional literature on the ways of remembrance in the Bible and Book of Mormon, see also Louis Midgley and Gary Novak, "Remembrance and the Past," *FARMS Review* 19/2 (2007): 37–66.

Kingdom of God and hence the faith of the Saints is required from all in the sacred covenants made with the Lord.

It seems that those who followed the *way* of the Lord later came to be known as "Christians" in much the same way that soon after 1830 the label *Mormon* came to identify the members of the fledgling Church of Christ. Both of those labels were originally derisive nicknames for those who follow the *way* of the King, whose obedient servant/slave a faithful disciple must be.[4] In addition, those opposed to the new covenant people of God—the often despised Mormons—were also soon calling themselves *anti*-Mormons (the prefix *anti*- being the common way in English of signaling that someone is against or opposed to something).[5]

This same dynamic also explains why the label *antichrist* turns up in letters in the New Testament (1 John 2:18–26; 4:1–6; compare 2 John 1:7–15), where it is said that there were those who had gone "out from us" because "they did not belong to us; for if they had belonged to us, they would have remained with us. But by going out they made it plain that none of them belongs to us" (1 John 2:19 NRSV). Some on the fringes of the primitive church were antichrists because they denied that the Lord (even YHWH) had come in the flesh to vindicate Israel by opening the *way* leading to life and light (John 14:6).[6]

---

4. The Greek word *doulos* actually means "slave." Hence one can be a "slave to sin" (Romans 6:16–17 NIV), from which one is freed by faith (trust) in Jesus Christ, even though one then becomes a slave of Jesus Christ (see Romans 1:1; Galatians 1:10; Philippians 1:1 NASB). Being a slave to Jesus Christ and trusting His gospel obliges disciples to minister to the wants and needs of others as an act of love for the new Master, who may justify and thereby include faithful servants in His own family (or household).

5. For a detailed defense of the propriety of the labels *anti-Mormon* and *anti-Mormonism* in classifying especially strident critics and criticisms of the faith of Latter-day Saints, see Louis Midgley, "The Signature Books Saga," *FARMS Review* 16/1 (2004): 403.

6. Later, however, Christians began to identify a beast who would challenge God at the end times, and so we have a mythology of a demonic public figure

The King by both His words and deeds has made redemption from death available for all, and redemption from sin available for those who genuinely turn to Him for mercy. He did this by meekly allowing Himself to be killed by the then most visible demonic powers, after which He vanquished all such powers both on earth and in heaven by rising triumphantly from the grave. The now-enthroned King called His followers to seek righteousness and receive sanctification. This is at the heart of Christ's gospel (see 1 John 1:5; 3:11–16). The condition for citizenship in the Kingdom of God is that one must genuinely seek and accept sanctification by undergoing what is sometimes called the baptism of fire or of the Holy Spirit (see Matthew 3:11, and compare 2 Nephi 31:13, 14; D&C 20:41; 33: 11; 39:6).

The departure of many from the primitive community of Saints showed that they were not genuinely the covenant people (or household) of God; they belonged instead to what is described as the world (or the evil, falsehood, and darkness of the age), thus remaining in carnal bondage to sin. Those who have turned away from the Lord often deny that there is sin (1 John 1:8, 10), though they might grant that there are mistakes, shortcomings, or miscalculations in seeking pleasure. The faithful turn to God and confess their sins—understood as offenses against God—and seek the companionship of the Holy Spirit and thereby the service of an Advocate with the Father. The death and subsequent resurrection of Jesus marked the victory over death and also the liberation of sin-laden souls from their previous bondage (on condition of faithfulness to Him as their King). The sign of being one with Christ (or loving God) is faith and faithfulness in keeping His commandments (1 John 2:3)

who will suddenly turn up and usher in the final scene of world history. This has led to much bizarre speculation.

and following his example of selfless love thus living as Jesus did, fully obedient to His (and our) Father (1 John 2:6).[7]

There are ultimately only two worlds and hence only two ways—that of light and a fullness of life and that of darkness and spiritual death, between which there is an inevitable clash taking place here below. The ancient war in heaven goes on around us and in our own souls as we struggle with temptations and doubts. But Jesus's true disciples can be of good cheer since His victory over the demonic powers has made available light and life and righteousness in the eyes of God through faith and faithful obedience. Paul's famous salutation "grace and peace" is the right way to see the heavenly gifts available to us. There can be no compromise with the darkness of this world. The Messiah (or Christ) has won a decisive victory over the world (1 John 2:12–14).[8]

Turning Away from God

A glance at the Internet shows a host of people filled with malice and even hatred toward the King and His Kingdom. Latter-day Saints currently encounter an array of striking examples of this on message boards and in podcasts. Hence here and now—just as then and there—unfortunately there are Saints who have gone missing. The most troublesome of these are in the business trying to pull the community of Saints from its crucial historical foundations and thereby offering reasons for their not remaining faithful to their covenants with God. They constitute a new generation of "alternate voices" against

---

7. What constitutes such love is partly defined in 1 John 3:17–18, and more fully explained elsewhere in the scriptures.

8. In this context *world* denotes not the created order of the earth (or the entire cosmos) but that which challenges the light, life, and righteousness of those desiring to be genuine Saints.

which Elder Dallin H. Oaks once warned the Saints.[9] Going far beyond rejecting Joseph Smith's prophetic ministry or the Book of Mormon, they deny that Jesus is the Messiah (or Christ), or they brush aside or ridicule the notion that he carried out an expiation for sin with a final victory over every kind of death. (Some may even question or deny that there ever was such a person as Jesus of Nazareth. I will say more on this later.)

In the Book of Mormon, Korihor, one of those who challenged the doctrine of Christ, is described as an antichrist because "he began to preach unto the people against the prophecies which had been spoken by the prophets, concerning the coming of Christ" (Alma 30:6; see also v. 12). He described belief in Christ as an unnecessary bondage to "a foolish and a vain hope" (Alma 30:13). Sherem also insisted "that there should be no Christ" (Jacob 7:1) and sought to "overthrow the doctrine of Christ" (Jacob 7:2), though he is not explicitly labeled an antichrist and may not, much like some recent exemplars of such a stance, have identified himself as such. With some now boasting that they see no reason for faith in God or little reason for believing that there even was a Jesus of Nazareth, it seems odd to me that one so clearly against the doctrine of Christ would not be proud to carry the label *anti-Mormon* as the badge of their new aggressive *un*faith. By the same token, why would an inveterate critic of the Church of Jesus Christ not insist on being known as *anti-Mormon*, unless he is covertly trying to spread his ideology among the community of Saints?

Green Cheese Anyone?

If the label *antichrist* were not so profoundly potent so as to make the Saints uncomfortable, thus preventing its use even when fully justified, it would seem to fit those who

---

9. For Elder Oaks remarks, see his "Alternate Voices," *Ensign*, May 1989, 27–30.

currently insist that there was no resurrected Christ because there is very little probability that there even was a Jesus of Nazareth. (If there was no historical Jesus, then what we call the Atonement makes no sense at all.) That there are people who have profoundly scrubbed Jesus from history may come as something of a surprise to most Latter-day Saints. However, there are some cultural Mormons and their secular associates who now hold this opinion.

Inhabiting certain Internet boards, producing podcasts or publishing books are those who, in addition to mocking the founding narrative upon which the faith of the Saints rests, also insist that the Jesus Christians worship never existed. One of these, Robert M. Price, a favorite of certain cultural Mormons, describes himself as a "Christian atheist."[10] But even among the most radical New Testament scholars (e.g., the so-called Jesus Seminar), those who insist that there is no reliable textual evidence of a Jesus of Nazareth are marginal figures who operate with their own cant in a bizarre underworld.

N. T. Wright, currently the leading New Testament scholar, tells the following story in which he sets out his witty response to a book by two such authors.[11] Wright indicates that he received

> a phone call from the BBC's flagship "Today" programme: would I go on air on Good Friday morning to debate with the authors of a new book, *The Jesus Mysteries*? The book claims (so they told me) that everything in the Gospels reflects, because it was in fact

---

10. See Louis Midgley, "Atheist Piety: A Religion of Dogmatic Dubiety," *Interpreter* 1 (2012): 111–43 at 123–30; and Midgley, review of Price's 2011 collection of essays entitled *Latter-day Scripture: Studies in the Book of Mormon*, in *Interpreter* 1 (2012): 145–50, at http://www.mormoninterpreter.com/journal/volume-1-2012/.

11. See Timothy Freke and Peter Gandy, *The Jesus Mysteries: Was the "Original Jesus" a Pagan God?* (New York: Three Rivers, 2001). This is the American and not the British imprint of this book.

borrowed from, much older pagan myths; that Jesus never existed; that the early church knew it was propagating a new version of an old myth; and that the developed church covered this up in the interests of its own power and control. The producer was friendly, and took my point when I said that this was like asking a professional astronomer to debate with the authors of a book claiming the moon was made of green cheese.[12]

Another New Testament scholar asks,

What about those writers like . . . Timothy Freke & Peter Gandy (*The Jesus Mysteries*), who say that Jesus never existed, and that Christianity was an invented religion, the Jewish equivalent of the Greek mystery religions? This is an old argument, even though it shows up every 10 years or so. This current craze argues that Christianity was a mystery religion like these other mystery religions. The people who are saying this are almost always people who know nothing about the mystery religions; they've read a few popular books, but they're not scholars of mystery religions. The reality is, we know very little about mystery religions—the whole point of mystery religions is that they're secret! So I think it's crazy to build on ignorance in order to make a claim like this. I think the evidence is just so overwhelming that Jesus existed, that it's silly to talk

12. N. T. Wright, "Jesus' Self-Understanding," in *The Incarnation*, ed. Stephen T. Davis, Daniel Kendall, and Gerald O'Collins (Oxford: Oxford University Press, 2004), 48. This has become a popular anecdote. See, for example, Paul R. Eddy and Gregory A. Boyd, *The Jesus Legend: A Case for the Historical Reliability of the Synoptic Jesus Tradition* (Grand Rapids, MI: Baker Academic, 2007), 165, where they report that when "the BBC approached N. T. Wright, asking him to comment on *The Jesus Mysteries*, Wright indicated that 'this was like asking a professional astronomer to debate with the authors of a book claiming the moon was made of green cheese.'"

about him not existing. I don't know anyone who is a responsible historian, who is actually trained in the historical method, or anybody who is a biblical scholar who does this for a living, who gives any credence at all to any of this.[13]

And still another New Testament scholar points out that

the very logic that tells us there was no Jesus is the same logic that pleads that there was no   Holocaust.   On such logic, history is no longer possible. It is no surprise then that there is *no* New Testament scholar drawing pay from a post who doubts the existence of Jesus. I know not one. His birth, life, and death in first-century Palestine have never been subject to serious question . . . among those who are experts in the field. The existence of Jesus is a given.[14]

Has the Jesus-myth ideology had any impact on Latter-day Saints? Probably not, since most of the Saints who go missing do so for other than genuinely intellectual reasons. Their stereotyped exit-stories indicate that they look for intellectual support for their rejection of their faith only after they have made the decision not to be faithful to their covenants. However, those who, for whatever reason, have turned Joseph Smith into a liar and/or lunatic, and the Book of Mormon into a tale fabricated from ideas floating around his immediate environment, also seem to be tempted to see the accounts of Jesus in a somewhat similar light. Some of what is available on podcasts, blogs, and message boards indicates that some disaffected Saints now

13. Craig A. Evans, *Fabricating Jesus: How Modern Scholars Distort the Gospels* (Downers Grove, IL: InterVarsity, 2008), 25.

14. Nicholas Perrin, *Lost in Transmission?: What We Can Know about the Words of Jesus* (Nashville: Thomas Nelson, 2007), 32. See also Bart D. Ehrman, *Did Jesus Exist? The Historical Argument for Jesus of Nazareth* (New York: HarperCollins, 2012).

entertain the opinion that there was never a Jesus of Nazareth. Removing the divine entirely from history also necessarily removes the last vestiges of hope one could have that the Holy One of Israel won a victory over the awful monster death and hell. Those who succumb to an atheist ideology also jettison all hope for genuine meaning to their endeavors. From my perspective, their trumpet gives a very uncertain sound.

A Publishing Renaissance

My early disillusionment with several publishing venues rested on the realization that they fostered what later came to be called "alternate voices." They became for me simply irrelevant. I longed for a venue in which I could use whatever scholarly gifts I might have to defend the faith and the Saints. Beginning in 1980, I made a conscious choice to make my scholarship strictly devotional (a kind of scholarly enterprise that Elder Maxwell called a form of worship and that, in the language of the scriptures, is one means of finding favor in the sight of God). Had I not, I reasoned, made a covenant to consecrate my efforts to sustain the Kingdom and hence also defend the King?

Such a venue eventually came on the scene in 1989 when Professor Daniel C. Peterson launched a publication dedicated to, among other things, defending the Book of Mormon. Beginning twenty-three years ago, I found an enchanted means of spending whatever intellectual gifts I might have defending the faith of the Saints. Be that as it may, Professor Peterson's earlier seemingly offbeat publishing adventure[15] immediately became the primary venue for solid Latter-day Saint scholarship defending the Book of Mormon, and it soon morphed into

---

15. For Professor Peterson's enlightening and also amusing account of the first twenty-two years of the *Review*, see his essay entitled "'To Cheer, to Raise, to Guide': 22 Years of the *FARMS Review*," *Mormon Studies Review* 23/1 (2011): vii–xvii.

a venue for those willing and able to defend the Church of Jesus Christ. Latter-day Saints have, of course, responded to attacks on the faith and the Saints. The following are some examples of this literature:

- seriously flawed accounts of the crucial generative events upon which the faith of the Saints must necessarily rest,[16]
- two recent efforts to revive versions of long-moribund explanations of Joseph Smith and the Book of Mormon.[17]
- flawed science to attack the Book of Mormon,[18]
- other efforts to explain away the Book of Mormon,[19]

---

16. For responses to Dan Vogel, ed., *The Word of God: Essays on Mormon Scripture*, see Louis Midgley, "More Revisionist Legerdemain and the Book of Mormon," *FARMS Review* 3/1 (1991): 261–311; and Stephen E. Robinson, *FARMS Review* 3/1 (1991): 312–18. For responses to Vogel's *Joseph Smith: The Making of a Prophet*, see Larry E. Morris, "'The Private Character of the Man Who Bore That Testimony': Oliver Cowdery and His Critics," *FARMS Review* 15/1 (2003): 311–51; Kevin Christensen, "Truth and Method: Reflections on Dan Vogel's Approach to the Book of Mormon," *FARMS Review* 16/1 (2004): 287–54; and Alan Goff, "Dan Vogel's Family Romance and the Book of Mormon as Smith Family Allegory," *FARMS Review* 17/2 (2005): 321–400.

17. For responses to a recent effort to revive the Spalding theory, see Matthew Roper, "The Mythical 'Manuscript Found,'" *FARMS Review* 17/2 (2005): 7–140; and Roper, "Myth, Memory, and 'Manuscript Found,'" *FARMS Review* 21/2 (2009): 179–223.

18. For responses to the claim that DNA studies have demonstrated that the Book of Mormon cannot be an authentic history, see Michael F. Whiting, "DNA and the Book of Mormon: A Phylogenetic Perspective," *Journal of Book of Mormon Studies* 12/1 (2000): 24–35; John M. Butler, "A Few Thoughts from a Believing DNA Scientist," *Journal of Book of Mormon Studies* 12/1 (2003): 36–37; D. Jeffrey Meldrum and Trent D. Stephens, "Who Are the Children of Lehi?," *Journal of Book of Mormon Studies* 12/1 (2003): 38–51; David A. McClellan, "Detecting Lehi's Genetic Signature: Possible, Probable, or Not?," *FARMS Review* 15/2 (2003): 35–90; and Butler, "Addressing Questions surrounding the Book of Mormon and DNA Research," *FARMS Review* 18/1 (2006): 101–8.

19. For a crushing refutation of a flawed effort to use stylometry to refute the Book of Mormon, see Paul J. Fields, G. Bruce Schaalje, and Matthew Roper, "Examining a Misapplication of Nearest Shrunken Centroid Classification to Investigate Book of Mormon Authorship," *Mormon Studies Review* 23/1 (2011):

· a noxious and bizarre claim from one presumably an "insider" that Joseph Smith was a fraud,[20]

· and, in addition to attacks on the Book of Mormon by its critics, some very bad science used to sell a fanciful geography.[21]

None of these (and many dozens of other similar essays) are, by any stretch of the imagination, "hit pieces," nor are they personal attacks on anyone, and they do not employ fallacious *ad hominem* arguments. Such unsubstantiated charges are diversionary efforts that replace solid arguments and supporting evidence with bald assertions and sarcasm. *Interpreter* now seems poised to become a fine source for both intellectual and spiritual nourishment, and as such it will genuinely honor Elder Maxwell. The existence of *Interpreter* dedicated to explicating and defending the Mormon scriptures provides solid evidence of Latter-day Saint disciple-scholars willing to defend the King and His Kingdom.

87–111; and Roper and Fields, "The Historical Case against Sidney Rigdon's Authorship of the Book of Mormon," *Mormon Studies Review* 23/1 (2011): 113–25.

20. For devastating reviews of Grant Palmer, *An Insider's View of Mormon Origins*, see Davis Bitton, "The Charge of a Man with a Broken Lance (But Look What He Doesn't Tell Us)," *FARMS Review* 15/2 (2003): 257–72; Steven C. Harper, "Trustworthy History?," *FARMS Review* 15/2 (2003): 273–308; Mark Ashurst-McGee, "A Onesided View of Mormon Origins," *FARMS Review* 15/2 (2003): 364; Louis Midgley, "Prying into Palmer," *FARMS Review* 15/2 (2003): 365–410; and James B. Allen, "Asked and Answered: A Response to Grant H. Palmer," *FARMS Review* 16/1 (2004): 235–86.

21. For a response to Rodney Meldrum's *Rediscovering the Book of Mormon Remnant through DNA*, see Gregory L. Smith, "Often in Error, Seldom in Doubt: Rod Meldrum and Book of Mormon DNA" *FARMS Review* 22/1 (2010): 17–161; for a response to Bruce H. Porter and Rodney Meldrum, *Prophecies and Promises: The Book of Mormon and the United States of America*, see Matthew Roper, "Joseph Smith, Revelation, and Book of Mormon Geography," *FARMS Review* 22/2 (2010): 15–85. And for a review by a geneticist of the relevant literature on DNA and the Book of Mormon, see Ugo Perego, "The Book of Mormon and the Origin of Native Americans from a Maternally Inherited DNA Standpoint," *FARMS Review* 22/1 (2010): 191–227.

Cultural Mormons wrongly believe that the faith of the Saints cannot be defended, while some Saints insist that it should not be defended. It seems that they both have a Mormon version of what is sometimes called *Judischer Selbsthaß* (Jewish self-hatred)—that is, an embarrassment at things Jewish because they are seen as both parochial and unnecessarily limiting. Something like this can be seen among cultural Mormons on various blogs, boards, and lists, or set out in podcasts in which disdain is expressed for embarrassing parochial concerns like testifying to or defending the faith of the Saints.

However, critics of Joseph Smith and the Book of Mormon seem to know that an effective defense of the faith is actually taking place. The unseemly invective directed especially at Professor Peterson by shady and anonymous former or cultural Mormons (some of whom self-identify as New Order Mormons or use similar labels in an effort to provide a kind of surrogate Internet community or "church") is actually solid evidence of the effectiveness of the defense of the faith and the Saints. If this were not so, critics would be insisting that faithful Saints read what those they denigrate as apologists publish, rather than doing their best to censor what is published[22] or otherwise discredit its contents.

There is currently some opposition to a defense of the faith on the grounds that engaging in such an undertaking constitutes dreaded "apologetics." The unexamined background assumption is that Latter-day Saint "apologists" fib and hide the past, while real scholars are presumably neutral, detached, balanced, and objective.[23] But the fact is that this way of seeing the situation rests on an obvious mistake. How so? Those who hold

---

22. The story of efforts to invoke censorship has yet to be told.

23. An instructive example is the apologia offered by Mark D. Thomas for his own efforts to explain away the Book of Mormon as merely some theological speculation by Joseph Smith. For details, see Midgley, "Atheist Piety: A Religion of Dogmatic Dubiety," *Interpreter* 1 (2012): 125–27, 137.

any opinion, if they are at all rational, at least to themselves, if not in public, will attempt to defend it as well as they can. Thus everyone is an apologist for those things they believe, even if it is merely their favorite sports team or beverage. Hence the question is not whether one is an apologist, but only what one is willing to defend and then how well one can do it. Appeals to so-called objectivity, especially when accounting for faith in God, or doing history, invoke a myth grounded on deep confusion about what is entailed in writing about such matters. Put another way, those who appeal to neutrality, balance, or objectivity are deceiving themselves and also their audience.[24]

From sectarian and secular critics of the church, and from some on the outer margins of the LDS intellectual world, one finds the complaint that scholarly Latter-day Saint efforts to defend the faith are merely so-called hit pieces—essentially personal or *ad hominem* attacks, rather than essays and reviews addressing genuine intellectual issues. Such assertions are flatly false; they are intended to discredit, without providing evidence and arguments, all efforts to defend the King and His Kingdom.

Making the Correct Delineation by Avoiding Idolatry

The Saints face doubts along their faith journey. The reason is that the choice to put our full trust in God and become His loving, faithfully obedient servants, and thereby enter into a world in which divine things are present in what otherwise is a world barren of ultimate meaning, necessarily comes before we have much understanding of either the natural world or solid grasp of the history of human things. So we all can expect to face a crisis of faith. A crisis is, of course, a turning point when a decision is made for better or worse–that is, the point at which

---

24. For a detailed treatment of this issue, see Louis Midgley, "Knowing Brother Joseph Again," *FARMS Review* 18/1 (2006): xiv–lx.

one affirms whether they will go onward or turn away. The fact is that we all face many such choices. It is often, however, such a crisis that brings people to genuine faith in Jesus Christ. Be that as it may, such decisions are essentially moral and not merely intellectual. They are never fully informed choices. God is not testing our intellect, and He is not on trial, which is our lot in life. The Lord does not force us to enter His Kingdom, but he invites us to come willingly to feast at his table and thereby nurture the seed of faith. We are here on probation and hence are both being tested and, if we are willing, taught line upon line.

Even though the final victory over demonic forces was won by Jesus of Nazareth, the war in heaven is not over. This victory over demonic powers was not with armies and firepower, as perhaps even the close disciples of Jesus may have expected, but with meekness, mercy, and love. But for us this war still continues. We can sense this is the case if we are honest about what goes on within our own souls. We all struggle with temptation and hence always need to repent. The victory over both physical and spiritual death is for mortals "already but not quite yet," since Jesus was resurrected and thereby completed the Atonement, and yet here and now we remain on probation. We must remain true and faithful to be cleansed, purified, purged and eventually sanctified through what our scriptures call the baptism of fire (or of the Holy Spirit). For this to happen we must be genuine Saints and not merely cultural Mormons.[25] But from the perspective of those who scorn and mock, faith in God is a rude scandal, perhaps explained away as delusional or illusional.

The truly terrible moral evils that we see around us or that tempt us are the product of common and insidious forms of

---

25. These are currently identified by such labels such as New Order-, Uncorrelated-, Internet-, Never-, DNA-, and Post-, Former-, or so-called Recovering Mormons. If the Saints insist on employing the label *Mormon*, the word should identify genuine faith in God and it should not be used to position oneself in opposition to the faith of the Saints.

idolatry. Our scriptures warn us of our urge to fashion our own gods with which we justify our avarice and ambition, as well as our carnality and self-righteousness—vices that are often driven by base mercenary motives, the desire for power, or the lusts of the flesh and so forth, or the devastating but seemingly less overtly demonic temptation to focus our lives on such things as golf or gardening and not on God. People who will not listen to the Lord, and especially those who knowingly stray from ordinances and break solemn covenants, "seek not the Lord to establish his righteousness, but . . . [walk] in their own way, and after the image of [their] own god, whose image is in the likeness of the world, and whose substance is that of an idol" (D&C 1:16). Idolatry is therefore not something that merely afflicts primitive people with icons. When our hearts are upon our treasures, then our treasure, whatever it might be, becomes our god (see 2 Nephi 9:30).

As responsible moral agents, we must choose to either put our trust in God or follow the easier "broad way" (Matthew 7:13). We are all being tested by God to see if we will trust Him and follow His *way*, and not to see how clever we are in figuring out human and divine things. Faith is, of course, possible only with some awareness of the alternatives and their moral implications. While here on probation the Saints live by faith and not by sight. But the decision to covenant with God, then to remain faithful to those covenants, and to renew them often is not made in the light of full knowledge and absolute certainty. It is a mistake to hold that we need a final proof before we nurture the seed of faith and begin to grow the tree of life in the hope of eventually tasting (or becoming) its delicious fruit (see Alma 32:26–43). Nurturing faith requires choices about what one most ardently hopes to be a manner of life that will find favor in the sight of the Lord and bring blessings to the one making such decisions, as well as to the community of Saints.

Of course no one wants the grounds or contents of their faith to be merely wishful thinking. This explains why we all look for confirmation that we are following the right *way* in our journey here below. In approaching sources of information and modes of understanding we should question whether our doubts have gone far or deep enough. The questions we entertain should be driven through the solvent of radical doubt about our own abilities, unaided, to fathom much of anything with any real confidence, given the intellectual trends that surround us (the source and history of which we hardly understand) and the socializing that often takes the form of mockery or flattery. Hence honest doubts especially about ourselves and our grasp of both this world and divine things can open the heart and mind to the possibility of genuine faith and open for us an enchanted and enchanting world in which we can participate if and only if we are not the center of attention but fellow citizens in a community governed by love. Those who seek the Kingdom of God must be willing to testify in both word and deed—that is, to defend and sustain the King and His Kingdom as well as they possibly can. We all should answer the clear call of the trumpet of the Lord, and not be toying with the silly question "why stay"?

Louis Midgley (PhD, Brown University) is an emeritus professor of political science at Brigham Young University. Dr. Midgley has had an abiding interest in the history of Christian theology. He wrote his doctoral dissertation on Paul Tillich, the then-famous German-American Protestant theologian and political theorist/ religious-socialist activist. Midgley also studied the writings of other influential Protestant theologians such as Karl Barth. Eventually he took an interest in contemporary Roman Catholic theology, and was also impacted by the work of important Jewish philosophers, including especially Leo Strauss and his disciples.

THE APOCRYPHAL ACTS
OF JESUS

John Gee

Abstract: *Numerous noncanonical accounts of Jesus's deeds exist. While some Latter-day Saints would like to find plain and precious things in the apocryphal accounts, few are to be found. Three types of accounts deal with Jesus as a child, his mortal ministry, or after his resurrection. The Jesus of the infancy gospels does not act like the Jesus of the real gospels. The apocryphal accounts of Jesus's ministry usually push a particular theological agenda. The accounts of Jesus's post-resurrection teaching often contain intriguing but bizarre information. On the whole, apocryphal accounts of Jesus's ministry probably contain less useful information for Latter-day Saints than they might expect.*

Apocrypha and Apocryphal Acts of Jesus

Jesus reserved his highest and holiest teachings for a close few,[1] to whom he spoke most plainly after his resurrection.[2] Those so privileged to receive this hidden treasure of knowledge prized it most highly[3] but shared it with few if

---

1. Matthew 13:11–16; 19:11; Mark 4:2, 33; Luke 18:34; 22:67; John 3:12; 6:60–61; 8:43; 10:27; 16:12, 18, 25; Acts 10:41. Indicative of this are the fifty-three parables of Jesus preserved in the Gospels, of which only three have interpretations, all of the interpretations being given behind closed doors to a chosen few (this was noted in ancient times in the Apocryphon of James I.8.4–10, listing some previously unknown parables as well).

2. Before the resurrection Jesus spoke in parables (John 16:25), and it was after the resurrection that he spoke more plainly (Luke 24:44–48; Acts 1:2–3; 3 Nephi 15:12–20).

3. Tertullian, *De Praescriptione Haereticorum* 20–22.

any others.[4] The situation is most poignantly explained by Ignatius of Antioch (d. ca. 110)[5] as he was led off to his death:

> Could I not write you the celestial matters? But I fear lest I might set harm before you, since you are but babes; so pardon me, lest, if you are unable to make room, you be suffocated; for although I am bound and am able to comprehend the celestial matters and the angelic orders and the principal revelations,[6] seen and unseen, nonetheless I am not yet a disciple.[7]

These hidden things were called by the Greek word for such, *apokrypha*.[8]

---

4. 1 Corinthians 3:1–2; 2 Corinthians 12:4; Colossians 1:26; Hebrews 5:11; 2 John 1:12. See also Elaine Pagels, *The Gnostic Gospels* (New York: Random House, 1979), 17–18; Hamblin, "Aspects of an Early Christian Initiation Ritual," 208–10.

5. Ignatius was thought to have been a disciple of John; J. B. Lightfoot, *The Apostolic Fathers*, 2 parts in 5 vols. (Peabody, MA: Hendrickson, 1989), 2.1:29–30.

6. Greek *tas systaseis tas archontikas*. Though Ignatius does use the word *systasis* in other senses (see Ignatius, *Epistle to the Romans*, 5), here it seems to be used in a more technical sense of oracular inquiry, the equivalent of the Demotic *p-ntr*; see Janet H. Johnson, "Louvre E3229: A Demotic Magical Text," *Enchoria* 7 (1977): 90–91.

7. Ignatius, *Epistle to the Trallians* 5. Unless specified, all translations are the author's own. This list of characteristics of the secret teachings makes its way into the magic tradition eventually to end up in an English fairy tale as the content of the magician's "one big book bound in black calf and clasped with iron, and with iron corners;" see "The Master and his Pupil," in Joseph Jacobs, coll., *English Fairy Tales* (London: Putnam's Sons, 1898, repr. New York: Dover, 1967), 73–74. These matters are also the principal subject of the books of 1 Jeu and 2 Jeu as well as much of the Jewish Hekalot literature.

8. For the usage of the term, as well as a similar explanation of it, see Clement of Alexandria, *Stromateis* I,12 (55.1–56.3); cf. Johannes Quasten, *Patrology* 4 vols. (Utrecht: Spectrum, 1950, repr. Westminster, MD: Christian Classics, 1990–92), 1:106: "An apocryphal book was in the beginning one too sacred and too secret to be known by everybody. It must be hidden (*apocryphos*) from the public at large and restricted to the initiates of the sect."

An object of ridicule by the Greeks and Romans,[9] these hidden teachings were counterfeited by those ambitious to lead the Church,[10] causing the meaning of *apocrypha* to change from hidden to "spurious, false, to be rejected."[11] In general, the motivations to alter the text of scriptures both canonical and noncanonical[12] match those Nephi gave:

> After the book hath gone forth through the hands of the great and abominable church, . . . there are many plain and precious things taken away from the book (1 Nephi 13:28).

> Behold the gold, and the silver and the silks, and the scarlets, and the fine-twined linen, and the precious clothing, and the harlots, are the desires of this great and abominable church (1 Nephi 13:8).

While not all second century Christians were consumed by these desires, some clearly were.[13] Another reason for the creation of pseudepigraphic literature is the desire to supplement

---

9. For the ridicule, see Lucian, *De Morte Peregrini* 11–12. Pliny, noting their perseverance in their secretive meetings and traditions, says that the Christians' recalcitrance and pigheadedness deserves to be punished ("*pertinaciam certe et inflexibilem obstinationem debere puniri*"); Pliny, *Epistulae* X.96.3, 7–8.

10. Hegesippus, quoted in Eusebius, *Historiae Ecclesiasticae* III.32.7; Irenaeus, *Contra Haereses* I.25.5; Tertullian, *De Praescriptione Haereticorum* 20–22, 25–27; Pagels, *Gnostic Gospels*, 25–27.

11. Quasten, *Patrology* 1:106.

12. See John Gee, "The Corruption of Scripture in Early Christianity," in *Early Christians in Disarray: Contemporary LDS Perspectives on the Christian Apostasy*, ed. Noel B. Reynolds (Provo, UT: FARMS, 2005), 163–204; also Tertullian, *De Praescriptione Haereticorum* 38–40; other categories and examples given in Robinson, "Lying for God," 144–46.

13. 1 Clement 44:1; Hegesippus, quoted in Eusebius, *Historiae Ecclesiasticae* III.32.7; *Second Treatise of the Great Seth* VII.59.19–61.24. The urge to usurp authority might have been the cause of the anonymous accusations attested in Pliny, *Epistulae* X.96.5.

the scarce sources.[14] (The desire to supplement or revise details from the canonical gospels has continued to the present with a number of recent forgeries and fictions,[15] from accounts designed to make a quick buck[16] or advance a position,[17] to honestly intended but nevertheless hypothetical and artificial scholarly constructs.)[18]

14. "Certain episodes in the life of Jesus were extracted from the canonical Gospels and further elaborated. This group . . . is heavily stamped with secondary legendary elements. Christians have fastened their pious interest upon the figure of Jesus and upon the persons who in the canonical Gospels are mentioned in association with Him, and fantasy has taken possession of them. Legends of every kind normally met with in folk-literature are transferred to Jesus and these other figures." Thus Wilhelm Schneemelcher, in *NTA* 1:83; see also Robinson, "Lying for God," 143–44.

15. Richard Lloyd Anderson, "Imitation Gospels and Christ's Book of Mormon Ministry," in C. Wilfred Griggs, ed., *Apocryphal Writings and the Latter-day Saints* (Provo, UT: Religious Studies Center, 1986), 53–75 surveys the Aquarian Gospel, the Archko Volume, the Crucifixion and the Resurrection of Jesus by an Eyewitness, the Death Warrant of Jesus Christ, (yet another) Gospel of Barnabas, the Gospel of the Holy Twelve, the Essene Gospel of Peace, the letter of Benan, the Letter of Lentulus, Oahspe, the Occult Life of Jesus of Nazareth, the Sorry Tale, the Unknown Life of Jesus Christ, and the Urantia Book. See further, Richard Lloyd Anderson, "The Fraudulent Archko Volume," *BYU Studies* 15/1 (1974): 43–64. Forgeries of Mormon historical documents follow similar patterns with the same financial and revisionist motivations; see Richard E. Turley, Jr., *Victims: The LDS Church and the Mark Hofmann Case* (Urbana: University of Illinois Press, 1992).

16. See, for example, the financial motivations of William D. Mahan in forging the Archko Volume in Anderson, "Fraudulent Archko Volume," 43–45. Mark Hofmann's financial motivations are well known; see Turley, *Victims*, 131–44; Edward L. Kimball, "The Artist and the Forger: Han van Meegeren and Mark Hofmann," *BYU Studies* 27/4 (1987): 6–7, 12.

17. See Turley, *Victims*, 9–23, 316, Kimball, "The Artist and the Forger," 6–7. So also Morton Smith's forgery of the secret Gospel of Mark; Stephen C. Carlson, *The Gospel Hoax: Morton Smith's Invention of Secret Mark* (Waco, TX: Baylor University Press, 2005); Peter Jeffery, *The Secret Gospel of Mark Unveiled: Imagined Rituals of Sex, Death, and Madness in a Biblical Forgery* (New Haven, CT: Yale University Press, 2006).

18. The most notable scholarly construct is Q. Most New Testament scholars think that the canonical gospels were not written by Matthew, Mark, Luke, and John. They posit an otherwise unattested source Q, which the authors of Matthew and Luke are conjectured to have used along with Mark in the compo-

By the early second century, Christianity had fragmented into dozens of splinter groups[19] with each group charging that the other possessed both forged and corrupted texts.[20] Since

---

sition of their gospels. A brief survey of the problem by Wilhelm Schneemelcher may be found in *NTA* 1:75–80; Thiessen, *Introduction to the New Testament*, 101–29; John S. Kloppenborg, *Q Parallels: Synosis Critical Notes & Concordance* (Sonoma, CA: Polebridge, 1988), 204–5 provides a history of the early scholarship on Q. For reasons why the Q hypothesis need not be followed, see Austin M. Farrer, "On Dispensing with Q," in Dennis E. Nineham, *Studies in the Gospels: Essays in Memory of R. H. Lightfoot* (Oxford: Basil Blackwell, 1967), 55–66; Wenham, *Redating Matthew, Mark and Luke*; note also the surprisingly sympathetic review by J. K. Eliot in *Novum Testamentum* 34/2 (1992): 200–1. A different approach is taken by Ronald V. Huggins, "Matthean Posteriority: A Preliminary Proposal," *Novum Testamentum* 34/1 (1992): 1–22, note especially the demonstration on p. 15 that much scholarship on Q rests on circular reasoning. The Q hypotheses has been effectively satirized in Robert Alter, *The Art of Biblical Narrative*, (New York: Basic, 1981), 48. Unlike any of the other documents discussed in this essay—outside those mentioned in the last two notes—there is no mention of Q before the nineteenth century when Weiss fabricated it, nor has a single ancient manuscript of this mythical text ever been discovered, nor do we have a complete text to work with. Acceptance of Q is a matter of belief—not scholarship. I have found no compelling reason to believe in the Q hypothesis.

19. Tertullian, *Scorpiace* 1; Irenaeus, *Contra Haereses* I.28.1, 29.1 describes them as popping up like mushrooms; more poignantly, Mārūtā, the bishop of Maipherqat, says that there was only one ear of wheat left in all the tares; see Mārūtā, *Against the Canons from the Synod of 318*, 5, in Arthur Vööbus, *The Canons Ascribed to Mārūtā of Maipherqat and Related Sources*, 2 vols., *CSCO* 439–40 (series *Scriptores Syri* 191–92) (Louvain: Peeters, 1982), 1:22. See also Henry Chadwick, *The Early Church* (Harmondsworth, Middlesex: Penguin, 1967), 34; W. H. C. Frend, *The Rise of Christianity* (Philadelphia: Fortress, 1984), 201–3; Pagels, *Gnostic Gospels*, 7–8.

20. Acts 20:30 (Paul prophesying the coming corruption of the teachings; cf. Kent P. Jackson, "'Watch and Remember': The New Testament and the Great Apostasy," in Lundquist and Ricks, eds., *By Study and Also By Faith*, 1:85; 2 Peter 3:15–16 (showing the process starting in apostolic times); Justin Martyr, *Dialogus cum Tryphone* 73 (accusing the Jews); Irenaeus, *Contra Haereses* I.7.3, 8.1, 9.4, 18.1, 19.1, 20.1–2, 22.1–3, 26.2, 27.2, 4; V.30.1 (accusing various groups); III.2.1 (for the counter charges); Tertullian, *De Baptismo* 17 (discussing well-intentioned but nonetheless misguided tampering with Paul); Tertullian, *Adversus Marcionem* IV.2.2–5 (charging Marcion with corrupting Luke); Tertullian, *De Praescriptione Haereticorum* 16–19, 38–40 (the charges run both ways); Mārūtā, *Against the Canons from the Synod of 318*, 5, in Vööbus, *Canons*

the secret teachings were the least known, they were the most subject to corruption. Some of the types of changes made in the texts are clearly enumerated by the very people responsible for preserving them. For example Rufinus says of the earlier Christian texts he is copying:

> Wherever, therefore, we have found in his books anything contrary to that which was piously established by him about the Trinity in other places, either we have *omitted* it as corrupt and interpolated, or edited it according to that pattern that we often find asserted by himself. If, however, speaking to the trained and learned, he writes obscurely because he desires to briefly pass over something, we, to make the passage plainer, have *added* those things that we have read on the same subject openly in his other books. . . . All who shall copy or read this . . . shall neither add anything to this writing, nor remove anything, nor insert anything, nor change anything.[21]

Ascribed to Mārūtā of Maipherqat, 1:22–23, 25–26 (with a long list of groups); Mārūtā, *The Seventy Three Canons* 1, in ibid., 1:57–58, cf. 135; The *Apocalypse of Peter* VII.76.24–78.31 (no specific sect specified); The *Apocalypse of Adam* V.77.18–82.25 lists thirteen different views of Christ, twelve of which—including the "orthodox" one—are labeled as being in error; see also *NTA* 1:31–34; Pagels, *Gnostic Gospels*, 20–21. Though from the fourth century, Epiphanius, *Panarion* 30.13.1, 14.1; 42.9.1–2 accuses the second century figures Ebion, Cerinthus, Carpocrates, and Marcion of corrupting the text of the Gospel of Matthew; Epiphanius, however, is not necessarily a reliable source. See also Gee, "The Corruption of Scripture in Early Christianity," 163–204.

21. Rufinus, preface to Origen, *Peri Archon*, 2–4, in *Patrologiae Graecae* 11:113–14; cf. G. W. Butterworth, trans., *Origen On First Principles* (Gloucester, MA: Peter Smith, 1973), lxiii–lxiv. This particular work of Origen's is preserved only through Rufinus's Latin translation and a few fragments quoted by Greek authors. Rufinus's unreliable translations of this and other works were known both to his contemporaries and to modern scholars as "vitiated and confused" if not "very hasty and careless" since "he frequently paraphrases and misinterprets his original," see Quasten, *Patrology*, 1:61, 170; 2:37, 49, 58, 146; 3:172, 240, 315, 341, 533.

In this Rufinus is explicitly following the example of his predecessors,[22] while simultaneously and almost hypocritically pleading that others not do to him what he has done to others. Deleting,[23] altering, and even adding to works have been a problem in antiquity,[24] in the Renaissance,[25] and even in the present day.[26] But other types of corruptions also affect the text.

---

22. Specifically the example of Macarius "who when he translated over seventy works of Origen, which are called homilies, and also several of his writings on the apostle into Latin, in which are found several offensive passages, therefore he *removed or cleaned up all of these* when he translated, so that a Latin reader would find nothing in them that disagrees with our belief. *This, therefore, we follow* even if we are not so eloquent, nevertheless as much as we can, by the same rules, watching to be sure not to reveal those passages in the books of Origen that disagree and contradict with himself." Rufinus, preface to Origen, *Peri Archon*, 2, in *PG* 11:112–13, italics added.

23. See Rufinus's preface to pseudo-Clement, *Recognitiones*, in Alexander Roberts, and James Donaldson, eds., *The Ante-Nicene Fathers*, 10 vols. (Grand Rapids, MI: Eerdmans, 1986), 8:75, and n. 3. "The most common scribal error (I think) is haplography, that is, reading two identical sequences of letters as one and omitting whatever intervenes;" P. Kyle McCarter, *Textual Criticism: Recovering the Text of the Hebrew Bible* (Philadelphia: Fortress, 1986), 17.

24. An excellent introduction to the problems involved may be found in Hugh Nibley, "The Way of the Church," *CWHN* 4:209–63. An awareness of the problems of textual tampering appears very early in human history; see, for example, Ur-Nammu (2112–2095 B.C.), the first king of the Ur III Dynasty, *lú mu-sar-ra-ba šu bí-íb-ùr-a* ^{d}*Bìl-ga-mes-e nam a-ba-da-ku$_5$-e* "may Gilgamesh curse whosoever alters this inscription;" Urnammu 41, in Ilmari Kärki, *Die Königsinschriften der dritten Dynastie von Ur*, vol. 58 of *Studia Orentalia* (Helsinki: Finnish Oriental Society, 1986), 26; similar imprecations spanning the length of Babylonian history may be found in Hermann Hunger, *Babylonische und assyrische Kolophone*, vol. 2 of *Alter Orient und Altes Testament* (Kevelaer: Butzon & Bercker, 1968); for the spread of this curse formula into Hittite culture at the beginning of its written history, see O. R. Gurney, *The Hittites* 4th ed. (Harmondsworth, Middlesex: Penguin, 1990), 141 (1st ed., 1952), p. 170.

25. See A. E. Housman, *M. Manilii Astonomicon*, 5 vols. (Cambridge: Cambridge University Press, 1937), 1:xiv–xxii; for an estimate of Renaissance and previous Byzantine textual work, see Alexander Hugh McDonald, "Textual Criticism," *OCD* 1049.

26. On the modern rewriting of Polybius, see Robert K. Ritner, "Implicit Models of Cross-Cultural Interaction: A Question of Noses, Soap and Prejudice," in Janet H. Johnson, ed., *Life in a Multi-Cultural Society: Egypt from Cambyses to Constantine and Beyond*, *SAOC* 51 (Chicago: Oriental Institute, 1992), 287–88.

One is the process by which the texts are reinterpreted in a nonliteral or allegorical framework.[27] Another is the changing of the meanings of words, such as occurred during the second sophistic period.[28]

This central point in Ritner's argument, was itself omitted in the original published version and the errata sheet must be checked. Ritner himself is not above rewriting sources; see Kerry Muhlestein, "The Book of Breathings in its Place," *FARMS Review* 17/2 (2005): 482–86. Another egregious example of rewriting the sources is Morton Smith's *Jesus the Magician* (San Francisco: Harper and Row, 1978): On p. 53, Smith claims to take Pliny's *Epistulae* X.96 "as it is usually taken, at face value" and then proceeds to introduce magical spells, demons, and cannibalism into a text which actually lacks all of these elements.

27. See Richard Lloyd Anderson, *Understanding Paul* (Salt Lake City: Deseret, 1983), 376–77; Layton, *Gnostic Scriptures*, 317. For an exhaustive analysis of the switch in interpretation in one passage of scripture, see Thomas W. Mackay, "Early Christian Millenarianist Interpretation of the Two Witnesses in John's Apocalypse 11:2–13," in Lundquist and Ricks, eds., *By Study and Also By Faith*, 1:222–331. For the use of the allegorical approach in Rabbinic Judaism, see Jacob Neusner, "The Case of Leviticus Rabbah," in Lundquist and Ricks, eds., *By Study and Also By Faith*, 1:366–70. For a historical discussion of allegory, see C. S. Lewis, *The Allegory of Love: A Study in Medieval Tradition* (Oxford: Oxford University Press, 1936), 44–111. For recent attempts to bring about a similar switch in interpretation among the Latter-day Saints, see Louis Midgley, "More Revisionist Legerdemain and the Book of Mormon," *RBBM* 3 (1991): 261–311; Stephen E. Robinson, review of Dan Vogel, ed., *The Word of God: Essays on Mormon Scripture*, in *RBBM* 3 (1991): 312–18; Daniel C. Peterson, "Questions to Legal Answers," *RBBM* 4 (1992): xl–lxxiii.

28. In general, this topic has not received the treatment it deserves. Preliminary steps in this direction are Nibley, "Evangelium Quadraginta Dierum," 33 n. 61; Welch, *The Sermon at the Temple and the Sermon on the Mount*, 88; John W. Welch, "New Testament Word Studies," *Ensign* 23/4 (April 1993): 28–30; John Gee, "The Grace of Christ," *The FARMS Review* 22/1 (2010): 247–59. For analysis of some of the dynamics involved, see Hugh Nibley, "Victoriosa Loquacitas: The Rise of Rhetoric and the Decline of Everything Else," *CWHN* 10:243–86.

Between the time of writing the New Testament and the end of the second century, the meanings of several of the words changed. Examples included the change of the principal meanings of *pistis* from "collateral, guarantee" to "belief" (*LSJ* 1408); of *homologein* from "to agree, accept an agreement, promise" to "to confess" (*LSJ* 1226); of *mystērion* from "(initation) rite" to "secret" (*LSJ* 1156). Because the New Testament is usually read with meanings of the second sophistic period and later—meanings which have often changed—the understanding of the text can be drastically changed. Unfortunately, many books by New Testament scholars

Accounts of Jesus's life were not immune from this propensity.[29] Thus we have both fragments and entire works purporting to tell what Jesus said and did (1) in his infancy,[30] (2) in his ministry,[31] and (3) after his resurrection.[32] Many were well-known in ancient times, but in some cases, scarcely little more than the name survives.[33] How reliable these works are can best be shown by contrasting them to the canonical gospels.

---

will not help the average reader remove this obfuscation because the scholars who write many of the books, have read little in Greek other than the New Testament or occasionally philosophical writings and thus, by training, reflect the viewpoint after the second sophistic period.

29. As they are not in modern times; see Smith, *Jesus the Magician*, 42 where he changes *planos* from "deceiver" to "magician" in Matthew 27:63; the admission of the legerdemain is buried in the notes on p. 177.

30. See Appendix I.

31. See Appendix II.

32. See Appendix III.

33. The following list of apocryphal gospels is culled from lists of canonical and noncanonical books. Some, but not all, of these works duplicate those in the previous lists. The source of the listing is included in parentheses after the name of the book:

The Book about the birth of the Redeemer and about Mary or the midwife (Decretum Gelasianum)

The Book of the Regions of the World (Mārūtā, *Against the Canons from the Synod of 318*, 5, in Vööbus, *Canons Ascribed to Mārūtā of Maipherqa*, 1:22–23, 25–26)

Cento about Christ (Decretum Gelasianum)

Epistle of Jesus to Abgar (Decretum Gelasianum)

The Gospel of Andrew (Decretum Gelasianum)

The Gospel of the Apostle Peter (Decretum Gelasianum)

The Gospel of Barnabas (Decretum Gelasianum, Canon Catalogue)

The Gospel of Bartholomew (Decretum Gelasianum)

The Gospel of Eve (Epiphanius, *Panarion* 26.2.6, 3.1, 5.1)

The Gospel which Hesychius forged (Decretum Gelasianum)

The Gospel of James the Younger (Decretum Gelasianum)

The Gospel which Lucian forged (Decretum Gelasianum)

The Gospel of Matthias (Decretum Gelasianum, Canon Catalogue)

The Gospel of Perfection (Epiphanius, *Panarion* 26.2.5)

The Gospel of Thomas (Decretum Gelasianum, Nicephorus)

Translations of the Decretum Gelasianum (6th cent. A.D.), the Stichometry of Nicophorus (ca. A.D. 850), and the Catalogue of the 60 Canonical Books may be found in *NTA* 1:47–52. Other lists are given in Quasten, *Patrology*, 1:128.

Authenticity

The authenticity of the canonical gospels can be seen from the writings of others telling about or quoting the gospels.[34] Most notably, all varieties of Christian sects from the first and second century—both those who would later be termed "orthodox" and those who would later be termed "heretical"—used the canonical gospels and considered them authoritative.[35] Thus the Gospel according to Matthew is quoted by the *Didache* (ca. 35–45),[36] Luke,[37]

---

34. See also the approach in Robert L. Millet, "'As Delivered from the Beginning': The Formation of the Canonical Gospels," in *Apocryphal Writings and the Latter-day Saints*, 204–8; and Henry Clarence Thiessen, *Introduction to the New Testament* (Grand Rapids, MI: Eerdmans, 1943), 130–33, 140–42, 150–54, 162–64.

35. One large caveat needs to be noted here. Some sects considered some of the canonical gospels authentic but jettisoned others as spurious or interpolated. Thus Marcion considered Luke authoritative, although he used a different version, but he considered Matthew, Mark and John to be spurious—as he would have all the apocrypha here considered; see Irenaeus, *Contra Haeresis* I.27.2, 4; Epiphanius, *Panarion* 42. What we are examining here is the general consensus that the four canonical gospels were part of the Christian scripture. For an examination of the problems with the canon in the larger Christian world, see Stephen E. Robinson, *Are Mormons Christian?* (Salt Lake City: Bookcraft, 1991), 45–56; Daniel C. Peterson and Stephen D. Ricks, *Offenders for a Word: How Anti-Mormons Play Word Games to Attack the Latter-day Saints* (Salt Lake City: Aspen, 1992), 117–28.

36. *Didache* 8:2 quotes Matthew 6:9–13; *Didache* 11:3 alludes to Matthew 6:19–34; 7:15–20; 10:5–15; *Didache* 15:3 alludes to Matthew 5:21–26; 18:15–17; *Didache* 15:4 alludes to Matthew 6:1–18. I will not justify the dating here.

37. Since Luke admits (Luke 1:1–2) that he has used earlier sources including many who had already tried to write narratives (*polloi epecheirēsan anataxasthai diēgēsin*), and eyewitnesses (*autoptai*), it is simpler to view Luke as using both Matthew and Mark to explain the material they share than to postulate some other unidentifiable source. Origen (*Homilia in Lucam* I) takes this passage differently: "Matthew did not 'take in hand' but wrote from the Holy Ghost, likewise also Mark and John and equally Luke. Those who composed the gospel ascribed to the Egyptians and the gospel ascribed to the Twelve, 'took in hand.' Even Basilides had already dared to write the gospel according to Basilides. 'Many have taken in hand.' It also refers to the Gospel according to Thomas and that according to Mathias, and many others. These are those who took in hand; but the church of God prefers the four only." The argument is important in this

the *Epistle of Barnabas* (ca. 70–138),[38] Polycarp (d. 156),[39] and Justin Martyr (ca. 148–61).[40] Additionally, Papias (ca. 130),[41] Irenaeus (ca. 185),[42] Tertullian (ca. 155–220),[43] Origen (ca. 185–253),[44] and Eusebius of Caesarea (ca. 263–340)[45] all attribute this gospel to Matthew and note that it was originally written in Hebrew.[46] The

---

context because it explicitly contrasts the canonical gospels with the apocryphal ones circulating in his day. The anachronism of Basilides (fl. 120–145) writing before Luke is a problem even for those who date Luke late. Origen might be stretching the Greek again, as he does with Matthew 5:8 in *Peri Archon* I.1.9.

38. *Epistle of Barnabas* 4:14 and 5:9 quote from Matthew 22:14; 9:13 respectively.

39. Polycarp, *Epistula ad Philippenses* 2:3 quotes from Matthew 7:10 and 5:3, 10; Polycarp, *Epistula as Philippenses* 7:2 quotes from Matthew 6:13 and 26:41; see also Frend, *Rise of Christianity*, 135. Polycarp was also thought to be a disciple of John; see Lightfoot, *Apostolic Fathers*, 2.1:29, 440–41.

40. Justin's numerous quotations of and allusions to Matthew are listed in Roberts and Donaldson, eds., *Ante-Nicean Fathers* 1:591.

41. Papias, fragment 2, in Eusebius, *Historiae Ecclesiasticae* III.39.16; for the date, see Quasten, *Patrology*, 1:82. Irenaeus (*Contra Haereses* V.33.4) said that Papias was a disciple of John but this was denied by Eusebius (*Historiae Ecclesiasticae* III.39.1–14); for a discussion, see Lightfoot, *Apostolic Fathers*, 2.1:29, 442; and R. H. Gundry, quoted in John Wenham, *Redating Matthew, Mark and Luke* (London: Hodder & Stoughton, 1991), 121–22, with a dating of A.D. 100–10.

42. Irenaeus, *Adversus Haereses* III.1.1. Quasten (*Patrology*, 1:287) dates Irenaeus' trip to Rome at 177 and the *Adversus Haereses* cannot have been composed before then; the date given is taken from Frend, *Rise of Christianity*, 921.

43. Tertullian, *Adversus Marcionem* IV.2.2.

44. Origen, *Commentary in Matthew* I, quoted in Eusebius, *Historiae Ecclesiasticae* VI.25.3–6.

45. Eusebius, *Historiae Ecclesiasticae* III.24.6.

46. This Hebrew version has recently been recovered through the diligent researches of Howard, *Gospel of Matthew according to a Primitive Hebrew Text*; cf. George Howard, "A Primitive Hebrew Gospel of Matthew and the Tol'doth Yeshu," *New Testament Studies* 34 (1988): 60–70; George Howard, "A Note on Codex Sinaiticus and Shem-Tob's Hebrew Matthew," *Novum Testamentum* 34/1 (1992): 46–47; ibid., 46 n. 2 has further bibliography. Wenham, *Redating Matthew, Mark and Luke*, 117–19 discusses the patristic evaluations of authorship. Note that this text cannot be the original Hebrew version but is a back translation as the use of the term קריס׳טוס "Christ" instead of משיח "Messiah" in, e.g. Matthew 1:16 shows.

Gospel according to Mark is quoted by Justin Martyr,[47] and perhaps by Clement of Rome (d. 156).[48] Papias,[49] Irenaeus,[50] Clement of Alexandria,[51] and Tertullian[52] attribute this gospel to Mark, who got his material from Peter.[53] The Gospel according to Luke is quoted by Clement of Rome,[54] Polycarp,[55] Justin Martyr,[56] and the *Apocalypse of Peter*,[57] and is even used by Marcion.[58] Irenaeus[59] and Tertullian[60] attribute this gospel to Luke. The Gospel according

---

47. Justin Martyr, *Apologia* I.16 quotes from Mark 12:30.

48. If 1 Clement 46:8 is a quotation of Mark 9:42 then one or the other has been tampered with. The date is from Quasten, *Patrology*, 1:77. One of the reasons it is difficult to find quotations of Mark in patristic writers is that there is so little in Mark that can only be Mark and much that is just as likely to be from Matthew or Luke; this was recognized in ancient times; see Eusebius, *Epistula ad Carpianum et Canones I-X* in Eberhard Nestle, et al., *Novum Testamentum Graecae*, 26th ed. (Stuttgart: Deutsche Bibelgesellschaft, 1979), 73*–78*.

49. Papias, fragment 2, in Eusebius, *Historiae Ecclesiasticae* III.39.15.

50. Irenaeus, *Contra Haereses* III.1.1.

51. Clement of Alexandria, *Adumbrationes* ad 1 Peter 5:13; Clement of Alexandria, *Hypotyposeis* VI, quoted in Eusebius, *Historiae Ecclesiasticae* II.15.1–2, and VI.14.5–7.

52. Tertullian, *Adversus Marcionem* IV.2.2, 5.3.

53. Clement of Alexandria, *Adumbrationes* ad 1 Peter 5:13; Clement of Alexandria, *Hypotyposeis* VI, quoted in Eusebius, *Historiae Ecclesiasticae* II.15.1–2, and VI.14.5–7; Tertullian, *Adversus Marcionem* IV.5.3. Justin Martyr (*Dialogus cum Tryphone* 106.3) even attributed Mark's Gospel to Peter.

54. 1 Clement 13:2 quotes Luke 6:31, 37–38; 1 Clement 46:8 quotes Luke 17:2; 2 Clement 6:1 quotes Luke 16:13 and 2 Clement 13:4 quotes Luke 6:32–33.

55. Polycarp, *Epstula ad Philippenses* 2:3 quotes Luke 6:20, 37; see also Frend, *Rise of Christianity*, 135.

56. Justin's quotations of and allusions to Luke are listed in Roberts and Donaldson, eds., *The Ante-Nicean Fathers* 1:591; in particular, Justin Martyr, *Dialogus cum Tryphone* 106.1 is a clear reference to Luke 24:26–27, 44–45 and cannot derive from any of the other canonical gospels.

57. *Apocalypse of Peter* VII.76.4–8 quotes Luke 6:44.

58. Irenaeus, *Contra Haereses* I.27.2.

59. Irenaeus, *Contra Haereses* III.1.1.

60. Tertullian, *Adversus Marcionem* IV.2.2.

to John is quoted by Ignatius,[61] Polycarp,[62] and the *Gospel of the Egyptians*.[63] Fragments of manuscripts date from as early as the late second century.[64] Papias,[65] Irenaeus,[66] Clement of Alexandria,[67] and Tertullian[68] attribute this gospel to John. Thus, though the support is not unanimous, the canonical gospels were seen as authoritative by most groups of Christians in the second century.

In contrast, many of the other "gospels" were condemned as forgeries by the fourth century. For example, the Gospel of Thomas was identified as spurious by Origen,[69]

---

61. Ignatius, *Epistula ad Philadelphenos* 7:1 quotes John 3:8; Ignatius, *Epistula ad Magnesios* 8:2 alludes to John 8:29; and Ignatius, *Epistula ad Ephesios* 17:1 alludes to John 12:3.

62. Frend, *Rise of Christianity*, 135.

63. *The Gospel of the Egyptians* (Nag Hammadi Version) III.49.10–12 = IV.61.12–14 quotes John 1:3.

64. Papyrus Rylands 457 (also known as P[52]) derives from Egypt and dates to the late second century and contains fragments of John 18:31–33, 37–38 (a photograph of said papyrus may be found in J. Reuben Clark, Jr., *Why the King James Version* [Salt Lake City: Deseret Book, 1956], 8); for the date, see Roger Bagnall, *Early Christian Books in Egypt* (Princeton: Princeton University Press, 2009), 12–24. It joins the other earliest New Testament manuscripts (Papyrus Berlin 11765 = *0189 containing Acts 5:3–21 and Papyrus Chester Beatty II + Papyrus Michigan 6238 = P[46] containing portions of the Pauline Epistles) dating from the end of the second century at earliest. This means that all of our New Testament manuscripts date from after the period when the Christians accused each other of tampering with the text, while the only manuscript previous to that time contains a mere five verses imperfectly preserved; see also John Gee, review of Wilford A. Fischer and Norma J. Fischer, *A Book of Mormon Guide: A Simple Way to Teach a Friend* (n.p.: n.p., 1988), in *RBBM* 2 (1990): 85 n. 14.

65. Papias, fragment 18 in Oscar de Gebhardt, Adolf Harnack and Theodor Zahn, *Patrum Apostolicorum Opera* (Leipzig: Hinrichs, 1906), 77.

66. Irenaeus, *Contra Haereses* III.1.1.

67. Clement of Alexandria, *Hypotyposeis* VI, quoted in Eusebius, *Historiae Ecclesiasticae* VI.14.7.

68. Tertullian, *Adversus Marcionem* IV.2.2.

69. Origen, *Homilia in Lucam* I.

Eusebius of Caesarea,[70] and Hippolytus (d. 236)[71] and others.[72] Unfortunately the situation is complicated by the existence of several different works all called the Gospel of Thomas.[73] The Protevangelium of James is clearly an ancient forgery,[74] and was identified as such in the fourth century.[75] Another forgery identified as such in ancient times was the *Sophia Jesu Christi*. Comparison of the *Sophia Jesu Christi* with the epistle of *Eugnostos the Blessed* reveals how Eugnostos's pagan philosophical speculations on deity are reworked and dressed in a forty-day frame story to produce the *Sophia Jesu Christi*.[76] That this instance of the dressing up of the philosophies of men as scripture was recognized in ancient times is presumably why the two tractates are placed back to back in Codex III from Nag Hammadi. The addition of forty-day window dressing can explain many documents, including the *Apocryphon of John*.

70. Eusebius, *Historiae Ecclesiasticae* III.25.6.

71. Hippolytus *Refutatio* 5.7.20, 8.32. For the date of Hippolytus, see Quasten, *Patrology*, 2:164.

72. For others, see *NTA* 1:278–79; Harold W. Attridge, "The Greek Fragments," in Bentley Layton, ed., *Nag Hammadi Codex II,2–7*, 2 vols., *NHS* 20–21 (Leiden: E. J. Brill, 1989), 103–9.

73. See Quasten, *Patrology*, 1:123–25; *NTA* 1:278–82.

74. The plot comes from 1 Samuel 1; Matthew 1–2 and Luke 1–2. The story that Zacharias was a martyr may be a true story preserved in a very embellished form in this account; see Editor [John Taylor?], "Persecution of the Prophets," *Times and Seasons* 3/21 (1 September 1842): 902; the last is the source of Joseph Fielding Smith, comp., *Teachings of the Prophet Joseph Smith* (Salt Lake City: Deseret, 1976), 261. "The author is not familiar with Jewish life or usages" (James, *Apocryphal New Testament*, 38) and "shows an astonishing ignorance of the geography of Palestine;" Quasten, *Patrology*, 1:121. For the estimation of other elements in the story in the *Protevangelium of James*, see Hugh Nibley, "Early Accounts of Jesus' Childhood," in *CHWN* 4:6–7.

75. Epiphanius, *Panarion* 26.12.1; perhaps it is also referred to Clement of Alexandria, *Stromateis* VII.93.

76. Douglas M. Parrott, "Eugnostos the Blessed (III,3 and V,1) and The Sophia of Jesus Christ (III,4 and BG 8502,3)," in Robinson, *Nag Hammadi Library* (1988), 220–21; *NTA* 1:243–48. Gerald Jones, "Man of Holiness," in Ludlow, ed., *Encyclopedia of Mormonism*, 3:852 wrongly identifies *Eugnostos the Blessed* as "pre-Christian;" it is not pre-Christian but rather non-Christian.

Looking over the material years ago, Hugh Nibley declared, "Most of them are pretty poor stuff and all of them are copies of copies."[77] The early church fathers did use noncanonical sources, some of which were thought to be authoritative,[78] but those considered authoritative have generally *not* been found in the mass of apocryphal literature.[79]

Though the number of works that all parade under the same title demonstrates the existence of ancient forgers "lying for God,"[80] for the historian and layman arriving on the scene thousands of years later there would seem to be no clear way of determining which, if any, of the works parading under a given title is authentic. Authenticity can often be a very tricky question; it must be done on a case by case basis, and even in a false work there might still be an element of truth. This means that it requires some amount of discernment to separate the truth from the lies. This same discernment needs to be used in dealing with the apocryphal accounts of Jesus.[81]

For historical documents, the standard method of determining authenticity is either to assume the document is genu-

77. Hugh Nibley, "The Expanding Gospel," *BYU Studies* 7 (Autumn 1965), 27; reprinted in Hugh Nibley, *Nibley on the Timely and the Timeless* (Provo, UT: Religious Studies Center, 1978) 40; reprinted again in Hugh Nibley, *Temple and Cosmos: Beyond This Ignorant Present*, CHWN 12 (Salt Lake City: Deseret Book, 1992), 203; quoted in Hugh Nibley, *Of All Things! Classic Quotations of Hugh Nibley*, Gary P. Gillum, comp. and ed., 2nd ed., (Salt Lake City: Deseret Book, 1993), 85.

78. Ignatius, *Epistula ad Smyrnaeos* 3:2. For discussion, see Hugh Nibley, "Evangelium Quadraginta Dierum: The Forty-day Mission of Christ—The Forgotten Heritage," in *CWHN*, 4:25, n. 29. In fact, since many of the documents, especially those from Nag Hammadi, are docetic and deny the resurrection of Christ, it is not surprising that the source has not shown up. Another example is given in Catherine Thomas, "Refuge in God's Love," in *Acts to Revelation*, 250–51.

79. The biggest exception being the Book of Enoch, for which see Hugh Nibley, "A Strange Thing in the Land," in *CWHN* 2:95–99; James H. Charlesworth, "Enoch: Ancient Sources," in Ludlow, ed., *Encyclopedia of Mormonism*, 2:459–60; E. Isaac, "1 (Ethiopic Apocalypse of) Enoch," *OTP* 1:8–10.

80. The term comes from Stephen E. Robinson, "Lying for God: The Uses of the Apocrypha," in *Apocryphal Writings and the Latter-day Saints*, 133–54.

81. See D&C 91:1–6; 9:7–9; 46:27–30.

ine and try to determine whether it reflects the milieu claimed for itself,[82] or assume that it is a forgery and allow nothing to change one's mind. This may not be sufficient in all cases; for example, for years the treatise *On Virginity* was listed among the works attributed to Basil of Caesarea and said to be spurious, for although it reflected his time period (because it was really written by his contemporary Basil of Ancyra) it did not match his style.[83] Stylistic analysis, however, is notoriously difficult and subjective. Individual tests for forgery are seldom "ever sufficient to guarantee results."[84] These tests are negative tests, meaning that they can determine that a document is a forgery but cannot determine that it is genuine.

In addition to the tests of the scholars, Latter-day Saints looking for a litmus test to determine whether any "plain and precious things"[85] are to be found in any given apocryphal work might also

---

82.　Friedrich Blass, "Hermeneutik und Kritik," *Einleitende und Hilfsdiszipline*, vol. 1 of *Handbuch der klassischen Altertumswissenschaft* (Nördlingen: Beck, 1886), 268–72; ANT 38; Thomas W. Mackay, "Content and Style in Two-Pseudo-Pauline Epistles (3 Corinthians and Epistle to the Laodiceans)," *Apocryphal Writings and the Latter-day Saints*, 234–36.

83.　Quasten, *Patrology*, 3:203.

84.　George J. Throckmorton, "A Forensic Analysis of Twenty-One Hofmann Documents," in Linda Sillitoe and Allen Roberts, *Salamander: The Story of the Mormon Forgery Murders* (Salt Lake City: Signature, 1988), 533.

85.　1 Nephi 13:26–29. On the "plain and precious" things, see also Robinson, "Lying for God," 135; Stephen E. Robinson, "Early Christianity and 1 Nephi 13–14," in Monte Nyman and Charles Tate, eds., *First Nephi: The Doctrinal Foundation* (Provo, UT: BYU Religious Studies Center, 1988), 177–91; Daniel C. Peterson, review of Nyman and Tate, eds., *The Doctrinal Foundation*, in RBBM 1 (1989): 127–28; Stephen E. Robinson, "Bible Scholarship," in Ludlow, ed., *Encyclopedia of Mormonism* 1:113; Stephen E. Robinson, review of Dan Vogel, ed., *The Word of God*, in RBBM 3 (1991): 318; John W. Welch, "The Plain and Precious Parts," in *Reexploring the Book of Mormon* (Salt Lake City: Deseret, and Provo, UT: FARMS, 1992), 37–40; John W. Welch, *The Sermon at the Temple and the Sermon on the Mount* (Salt Lake City: Deseret and Provo, UT: FARMS, 1990), 88–89; Richard D. Draper, *Opening the Seven Seals: The Visions of John the Revelator* (Salt Lake City: Deseret, 1991), 14–15, 190; Gee, review of Fischer and Fischer, *Book of Mormon Guide*, 85 and notes.

ask themselves how the first principles of the gospel[86] fare in that work.[87] If we take what the secular scholars consider to be the earliest gospel and hymn as our guides,[88] we find that the emphasis on the first principles is there in the earliest Christian texts. The Gospel of Mark begins: "The first principle of the gospel of Jesus the anointed son of God . . . was John baptizing in the desert and preaching a baptism of repentance for a remission of sins" (Mark

---

86. For discussion, see Noel B. Reynolds, "The Gospel of Jesus Christ as Taught by the Nephite Prophets," *BYUS* 31/3 (Summer 1991): 31–47; Louis Midgley, "Prophetic Messages or Dogmatic Theology? Commenting on the Book of Mormon: A Review Essay," *RBBM* 1 (1989): 99–104; Noel B. Reynolds, "Gospel of Jesus Christ," in Ludlow, ed., *Encyclopedia of Mormonism*, 2:556–60; Marie Kartchner Hafen, "First Principles of the Gospel," in Ludlow, ed., *Encyclopedia of Mormonism*, 2:514–15; Jeffrey R. Holland, "Atonement of Jesus Christ," in Ludlow, ed., *Encyclopedia of Mormonism*, 1:82–86; John W. Welch, "Book of Mormon Religious Teachings and Practices," in Ludlow, ed., *Encyclopedia of Mormonism*, 1:201–5; M. Gerald Bradford and Larry E. Dahl, "Doctrine: Meaning, Source, and History of Doctrine," in Ludlow, ed., *Encyclopedia of Mormonism*, 1:393–97; William S. Bradshaw, "Remission of Sins," in Ludlow, ed., *Encyclopedia of Mormonism*, 3:1210–11; Ivan J. Barrett, "Church of the Firstborn," in Ludlow, ed., *Encyclopedia of Mormonism*, 1:276; Gee, review of Fischer and Fischer, *Book of Mormon Guide*, 79 and n. 5; Daniel C. Peterson, "Questions to Legal Answers," *RBBM* 4 (1992): lxii–lxxiii.

87. This research method is not unique: "From the point of view of the restored gospel, Latter-day Saints can usually justify a rather straightforward method of identifying doctrines and teachings which derive not only from Jesus' era but more notably from the earlier period of the patriarchs and prophets. This procedure consists in isolating those elements which harmonize with the basic teachings of the restored gospel. But while this method of identifying parallels between LDS beliefs and those mirrored in ancient literatures has its attractions, one must still employ considerable caution when treating the issue of what may have genuinely come from Jesus and his followers and what may not." S. Kent Brown, "The Nag Hammadi Library: A Mormon Perspective," *Apocryphal Writings and the Latter-day Saints*, 257.

88. Using these passages in this way does not mean that I agree with the scholars' assessments. Because Latter-day Saints need to "be ready always to give an answer [*apologian*, defense] to every man that asketh you a reason of the hope that is in you" (1 Peter 3:15 KJV), I give this as a way of showing why, even by the secular scholars' standards, the first principles of the gospel can be seen as a fundamental element of the earliest Christian tradition. We tend to forget that apologetics are not only a Christian, but especially a Mormon duty (see Mosiah 18:9; D&C 123:4–15).

1:1–4, author's translation). In what is thought to be a quotation of the earliest Christian hymn, we learn of Jesus "who was born like men and, finding himself in the form of a man, humbled himself by becoming obedient unto death, even crucifixion; therefore God also exalted him and granted him the name which is above every name, that in the name of Jesus every knee should bow, of beings celestial, terrestrial and telestial, and every tongue acknowledge to the glory of God the Father that Jesus Christ is Lord" (Philippians 2:7–11, author's translation). Thus if we take the first four Articles of Faith and examine how any given apocryphal work deals with these themes (God, Christ, the Holy Ghost, accountability, atonement, obedience, faith, repentance, baptism), that might give some idea about how likely one is to find "plain and precious things" in that apocryphal work. Most apocryphal works fail this test.

Infancy Gospels

Many of the Apocryphal Acts of Jesus may be found in what are called Infancy Gospels because they tend to deal exclusively with the exploits of Jesus before the end of his thirteenth year. These are first known and condemned in the second century, when knowledge of Jesus's life appears to have been at a minimum.[89] In lieu of actual accounts, interest in the exploits of Jesus' childhood provoked a rash of accounts supplementing the gospel accounts. The Infancy Gospels tend to expand and become more and more miraculous with time and gather more and more stories. If we assume a tendency toward textual accretions, then one can construct a stemma of the various versions:

---

89. Irenaeus (*Contra Haereses* II.22.6) actually maintains that Jesus could not have lived less than fifty years.

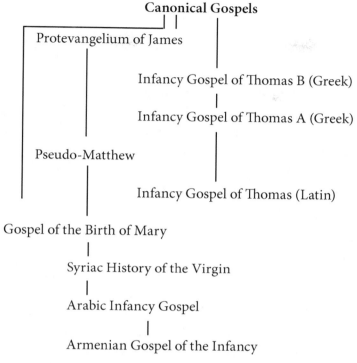

Canonical Gospels

Protevangelium of James

Infancy Gospel of Thomas B (Greek)

Infancy Gospel of Thomas A (Greek)

Pseudo-Matthew

Infancy Gospel of Thomas (Latin)

Gospel of the Birth of Mary

Syriac History of the Virgin

Arabic Infancy Gospel

Armenian Gospel of the Infancy

At the very time that miracles ceased from the church,[90] they swarmed among the infancy gospels, the literary accounts of the saints' lives (called hagiographies),[91] and in the apocrypha.[92] For the apocryphal baby Jesus, miracles begin at an early age: "Jesus talked when he was in the crib[93] and said to Mary, his mother: I am Jesus, the son of God, the Word whom you

---

90. For the loss of miracles in the second century, see Hugh Nibley, *The World and the Prophets*, CWHN 3:141–42. If revelation be counted a miracle, then see also Chadwick, *Early Church*, 52–53; the loss of prophecy was noted in the Apocryphon of James I.6.21–7.10.

91. On the miracles in the hagiographies, see Ritner, *Mechanics of Ancient Egyptian Magical Practice*, 89–91. Ritner makes a good case for some later miracle stories being borrowed from pagan miracle stories. See also Hugh Nibley, "Baptism for the Dead in Ancient Times," *CWHN* 4:108–9.

92. Quasten, *Patrology*, 1:106, 124.

93. *Mahd* "crib" not *mid̲h̲wad* "manger".

bore just as Gabriel, the angel, announced to you, and my father sent me to save the world."[94]

On the trip to Egypt, Joseph, Mary and the baby encounter several serpents:

> The little infant Jesus himself walked in front of them so that nothing would hurt them. But Mary and Joseph were intensely scared lest perchance the little infant would be injured by a serpent, to which Jesus said, "Don't worry! Do not even consider me your son, for I always was and am a perfect man. Besides, it is necessary as all the beasts of the forests become tame before me."[95]

The mention of forests in Sinai and Egypt shows that the European who retold this story in Latin knew no more about the geography of the Holy Land than the author of the Christmas carol who saw three ships come sailing in to land-locked Bethlehem. We can identify the origin of this story, for the infant master of the animals who protects travellers from snakes, serpents, and scorpions is the Egyptian god Horus the child, or Harpocrates,[96] whose cult had spread through the Roman world and beyond.[97] Later Christians borrowed the ico-

---

94. Arabic Infancy Gospel 1.

95. Pseudo-Matthew 18:2.

96. Heike Sternberg-El Hotabi, *Untersuchungen zur Überlieferungsgeschichte der Horusstelen* (Wiesbaden: Harrassowitz Verlag, 1999); Robert K. Ritner, "Horus on the Crocodiles: A Juncture of Religion and Magic in Late Dynastic Egypt," in William Kelly Simpson, ed., *Religion and Philosophy in Ancient Egypt*, YES 3 (New Haven: Yale Egyptological Seminar, 1989), 103–16; Gun Björkmann, "Harsiese," in *LdÄ* 2:1018–20; Hellmut Brunner, "Götter, Kinder-," in Otto and Helck, eds., *LdÄ* 2:649–50.

97. See Vilmos Wessetzky, *Die ägyptischen Kulte zur Römerzeit in Ungarn*, EPRO 1 (Leiden: Brill, 1961), 25–27; Mario Floriani Squarciapino, *I Culti Orientali ad Ostia*, EPRO 3 (Leiden: Brill, 1962): 35–36; A. García y Bellido, *Les religions orientales dans l'Espagne romaine*, EPRO 5 (Leiden: Brill, 1962), 106–9; Eve and John R. Harris, *The Oriental Cults in Roman Britain*, EPRO 6 (Leiden: Brill, 1965), 81; Günter Grimm, *Die Zeugnisse ägyptischer Religion und Kunstelemente im römischen Deutschland*, EPRO 12 (Leiden: Brill, 1969),

nography of Isis with Harpocrates for Mary and her child,[98] and that of Harpocrates for Christ,[99] so it is not surprising that once again, Horus—who went "to ward off [any bit]ing snake" saying "I am Horus the Saviour (*šdw*) who ensures protection (*s3w*) for you"[100]—should be confounded with Christ in popular imagination.[101]

63; Regina Salditt-Trappmann, *Tempel der ägyptischen Götterin Griechenland und an der Westküste Kleinasiens*, EPRO 15 (Leiden: Brill, 1970), 22–23; V. Tran Tam Tinh, *Le Culte des divinités orientales a Heraculanum*, EPRO 17 (Leiden: Brill, 1971), 21–22, 68–74, Plates X-XIII; Anne Roullet, *The Egyptian and Egyptianizing Monuments of Imperial Rome*, EPRO 20 (Leiden: Brill, 1972), 89, Plate XCV; Michael Malaise, *Inventaire préliminaire des documents égyptiens découverts en Italie*, EPRO 21 (Leiden: Brill, 1972), 364; Michael Malaise, *Les conditions de* pénétration et de diffusion des cultes égyptiens en Italie, EPRO 22 (Leiden: Brill, 1972), 198–203; V. Tran Tam Tinh, *Le Culte des divinités orientales en Campanie*, EPRO 27 (Leiden: Brill, 1972), 48, 56, 72–74; Giulia Sfameni Gasparro, *I Culti Orientali in Sicilia*, EPRO 31 (Leiden: Brill, 1973), Plates 31, 45, 52; Martin Bommas, *Heiligtum und Mysterium: Griechenland und seine ägyptischen Gottheiten* (Mainz am Rhein: Philipp von Zabern, 2005).

98. G. A. Wellen, "Maria, Marienbild: I. Das Marienbild der frühchr. Kunst," in Engelbert Kirschbaum, ed., *Lexikon der christlichen Ikonographie*, 8 vols. (Freiburg: Herber, 1968–76), 3:158–59; V. Tran Tam Tinh, *Isis Lactans*, EPRO 37 (Leiden: Brill, 1973); Grimm, *Zeugnisse ägyptischer Religion und Kunstelemente im römischen Deutschland*, 143–44, 156–59, Tafeln 2–3, 76; Bellido, *Religions orientales dans l'Espagne romaine*, 119–20.

99. Ritner, "Horus on the Crocodiles," 114.

100. Standard cippus text A, in J. F. Bourghouts, *Ancient Egyptian Magical Texts*, vol. 9 of *Nisaba: Religious Texts Translation Series* (Leiden: Brill, 1978), 84–85 #123; also in Ritner, "Horus on the Crocodiles," 108; cf. *Book of the Dead* 37; P. Louvre 204, in Robert W. Daniel and Franco Maltomini, eds., *Supplementum Magicum Vol. I*, vol. 16.1 of *Papyrologica Coloniensia* (Opladen: Westdeutscher, 1989), 17–19. For the range of translation of the epithet "Horus the Savior," "Horus the Reciter," or "Horus the Enchanter," see Ritner, "Horus on the Crocodiles," 109; Ritner, *Mechanics of Ancient Egyptian Magical Practice*, 44–45.

101. Although many modern scholars may equate Christ with Osiris, the ancients equated Christ with Horus. For examples of the former position, see *inter alia* Joseph Campbell, *The Masks of God: Primitive Mythology* (New York: Viking, 1959), 143; Joseph Campbell, *The Masks of God: Oriental Mythology* (New York: Viking, 1962), 47–48; Joseph Campbell, *The Masks of God: Occidental Mythology* (New York: Viking,, 1964), 234, 338–39, 347, 362–63; James R. Harris,

Once again, a contrast of the apocryphal gospels with the canonical gospels reveals the former for what they are. Raising the dead, comparatively rare in the gospels,[102] is common in the infancy gospels.[103]

> Jesus was playing with some other children on the second story of a house and one of the children was pushed by another, and plummeting to the ground he died. And when his playmates saw they fled, and Jesus alone was left standing upon the roof whence the child had been flung headlong. And when the parents learned of their child's death, they ran weeping. And when they found the child lying dead on the ground, with Jesus standing above, they supposed that the child had been pitched down by him and glaring they blamed him. But Jesus seeing, immediately jumped down from the second story, and stood at the head of the deceased and said to him, "Zenon (the child was so called), did I throw you down? Stand and speak." And with that command the child arose, and worshiping Jesus said: Lord, you did not throw me down, but you made me alive, who was dead.[104]

The Facsimiles of the Book of Abraham: A Study of the Joseph Smith Egyptian Papyri (Payson, UT: James R. Harris, 1990); for examples of the ancient evidence, see Ritner, "Horus on the Crocodiles," 114; P. Berol. 8314, column 2, line 1 ("Jesus Horus son of Isis went upon a mountain to rest"), in Walter Beltz, "Die koptischen Zauberpapiere und Zauberostraka der Papyrus-Sammlung der Staatliche Museen zu Berlin," AfP 31 (1985): 67.

102. There are only three specific instances recorded: (1) the son of the widow of Nain (Luke 7:11–18), (2) Jairus' daughter (Matthew 9:18–19, 27–31; Mark 5:22–24, 35–43; Luke 8:41–42, 49–56), and (3) Lazarus (John 11:1–46).

103. The (Infancy) Gospel of Thomas A 9:3; 17:1; 18:1; B 8:3.

104. Infancy Gospel of Thomas B 8:1–3.

In the canonical gospels, Jesus refused to do miracles for his own convenience;[105] yet in the infancy gospels no miracle is too trivial if it is for Jesus's convenience.[106]

When this little child Jesus was five years old, he was playing at the ford of a rushing stream, and the flowing water gathered into pools, and with a single command he made them all clean. And after making some soft clay, he molded twelve sparrows. But it was the Sabbath when he did this, though there were many other children playing with him. And when a certain Jew saw what Jesus did while playing on the Sabbath, he went immediately and told his father Joseph, "Hey, your kid is at the brook, and he has taken some clay and made twelve sparrows and broken the Sabbath." And when Joseph came to the place and saw, he yelled at him, saying, "Why did you do what it isn't right to do on the Sabbath?" But Jesus clapped his hands together and cried out to the sparrows and told them, "Go!" And the sparrows fluttered and went off chirping.[107]

The Jesus of the canonical gospels is longsuffering, enduring torture and indignity in silence or with a dignified rebuke;[108] the Jesus of the infancy gospels is a spoiled brat who calls down immediate and terrible curses for the slightest offense.[109] "Later he was going through the village, and a running child crashed into his shoulder. And Jesus being bitter said to

---

105. E.g. Matthew 4:2–4; 27:39–44; Mark 15:29–32; Luke 4:1–4; 23:35–39.

106. *The (Infancy) Gospel of Thomas* A 2:1–3:2; 4:1; 9:3; 11:1–2; 13:1; 14:2; B 2:1–3; 3:2; 10:1; 11:2; Latin version 1; 4:1–2.

107. Infancy Gospel of Thomas A 2:1–4.

108. Matthew 26:55–27:50; Mark 14:48–15:37; Luke 22:47–23:47; John 18:1–19:30.

109. *The (Infancy) Gospel of Thomas* A 3:2–3; 4:1; 8:1–2; 14:2–3; B 2:2–3; 4:1; Latin version 4:3. Cf. Quasten, *Patrology,* 1:124: "Some of the miracles do not show much taste. The author seems to have had a queer concept of divinity, because he pictures the boy Jesus as using his power to take revenge."

him, 'You'll never finish your course.' And immediately he dropped dead."[110]

Perhaps the most telling difference between the Jesus of the canonical gospels and the *Wunderkind* of the infancy gospels, is who gets the glory from the miracles: In the infancy gospels the glory usually goes to the child Jesus,[111] in the canonical gospels it goes to God, his Father.[112]

This is not to suggest that everything in the infancy gospels is, of necessity, wrong. There is one detail that occurs in several of the infancy narratives that is probably correct. The accounts inform us that Mary was engaged at the age of twelve and bore Jesus somewhere between the ages of fourteen and sixteen.[113] This seems young to us, but was normal at the time.[114]

The Apocryphal Ministry

After the Infancy Gospels, we hear nothing about Jesus as a young man in the extra-canonical books until the time of his ministry, which is both a mixed bag and a small one. The main reason for the paucity is that those accounts that do cover the mortal ministry are fragmentary: some are preserved only in

---

110. Infancy Gospel of Thomas A 4:1.

111. *The (Infancy) Gospel of Thomas* A 9:3; 10:2; 17:1–2; 18:1.

112. Matthew 5:15–16; 9:2–8; 15:29–31; Mark 2:1–12; Luke 5:18–26; 13:11–13; 17:11–19; 18:35–43; John 7:39; 8:54–55; 11:1–4; 12:16, 23–28; 13:31–32; 14:13–14; 15:5–8; 16:13–14; 17:1–10; 21:18–19; but note Luke 4:14–15. Compare Moses 4:1–2.

113. Protevangelium of James 8:2–3, 12:3; History of Joseph the Carpenter, Arabic version 3:1, Coptic version 5:1.

114. Roger S. Bagnall and Bruce W. Frier, *The Demography of Roman Egypt* (Cambridge: Cambridge University Press, 1994), 112. Morris Jastrow, *A Dictionary of the Targumim, the Talmud Babli and Yerushalmi, and the Midrashic Literature* (New York: Traditional Press, n.d.), 137–38, 922, 1350. Raphael Taubenschlag, *The Law of Greco-Roman Egypt in the Light of the Papyri 332 B.C.-640 A.D.*, 2nd ed. (Warsaw: Państwowe Wydawnictwo Naukowe, 1955), 112: "As a rule Greek and Egyptian boys would marry at the age of 14 and girls at the age of 12."

fragments;[115] others, since they were simply alterations of the canonical gospels, have only been preserved in short, often derisive, quotations.[116]

Alterations of the apocryphal ministry usually advocate specific points of view on theological or behavioral issues. For example, one apocryphal account gives thirteen different ways of looking at Jesus's baptism, and concludes that the canonical version is wrong.[117] At other times, strange things appear, with an emphasis on the miraculous.[118] For example, in a fragment from the Gospel of the Hebrews, Jesus relates "suddenly, my mother, the Holy Ghost,[119] took me by the one of my hairs and brought me up to the great mountain of Tabor."[120]

Another story told of Jesus concerns his response to the Syrian king Abgar who wrote to him on account of his miracles. Abgar, we are told, heard that Jesus effected his cures "without magic or drugs," and thus decided that "either thou

---

115. For example, Papyrus Oxyrhynchus 840.

116. For example, the Gospel of the Ebionites, the Gospel of the Egyptians, the Gospel of the Hebrews, the Gospel of the Nazarenes, and Marcion's version of Luke (for which see Epiphanius, *Panarion* 42.11–12).

117. *The Apocalypse of Adam* V.77.18–82.25.

118. Narration of Joseph of Arimathea 5:4; Epistula Apostolorum 5.

119. The idea that the Holy Ghost was female and the consort of God the Father was a widespread idea in Sethian Gnostic circles; see Irenaeus, *Contra Haereses* I.30.1; Epiphanius, *Panarion* 39.2.3–4; 40.2.8. For the Valentinians, the Holy Ghost was the wife of Christ; Irenaeus, *Contra Haereses* I.2.6; cf. Gospel of Phillip II.55.23–26. The idea derived from the grammatical gender of the word "spirit" in Hebrew and other Semitic languages (feminine), though curiously, all our evidence for these groups comes from languages where the word for "spirit" is not feminine; i.e. Greek (*pneuma* is neuter), Latin (*spiritus* is masculine) and Coptic (*pneuma* is masculine).

120. Gospel of the Hebrews, fragment 5, cited in Origen, *Commentary on John* II.12.87, and in Origen, *Homilies in Jeremiah* 15.4, and in Jerome, *Commentary in Micah* 7:7, and in Jerome, *Commentary in Isaiah* 40:9. The first citation is the fullest and Jerome's citations seem dependent on Origen's; for which see also *ANT* 166; Erich Klostermann, "Einführung in die Arbeiten des Origenes zum Matthäus," in Erich Klostermann and Ludwig Früchtel, *Origenes Werke*, 12 vols. of *GCS* (Berlin: Akademie, 1953), 12.2:3–5.

art God and descending from heaven thou doest these things or thou art a son of God who does these things." So Abgar supposedly wrote Jesus a letter inviting him to come live under his protection.[121] Jesus politely refused the invitation in the following written response:

> Blessed art thou who believest in me, without having seen me. For it is written of me that those who have seen me have not believed in me, and those who have not seen me, they who should believe shall also live. Concerning coming to thee about which thou hast written me, it must needs be that I fulfill those things for which I have been sent, and after fulfilling to thus ascend to him who sent me. And because I shall ascend, I shall send thee certain of my disciples, that thy affliction might be healed and that life be provided for thee and those with thee.[122]

This intriguing set of documents is now thought to be a forgery, because (1) the king Abgar who lived at the time of Christ was known to have been a pagan as were his descendants, (2) the Syrian Christians had never heard of this story until the days of Constantine, and (3) the earliest Christians in Edessa were not followers of Thaddeus or Addai, as the Abgar legend requires, but followers of Marcion, Bardesanes and Mani.[123]

The Apocryphal Passion

Since, for Latter-day Saints, the most important act in history was the Atonement of Christ, perhaps it is significant that this act of Jesus does not usually have a central role in the apoc-

---

121. Letter from Abgar to Jesus, quoted in Eusebius, *Historiae Ecclesiasticae* I.13.6–8.

122. Epistle of Jesus to Abgar, quoted in Eusebius, *Historiae Ecclesiasticae* I.13.10.

123. See *NTA* 1:437–40.

ryphal acts, though this does not mean that it is absent. The picture presented is not consistent, for while in one apocryphal passion, Jesus gathers his disciples together and prays with them before his agony in Gethsemane,[124] in others the garden is omitted entirely.[125] One example of a fraudulent gospel is the *Acts of Pilate*. Following the narrative patterns of later fictionalized martyrdoms, the leaders of the Jews bring Jesus before Pilate and accuse him:

> "We have a law not to heal anyone on the Sabbath,[126] but this man has healed those lame, hunchbacked, withered, blind, paralyzed, deaf and possessed on the Sabbath by evil deeds." Pilate said to them: "What evil deeds?" They said to him: "He is a magician, and by Beelzebul the prince of demons, he casts out demons, and all are subject to him." Pilate said to him: "This casting out of demons is not by unclean spirits but by the god, Asklepios."[127]

As Pilate here deftly points out, magic is in the mind of the accuser.[128] As the trial goes on, all signs indicate that Jesus

124. Strasbourg Papyrus Coptic 5, in *NTA* 1:229–30.

125. Narration of Joseph of Arimathea 2:3–4; Apocalypse of Peter VII.80.23–81.25.

126. The laws against healing on the Sabbath specify that one is not to anoint with specific sorts of oil on the Sabbath: root oil (*šemen ʿiqqārīn*) and (depending on the legal authority) rose oil (*šemem wered*) are prohibited but other types of oil are permitted. See *Mishnah Shabbat* 14:3–4. The general ruling is that healing is permitted on the Sabbath only if one does not go out of one's way to do so. Broken bones were not allowed to be set.

127. Acts of Pilate 1:1. The charge of *maleficium*, "magic," is a common one in the martyrdoms. See, for example, the *Acts of Paul and Thecla* 15, 20; *The Martyrdom of Saint Serapion*, in *CSCO* 43:76.

128. Magic was a capital crime among the Hittites (Gurney, *Hittites*, 134; Johannes Friedrich and Annelies Kammenhuber, *Hethitisches Wörterbuch*, 2nd ed., 10 vols. to date [Heidelberg: Winter, 1975–], 1:64 s.v. *alanzatar*), and Babylonians (Codex Hamurabbi §2; *CAD* K 454–56), as well as the Romans, but objective definition of the term has eluded scholars; see, John Gee, "Abracadabra,

is God, and witnesses continually arise to testify of Jesus's innocence and the perfidy of the leaders.[129] Some apocryphal accounts of the passion, though professing the best of intentions,[130] betray elements of fictionalization that mark them as pious (or impious) frauds, such as adding the names of the brigands crucified with Jesus, Gestas and Demas, as well as lengthy biographies wherein we learn that Gestas was thoroughly reprobate, but Demas was something of an ancient Robin Hood: "He had pirated from the rich, but he did good to the poor."[131] The sobriety of the canonical accounts contrasts strikingly with the wild fantasies of the apocrypha.[132]

Some of the apocryphal accounts of the passion of Jesus maintain that Jesus did not really suffer and die on the cross but only seemed to. This doctrine was common in the first and second centuries of the Christian era and is called Docetism after the Greek word for "seeming" (*dokein*).[133] For example, the

---

Isaac and Jacob," in *RBBM* 7/1 (1995): 19–84; John Gee, "'An Obstacle to Deeper Understanding,'" in *FARMS Review of Books* 12/2 (2000): 185–224.

129. *Acts of Pilate* 1:1–9:3.

130. "Being an eyewitness, I write these things so that all might believe in the crucified Jesus Christ, our Lord and no longer observe the law of Moses, but believe on the signs and wonders that happened because of him, and so that believing we might inherit eternal life and be found in the kingdom of heaven." Thus the Narration of Joseph of Arimathea 5:4.

131. Narration of Joseph of Arimathea 1:2; other indications of speciousness include the translation of Demas in 4:1 and the slighting of the apostles in 5:2–3. The Narration of Joseph of Arimathea is also very anti-Semitic.

132. Significantly, in his discussion of the sources, Bernard Jackson does not even deign to dismiss the apocryphal versions in a footnote; Bernard S. Jackson, "The Trials of Jesus and Jeremiah," *BYUS* 32/4 (1992): 63–77. There is simply no historical veracity to the accounts.

133. Chadwick, *Early Church*, 37–38; Quasten, *Patrology* 1:65, 114; S. Kent Brown, "Whither the Early Church?" in Robert L. Millet, *Acts to Revelation*, vol. 6 in *Studies in Scripture* (Salt Lake City: Deseret, 1987), 281–82; *NTA* 1:401. Classic formulations of doceticism may be found in Irenaeus, *Contra Haereses* I.6.1, 7.2, 24.2, 4.

Gospel of Philip says: "Jesus took them all by fraud;[134] he did not appea[r] as he was, but as [they co]uld see him he appeared."[135] The *Apocalypse of Peter* takes a more extreme view: A substitute suffered on the cross while Jesus laughed.[136]

The Forty-Day Ministry

The culmination of Jesus' ministry is his resurrection from the dead into glory. As the most important event of history, the apocryphal acts do not pass this event by. The picture presented is best seen in overview.[137]

After rising from the dead, Jesus appears to the women gathered at the tomb and sends them to tell his disciples of his resurrection, but they will not believe the testimony of a woman.[138] So Jesus himself visits them and demonstrates the resurrection to the unbelieving eleven,[139] providing them hope for their own

---

134. Coptic *ⁿjioue*, "stealthily"; *CD* 794a. The basic meaning of *jioue* is "theft, fraud"; *CD* 794a. *Fit=* *ⁿjioue* is also used to translate the Greek *klepsōsin* "they might steal and *eklepsan* "they stole" at Matthew 27:64; 28:13 in the Mesokemic version of Matthew; see Hans-Martin Schenke, *Das Matthäus-Evangelium im Mittelägyptischen Dialekt des Koptischen (Codex Scheide)*, TU 127 (Berlin: Akademie, 1981), 89. The Coptic word *jioue* is the descendant of Late Egyptian *t3wt* "theft". The phrase *ⁿjioue* is a descendant of Late Egyptian *m-t3wt* "secretly"; e.g. *mky ib=i prt m t3wt* "behold, my mind goes forth secretly (like a thief)" in P. Anastasi IV, 4.11 in Alan H. Gardiner, *Late Egyptian Miscellanies*, vol. 7 of *Bibliotheca Aegyptiaca* (Bruxelles: Fondation Égyptologique Reine Élisabeth, 1937), 39. This passage from the Gospel of Philip has been rendered variously as "Jesus took them all by stealth;" Wesley W. Isenberg, "The Gospel According to Philip," in Layton, *Nag Hammadi Codex II,2–7*, 1:155; and Wesley W. Isenberg, "The Gospel of Philip (II,3)," in Robinson, *Nag Hammadi Library* (1988), 144; "Jesus tricked everyone;" Layton, *Gnostic Scriptures*, 334.

135. Gospel of Philip II.57.28–32.

136. *Apocalypse of Peter* VII.80.31–82.16.

137. The overview is taken from John Gee, "Jesus Christ: Forty-Day Ministry and Other Post-Resurrection Appearances of Jesus Christ," in Ludlow, ed., *Encyclopedia of Mormonism*, 2:735.

138. Epistula Apostolorum 9–10.

139. Epistula Apostolorum 2, 11–12. Perhaps most important here is the non-canonical source cited by Ignatius of Antioch (*Epistula ad Smyrnaeos* 3:2): "And when he [*scil.* Jesus] came to those around Peter, he said to them: 'Take, touch

resurrection as they follow their master.[140] Jesus prepares his disciples to be his witnesses and preach repentance to the nations by expounding the scriptures to the understanding of his disciples,[141] and responding to their questions.[142] He begins with the premortal life, the council in heaven,[143] the expulsion of the devil and his angels,[144] and the creation of the world,[145] and the garden story.[146] This life is a probationary state of choosing between good and evil so that those who choose good might return to the glory of God.[147] Jesus's explanation extends through the days of the apostles and on through the last days.[148] Jesus warns the disciples to prepare for tribulation, for they will be killed and the primitive church will be perverted after one generation.[149] Besides salvation for the living,[150] salvation for the dead is a

---

me and see, that I am not a bodyless demon.' And straightway they began to hold and they believed, grasping his flesh and spirit. Therefore they scorned even death, but were found superior to death."

140.   Epistula Apostolorum 19, 21; Apocryphon of James I.3.11–16.

141.   Luke 24:44–45; Acts 1:3; Papyrus Deir el-Bala'izah 52; Epistula Apostolorum 13–51; Discourse on Abbaton fol 6a-31a; Gospel of Bartholomew 5:6, 9; Apocalypse of Peter 14.

142.   Gospel of Bartholomew 1:1–7; Apocalypse of Peter 1; 1 Jeu 1–4.

143.   Discourse on Abbaton fol. 9a-13b; Apocryphon of James I.5.23–29. This theme is also dealt with in Joseph F. McConkie, "Premortal Existence, Foreordinations, and Heavenly Councils," *Apocryphal Writings and the Latter-day Saints*, 173–98, but the treatment is almost all from canonical scriptures and Old Testament apocrypha and pseudepigrapha except pp. 183–84 dealing with the Hymn of the Pearl from the Acts of Thomas.

144.   Papyrus Deir el-Bala'izah 27; Discourse on Abbaton fol. 13a-14b; Gospel of Bartholomew 4:7–60.

145.   Discourse on Abbaton fol. 9a-10a; Gospel of Bartholomew 4:28–35, 45, 47, 52–57.

146.   Discourse on Abbaton fol. 14b-21b; Gospel of Bartholomew 4:5.

147.   Epistula Apostolorum 24, 39, 43–44; Apocalypse of Peter 3, 13–14; Gospel of Bartholomew 4:67–68; 5:1–8.

148.   Epistula Apostolorum 16–19; Discourse on Abbaton fol. 25a-30b; Apocalypse of Peter 1–6; Gospel of Bartholomew 1:23–35.

149.   Epistula Apostolorum 36, 44, 52; Apocryphon of James I.10.26–11.4, 12.18–30.

150.   Epistula Apostolorum 19, 46–48; Discourse on Abbaton fol. 28b-29b.

major theme,[151] as are the ordinances: baptism,[152] receiving the Holy Ghost,[153] the sacrament,[154] the ordination of the apostles to authority,[155] and an initiation with an emphasis on washing,[156] anointing,[157] garments,[158] marriage,[159] sealings[160] and prayer circles.[161] These secret[162] accounts are often connected somehow to the temple,[163] or a mountain[164] that is sometimes compared to the Mount of Transfiguration,[165] as even the apostles are transfigured and ascend to heaven[166] or descend into the netherworld[167]

---

151. Epistula Apostolorum 26–28; Gospel of Bartholomew 1:8–9, 20–22.

152. Epistula Apostolorum 41–42; Discourse on Abbaton fol. 6b; Gospel of Bartholomew 5:8; Apocalypse of Peter 13; 2 Jeu 46–47.

153. 2 Jeu 47.

154. Epistula Apostolorum 15; Gospel of Bartholomew 2:18–19.

155. Papyrus Strasbourg Coptic 6; Discourse on the Abbaton fol. 6a; Epistula Apostolorum 41–42.

156. Gospel of Bartholomew 2:17.

157. Gospel of Bartholomew 4:65.

158. Epistula Apostolorum 21; Papyrus Strasbourg Coptic 6 verso; Discourse on Abbaton fol. 28b; Gospel of Bartholomew 4:18–22, 70; Apocalypse of Peter 13; 1 Jeu 4; 2 Jeu 47.

159. Epistula Apostolorum 43; Discourse on Abbaton fol. 27b; Gospel of Bartholomew 5:8 (definitely not the LDS concept).

160. Epistula Apostolorum 41; 1 Jeu 33–38; 2 Jeu 46–49.

161. 1 Jeu 41: "He said to the twelve: Circle around me all of you. They all surrounded him. He said to them: Repeat after me and give glory with me and I will give glory to my father." See also 2 Jeu 42, 47–48. The standard work is Hugh Nibley, "The Early Christian Prayer Circle," *CWHN* 4:45–99; but note especially Compton, review of Welch, *Sermon at the Temple and the Sermon on the Mount,* 322; see also now, Donald W. Parry, "Temple Worship and a Possible Reference to a Prayer Circle in Psalm 24," *BYUS* 32/4 (1992): 57–62.

162. Gospel of Bartholomew 2:4–5, 14, 22; 4:10, 66–68; 1 Jeu 1; 2 Jeu 43; Apocryphon of John II.31.32–32.1; Apocryphon of James I.1.8–2.15.

163. Apocryphon of John II.1.1–2.25.

164. Papyrus Strasbourg Coptic Papyrus 6 recto; Gospel of Bartholomew 4:1–2, 6; Apocalypse of Peter 1, 15; Apocryphon of John II.1.17–2.25.

165. Epistula Apostolorum 51; Papyrus Strasbourg Coptic 6 verso; Narration of Joseph of Arimathea 5:1; Apocalypse of Peter 15–17.

166. Narration of Joseph of Arimathea 4:2–3; Epistula Apostolorum 19; Apocalypse of Peter 17; Apocalypse of Paul prologue; 1 Jeu; 2 Jeu; Pistis Sophia.

167. Gospel of Bartholomew 4:12–5:5.

where they see marvelous things. Jesus gives his apostles the kiss of peace[168] before he ascends into the clouds.[169]

Nevertheless, all in the apocryphal accounts is not orthodox. The overview tends to obscure the discordant points in the accounts. Some of the apocryphal expositions show traces of Docetic,[170] Gnostic,[171] or Manichaean doctrine.[172] In the Gospel of Bartholomew, Jesus has Satan narrate the creation,[173] and elements are borrowed from the Egyptian Setne Khamwas cycle.[174] Certain elements appear, shadowy remembrances of half-forgotten things that were supposed to have been there,[175] yet these are not identical to what Latter-day Saints are familiar with. For example, one of the ascensions through one of the heavenly treasuries runs as follows:

> Again we, I and my order which encircled me, came out to the fifty-eighth treasury of *Eōzeōza*. [There are a total of sixty of these.] I said: Hearken now to the

168. Gospel of Bartholomew 4:71.

169. Gospel of Bartholomew 5:9; Apocryphon of James I.14.19–36.

170. *Apocalypse of Peter* VII.80.31–82.16.

171. The Apocryphon of John "contains one of the most classic narrations of the gnostic myth." Thus Layton, *Gnostic Scriptures*, 23.

172. E.g. the reference to the five trees of paradise in Papyrus Deir el-Bala'izah 52 41.31; *Gospel of Thomas* 19; cf. Samuel N. C. Lieu, *Manichaeism in the Later Roman Empire and Medieval China: A Historical Survey* (Manchester: Manchester University Press, 1985), 10–11.

173. Gospel of Bartholomew 4:28–57. Noted in Quasten, *Patrology* 1:127.

174. The view of the deep like a scroll in Gospel of Bartholomew 3:1–9 parallels the view of the deep by a scroll in Setna I 3/12–15, 3/35–4/5. While in the netherworld, pounding one's opponent into the earth up to his ears in Gospel of Bartholomew 4:22 parallels Setna I 4/27–31. The trip to the netherworld itself (Gospel of Bartholomew 3:1–5:6) has parallels in Setna II 1/25–2/27. For Setna I have used Wilhelm Spiegelberg, *Die demotischen Denkmäler*, 2 vols., CGC (Leipzig: Druglin, 1904–8), 2:plates 44–47; a serviceable translation may be found in Miriam Lichtheim, *Ancient Egyptian Literature*, 3 vols. (Berkeley: University of California Press, 1973–80), 3:125–51; see now Sara Goldbrunner, *Der verblendete Gelehrte* (Sommerhausen: Gisela Zauzich Verlag, 2006).

175. Compare the following quote from 1 Jeu 36 with the list of secret knowledge in Ignatius, *Epistula ad Trallianos* 5:2 quoted at the beginning of this essay.

layout of this treasury and everything which is within it, there being six places which surround it. Whenever you come to this place, seal yourself with this seal. This is its name: *Zaaiuzōaz*. Speak it only once having this number [or stone, *psēphos*],[176] 70122, in your hand, and speak this name three times also: *Eeeeeieēzēōzaaize* and the guards and the orders and the veils will always withdraw themselves until you enter the place of their father and he will give his seal and his name and you will cross over the gate into his treasury. This is the layout of this treasury and all those who are within it.[177]

While some Latter-day Saints might find some of these elements familiar, there is a bizarreness about it. Latter-day Saints, having their own authentic accounts of the teachings of the Savior after his resurrection in the Book of Mormon (3 Nephi 1–30)[178] would do well to use it as a touchstone for the apocryphal accounts.[179]

Conclusions

Often, when first presented with the stories from the apocryphal gospels, people's interests become piqued and sometimes they become excited. Sooner or later, "we learn to prize the heavenly; we look for revelation, that nowhere burns more

---

176. Compare John Gee, "Abraham in Ancient Egyptian Texts," *Ensign* 22/7 (July 1992): 60.

177. 1 Jeu 36.

178. Possibly D&C 45:16–59 can be another forty-day account depending on how the phrase "in the flesh" is understood. The general tendency is to take this as a reference to the mortal Jesus.

179. Comparisons of the Forty-day literature with the Book of Mormon are available in Hugh Nibley, "Christ among the Ruins," *CWHN* 8:407–34; and Gee, "Jesus Christ: Forty-day Ministry and Other Post-Resurrection Appearances of Jesus Christ," 735–36.

worthily or beautifully than in the New Testament."[180] Jesus' works cannot be separated from his words. Both are eternal. But we can separate the canonical from the apocryphal accounts of Jesus' acts and words. Reading the former helps us feel the Spirit, which we need to read the latter, for "whoso receiveth not by the Spirit cannot be benefitted" (D&C 91:6). Like cream-puffs, most apocryphal accounts of Jesus, though they look enticing, have little nourishment and are usually are not as good nor even as sweet as they look, being dusty pastry filled with imitation cream.

John Gee is the William (Bill) Gay Research Chair and a Senior Research Fellow at the Neal A. Maxwell Institute for Religious Scholarship at Brigham Young University.

---

180. Goethe, *Faust* 1216–19.

Abbreviations

AfP   *Archiv für Papyrusforschung*

ANRW *Aufstieg und Niedergang der römischen Welt* (Berlin: Walter de Gruyter)

AN   Montague R. James, *The Apocryphal New Testament* (Oxford: Clarendon, 1975)

BYU   *Brigham Young University Studies*

CA   *Chicago Assyrian Dictionary*, 21 vols. (Chicago: Oriental Institute, 195–)

CD   Walter E. Crum, *A Coptic Dictionary* (Oxford: Clarendon, 1939)

CGC   Catalogue Général des Antiquités égyptiennes du Musée du Caire

CSCO *Corpus Scriptorum Christianorum Orientalium*

CWHN *Collected Works of Hugh Nibley*, 12 vols. to date (Salt Lake City: Deseret, and Provo, Utah: FARMS, 198–)

FARMS Foundation for Ancient Research and Mormon Studies

GCS   *Die Griechische Christliche Schriftstelle* (Berlin: Akademie)

LdÄ   Eberhard Otto and Wolfgang Helck, eds., *Lexikon der Ägyptologie*, 7 vols. (Wiesbaden: Otto Harrassowitz, 197–90)

LSJ   Henry George Liddell, Robert Scott, Henry Stuart Jones, and Roderick McKenzie, *A Greek-English Lexicon*, 9th ed. (Oxford: Clarendon, 1968)

MIFAO Mémoires publiés par les Membres de l'Institut Français d'Archéologie Orientale, Cairo.

NHS   *Nag Hammadi Studies* (Leiden: Brill,)

NTA   Edgar Hennecke and Wilhelm Schneemelcher, eds., *New Testament Apocrypha*, 2 vols., trans. R. McL. Wilson (Philadelphia: Westminster, 196–65)

NTAP James H. Charlesworth, *The New Testament Apocrypha and Pseudepigrapha: A guide to publications with excurses on apocalypses* (Metuchen, NJ: American Theological Library Association, 1987)

OCD   N. G. L. Hammond and H. H. Scullard, eds., *The Oxford Classical Dictionary* 2nd ed. (Oxford: Clarendon, 1970)

OTP   James H. Charlesworth, *The Old Testament Pseudepigrapha*, 2 vols. (Garden City, New York: Doubleday, 198–85)

PG   J.-P. Migne, ed., *Patrologiae Graecae*, 161 vols. (Paris: Migne, 185–)

PO   R. Graffin and F. Nau, eds., *Patrologia Orientalis* (Paris: Firmin-Didot, 190–)

RBBM   *Review of Books on the Book of Mormon*

SAOC   *Studies in Ancient Oriental Civilization* (Chicago: Oriental Institute)

TU   *Texte und Untersuchungen zur Geschichte der altchristlichen Literatur*

YES   *Yale Egyptological Studies* (New Haven, CT: Yale Egyptological Seminar)

Appendix I

The text editions listed in the appendices may not be the latest or the most available; the bibliography will often give more recent editions.

The following may be counted as Infancy Gospels:

The Arabic Infancy Gospel. This seems to be an Arabic version of the Infancy Gospel of Thomas, large portions of this are included in the Syriac History of the Virgin. A Latin translation of the text may be found in Constantinus von Tischendorf, *Evangelia Apocrypha*, 2nd ed. (Leipzig: Hermann Mendelssohn, 1876), 18–209; selections translated in *NTA* 1:40–1, 40–9; bibliography in *NTAP* 21–14.

The Armenian Infancy Gospel. Bibliography in *NTAP* 215.

The Arundel Manuscript. Selections translated in *NTA* 1:41–14.

The (Infancy) Gospel of Thomas. This is not the same as the Gospel of Thomas found at Nag Hammadi and Oxyrhynchus which is a sayings gospel set among the forty-day literature. Text in Tischendorf, *Evangelia Apocrypha*, 14–63; translation in *NTA* 1:39–99; bibliography in *NTAP* 40–9.

The Latin Infancy Gospel. Text in Tischendorf, *Evangelia Apocrypha*, 16–80; bibliography in *NTAP* 21–17.

The Life of John according to Serapion. Selections translated in *NTA* 1:41–17.

The Protevangelium of James. Text in Tischendorf, *Evangelia Apocrypha*, –50; translation in *NTA* 1:37–88; bibliography in *NTAP* 21–28.

Pseudo-Matthew. Text in Tischendorf, *Evangelia Apocrypha*, 5–111; extracts translated in *NTA* 1:41–13; bibliography in *NTAP* 26–67.

Appendix II

The following may be classed under the head of Christ's ministry and passion:

Coptic Narratives of the Ministry and Passion. Text in E. Revillout, "Les apocryphes coptes," *PO* 2:11–98; bibliography in *NTAP* 19–97.

The Epistles of Abgar. Translation in *NTA* 1:44–44; bibliography in *NTAP* 17–85.

The *Evan Bohan*. This is a Jewish anti-Christian tract which preserves portions of earlier material including most of the original Hebrew version of the canonical gospel of Matthew. For a discussion, see George Howard, *The Gospel of Matthew according to a Primitive Hebrew Text*, (Macon, Georgia: Mercer University Press, 1987), ix.

The Fayyum Fragment. Translation in *NTA* 1:116.

The Gospel of the Ebionites. The text may be found in Erwin Preuschen, *Antilegomena: Die Reste der auserkanoischen Evangelien und urchristlichen Überlieferungen*, 2nd ed, (Gieszen: Alfred Töpelmann, 1905), 1–12; translation in *NTA* 1:15–58; bibliography in *NTAP* 19–201.

The Gospel of the Egyptians. This is different from the version found in two versions among the Nag Hammadi codices;

see *NTA* 1:36–62. Text in Preuschen, *Antilegomena*, –3; bibliography in *NTAP* 20–3.

The Gospel of Gamaliel. Text in Pierre Lacau, *Fragments d'apocryphes coptes, MIFAO* 9 (Cairo: Institut français d'archéologie orientale, 1904), 19; bibliography in *NTAP* 20–6.

The Gospel of the Hebrews. There is confusion of the fragments preserved of this work with both the Hebrew version of Matthew preserved in the *Evan Bohan* and with the Gospel of the Nazaraeans. Text in Preuschen, *Antilegomena*, –9; translation in *NTA* 1:16–65; bibliography in *NTAP* 20–11.

The Gospel of the Nazaraeans. There is much confusion of this with the Gospel of the Hebrews as well as the Hebrew version of Matthew. Translation in *NTA* 1:14–53; bibliography in *NTAP* 26–71.

The Gospel of Truth. Translation in Layton, *Gnostic Scriptures*, 25–64.

The Narrative of Joseph of Arimathea. Text in Tischendorf, *Evangelia Apocrypha*, 45–70; bibliography in *NTAP* 24–44.

Papyrus Cairensis 10,735. Translation in *NTA* 1:115.

Papyrus Oxyrhynchus 1224. Translation in *NTA* 1:114.

Appendix III

The following are examples of the Forty-Day genre:

Acts of Paul. Bibliography in *NTAP* 27–87.

Acts of Pilate. This is an expanded version of the Gospel of Nicodemus. Greek text in Tischendorf, *Evangelia Apocrypha* 21–332; Coptic text in E. Revillout, "Les Acta Pilati," *Patrologia Orientalis*, 9:5–140; translation in *NTA* 1:44–76; bibliography in *NTAP* 33–43.

Acts of Thomas. Bibliography in *NTAP* 36–72.

Apocalypse of Paul (This is a version of the Vision of Paul but is not identical with the Apocalypse of Paul among the Nag Hammadi codices). The text may be found in E. A. W. Budge, *Miscellaneous Coptic Texts* (Oxford, 1915); bibliography in *NTAP* 28–94.

Apocalypse of Peter. Translation in *NTA* 2:66–83; bibliography in *NTAP* 31–21.

Apocalypse of Thomas. Translation in *NTA* 2:79–803; bibliography in *NTAP* 37–74.

Apocryphon of James. Translation in Robinson, *Nag Hammadi Library* (1988), 3–37.

Apocryphon of John. Translation in Robinson, *Nag Hammadi Library* (1988), 10–23.

Book of the Resurrection of Christ. Text in E. A. W. Budge, *Coptic Apocrypha in the Dialect of Upper Egypt* (London: British Museum, 1913), –48, Plates I-XLVIII; translation in ibid., 17–215; discussion in James, *Apocryphal New Testament*, 18–86.

127 Canons of the Apostles. This selection of Church rules attributed to the apostles assumes a forty-day authority, but is not strictly speaking a forty-day text. Arabic text and French translation in Jean Périer and Augustin Périer, "Les '127 Canons des Apôtres," in *PO* 8:55–710.

Contendings of the Apostles. See E. A. W. Budge, *Contendings of the Apostles* (Oxford: Oxford University Press, 1935).

Dialogue between John and Jesus. This work is also known as Papyrus Bala'izah 52. Text and translation in Paul E. Kahle, *Bala'izah*, 2 vols. (Oxford: Griffith Institute, 1954), 1:47–77.

Dialogue of the Savior. Translation in Robinson, *Nag Hammadi Library* (1988), 24–55.

The Didache. Text in Oscar de Gebhardt, Adolf Harnack and Theodor Zahn, eds., *Patrum Apostolicorum Opera*, 5th ed. (Leipzig: J. C. Hinrichs, 1906).

Discourse on Abbaton. The text may be found in E. A. Wallis Budge, *Coptic Martyrdoms etc. in the Dialect of Upper Egypt* (London: British Museum, 1914); 22–49; translation in ibid., 47–96; bibliography in *NTAP* 156.

Epistula Apostolorum. This is the Coptic version of the Testament in Galilee. The text may be found in Carl Schmidt, *Gespräche Jesus mit seinen Jüngern nach der Auferstehung: Ein katholisch-apostolisches Sendschreiben des 2. Jahrhunderts*, *TU* 43 (Leipzig: J. C. Hinrichs, 1919); translation in *NTA* 1:19–227; bibliography in *NTAP* 16–71.

Freer Logion (version of Mark 16:14 in Codex
Washingtonianus). The text is available in Nestle, et al.,
eds., *Novum Testamentum Graece*, 148, or Kurt Aland,
et al., eds., *The Greek New Testament*, 3rd ed. (New York:
United Bible Societies, 1975), 197; translations available in
Bruce M. Metzger. *A Textual Commentary on the Greek New
Testament*, 2nd ed. (New York: United Bible Societies, 1975),
124, and *NTA* 1:189.

The Gospel of Bartholomew. This text is identical with the
Questions of Bartholomew; Text in E. Revillout, "Les
Apocryphes Coptes," *PO* 2:18–98; translation in *NTA*
1:48–503; bibliography in *NTAP* 17–77.

The Gospel of Mary. Text in Walter Till, *Die gnostischen
Schriften des koptischen Papyrus Berolinensis 8502, TU* 60
(Berlin: Akademie, 1955), 2–32; selections translated in *NTA*
1:34–44; bibliography (to 1961) in *NTA* 1:340.

The Gospel of Nicodemus. Bibliography in *NTAP* 27–77.

The Gospel of Peter (ANT); translation in *NTA* 1:18–87; bibliography in *NTAP* 32–327.

The Gospel of Philip. Text and translation in Bentley Layton,
ed., *Nag Hammadi Codex II,–7*, 2 vols., *NHS* 2–21 (Leiden:
E. J. Brill, 1989), 1:14–214, translation also in Robinson, *Nag
Hammadi Library* (1988), 14–60.

The Gospel of Thomas. This is the Coptic version found in
Nag Hammadi codex II. Text and translation in Layton, *nag
Hammadi Codex II.–7*, 1:5–93; translation also in Robinson,
Nag Hammadi Library (1988), 12–38; bibliography in *NTAP*
37–402.

The Gospel of the Twelve Apostles. Text in E. Revillout, "Les
Apocryphes Coptes," 13–84; bibliography in *NTAP* 41–13.

The History of Joseph the Carpenter. This is an infancy narrative set in a forty-day frame story. The Arabic text may
be found in Ioannis Caroli Thilo, *Codex Apocryphus Novi
Testament* (Leipzig: Wilhelm Vogel, 1832), –61; selections
of the Coptic text may be found in Thomas O. Lambdin,
Introduction to Sahidic Coptic (Macon, GA: Mercer
University Press, 1983), 19–208; bibliography in *NTAP*
24–248.

1 Jeu. The text and translation is most conveniently found in Carl Schmidt and Violet MacDermot, *The Books of Jeu and the Untitled Text from the Bruce Codex*, vol. 13 of *NHS* (Leiden: Brill, 1978), –123; Schmidt's reconstructed text is the standard even if it has not been checked by a codicological method, but MacDermot's English translation is often infelicitous to the Coptic.

2 Jeu. The text and translation in Schmidt and MacDermot, *Books of Jeu and the Untitled Text from the Bruce Codex*, 12–211; the same cautions apply to 2 Jeu as to 1 Jeu.

The Letter of Christ from Heaven. Bibliography in *NTAP* 18–88.

Oxyrhynchus Logia (see under Papyrus Oxyrhynchus 1 and 655).

Papyrus Bodmer X. This was cited as a forty-day text by Nibley, "Evangelium Quadraginta Dierum," 25 n. 27, 29 n. 43, 33 n. 61, 36 n. 73; and discussed by Thomas W. Mackay, "Content and Style in Two Pseudo-Pauline Epistles (3 Corinthians and the Epistle to the Laodiceans)," *Apocryphal Writings and the Latter-day Saints* (Provo, Utah: Religious Studies Center, 1986), 216. The papyrus contains a Coptic version of the Acts of Paul and Thecla (Greek versions also exist), which is a martyrdom or hagiography and not really a forty-day account. Tertullian (*De Baptismo* 17) condemns it as a second-century forgery. A translation may be found in *NTA* 2:35–64.

Papyrus Deir el-Bala'izah 28. This fragment is similar to the Discourse on Abaton. Text and translation in Kahle, *Bala'izah*, 1:40–4.

Papyrus Deir el-Bala'izah 52. This is another name for the Dialogue between John and Jesus.

Papyrus Oxyrhynchus 1. This is one manuscript of the Greek version of the Gospel of Thomas. Text in Layton, ed., *Nag Hammadi Codex II,–7*, 1:11–21; translation in ibid., 1:127; bibliography in ibid., 1:10–2, 11–12.

Papyrus Oxyrhynchus 654. This is another manuscript of the Greek version of the Gospel of Thomas. Text in Layton, ed., *Nag Hammadi Codex II,-7*, 1:11–17; translation in ibid., 1:12–27; bibliography in ibid., 1:10–2, 11–12.

Papyrus Oxyrhynchus 655. Yet another manuscript of the Greek version of the Gospel of Thomas. Text in Layton, ed., *Nag Hammadi Codex II,-7*, 1:117, 12–25; translation in ibid., 1:12–28; bibliography in ibid., 1:10–2, 11–12.

Papyrus Oxyrhychus 1081. This is a Greek version of the Sophia Jesu Christi.

Papyrus Strasbourg Coptic 5. Translation in *NTA* 1:22–30.

Papyrus Strasbourg Coptic 6. Translation in *NTA* 1:230.

Pistis Sophia. Text and Translation in Carl Schmidt and Violet MacDermot, *Pistis Sophia*, *NHS* 9 (Leiden: Brill, 1978). Schmidt's text is the standard, but MacDermot's English translation often leaves something to be desired.

Questions of Bartholomew (identical with the Gospel of Bartholomew)

Questions of Mary. Translation in *NTA* 1:339; bibliography in *NTAP* 26–64.

Revelation to Peter. Another name for the Apocalypse of Peter.

Sophia Jesus Christi. Translation in Robinson, *Nag Hammadi Library* (1988), 22–43.

Testament in Galilee. This is an Ethiopic version of the Epistula Apostolorum. Text in L. Guerrier, "Le Testament en Galilée de Notre-Seigneur Jésus-Christ," *PO* 9:14–236; translation in *NTA* 1:19–227.

Testamentum Domini Nostri Jesu Christi (the Syriac version of the Epistula Apostolorum). The text may be found in Ignatius Rahmani, *Testamentum Domini Nostri Jesu Christi* (Moguntiae: Kircheim, 1899); bibliography in *NTAP* 19–98.

The Vision of Paul (the Latin version of the Apocalypse of Paul). Bibliography in *NTAP* 30–9.

Additional bibliography on these items may be found in David M. Scholer, *Nag Hammadi Bibliography 194–1969*, vol. 1 of *Nag Hammadi Studies* (Leiden: E. J. Brill, 1971) and in the yearly updates in *Novum Testamentum*.

This article has a history. It was originally commissioned in the early 1990s as general overview and a companion piece to an article by Stephen Robinson on the apocryphal words of Jesus for a volume to be published by Brigham Young University's Religious Studies Center. That volume was cancelled after it was deemed too technical. John W. Welch then requested it to be submitted to *BYU Studies*. Robinson's article was published as Stephen E. Robinson, "The Noncanonical Sayings of Jesus," *BYU Studies* 36/2 (1996–1997): 74–91. The editors, however, rejected this article because it took too dim a view of apocryphal literature. In 2011, Kristian Heal requested the author to submit it to *Studies in the Bible and Antiquity*, but the editors rejected it on the grounds that it was a general overview. It has not been substantially updated.

Made in the USA
San Bernardino, CA
23 March 2016